Middle Class Union

CLASS : CULTURE

SERIES EDITORS
Amy Schrager Lang, Syracuse University, and Bill V. Mullen, Purdue University

RECENT TITLES IN THE SERIES:

Mark W. Robbins, *Middle Class Union: Organizing the 'Consuming Public' in Post–World War I America*

Marie A. Failinger and Ezra Rosser, Editors, *The Poverty Law Canon: Exploring the Major Cases*

M. Michelle Robinson, *Dreams for Dead Bodies: Blackness, Labor, and the Corpus of American Detective Fiction*

Benjamin Balthaser, *Anti-Imperialist Modernism: Race and Transnational Radical Culture from the Great Depression to the Cold War*

Clarence Lang, *Black America in the Shadow of the Sixties: Notes on the Civil Rights Movement, Neoliberalism, and Politics*

Andreá N. Williams, *Dividing Lines: Class Anxiety and Postbellum Black Fiction*

Liam Kennedy and Stephen Shapiro, Editors, The Wire: *Race, Class, and Genre*

Mark W. Van Wienen, *American Socialist Triptych: The Literary-Political Work of Charlotte Perkins Gilman, Upton Sinclair, and W. E. B. Du Bois*

John Marsh, *Hog Butchers, Beggars, and Busboys: Poverty, Labor, and the Making of Modern American Poetry*

Matthew H. Bernstein, Editor, *Michael Moore: Filmmaker, Newsmaker, Cultural Icon*

Lorraine M. López, Editor, *An Angle of Vision: Women Writers on Their Poor and Working-Class Roots*

Carole Srole, *Transcribing Class and Gender: Masculinity and Femininity in Nineteenth-Century Courts and Offices*

Pamela Fox, *Natural Acts: Gender, Race, and Rusticity in Country Music*

Clarence Lang, *Grassroots at the Gateway: Class Politics and Black Freedom Struggle in St. Louis, 1936–75*

Fran Leeper Buss, Editor, *Moisture of the Earth: Mary Robinson, Civil Rights and Textile Union Activist*

Marcial González, *Chicano Novels and the Politics of Form: Race, Class, and Reification*

# Middle Class Union

## Organizing the 'Consuming Public' in Post–World War I America

Mark W. Robbins

University of Michigan Press • Ann Arbor

Published in the United States of America by the
University of Michigan Press
Manufactured in the United States of America
♾ Printed on acid-free paper

2020 2019 2018 2017 4 3 2 1

A CIP catalog record for this book is available from the British Library.

Library of Congress Cataloging-in-Publication Data

Names: Robbins, Mark W., author.
Title: Middle class union : organizing the 'consuming public' in post–World War I America / Mark W. Robbins.
Description: Ann Arbor : University of Michigan Press, [2017] | Includes bibliographical references and index.
Identifiers: LCCN 2016047590| ISBN 9780472130337 (hardcover : alk. paper) | ISBN 9780472122790 (e-book)
Subjects: LCSH: Consumers—United States—History—20th century. | Consumers' leagues—United States—History—20th century. | Consumer cooperatives—United States—History—20th century. | Middle class—United States—History—20th century. | United States—Economic conditions—1918–1945.
Classification: LCC HC110.C6 R623 2017 | DDC 339.4/7097309042—dc23
LC record available at https://lccn.loc.gov/2016047590

*For Christine, Thomas, and Marian*

# Acknowledgments

It is my great pleasure to thank a number of people and institutions for their support in the research, writing, and publication of this book. I am grateful for the efforts and insights of LeAnn Fields, Christopher Dreyer, the staff at the University of Michigan Press, and the Class: Culture series editors, Amy Schrager Lang and Bill V. Mullen. I would also like to thank two anonymous reviewers, who improved the manuscript through their thoughtful and detailed feedback. As a graduate student at Brown University, I could not have asked for a more supportive group of mentors. I am truly grateful for Mari Jo Buhle's dedication, kindness, and insights while serving as my primary advisor, and for her continued support. Robert Self and Elliott Gorn generously helped me to think about this project in new ways and directed me to a number of fruitful lines of analysis. I am also indebted to Nancy Jacobs for her guidance and encouragement, and for exposing me to new theoretical concepts and writing strategies. A number of other people have supported this project in a variety of ways, ranging from commenting on earlier drafts of the work to assisting in the location of source materials. They include Erik Anderson, who always has been generous in sharing his knowledge and offering his encouragement, Gill Frank, Jim Klein, Gabriel Rosenberg, Paige Meltzer, Caroline Boswell, Christopher Brick, Robert Fleegler, Natalina Earls, Lara Couturier, Stacie Taranto, Jessica Foley, Nichole Eaton, Derek Seidman, Daniel Puskin, Kimberly Hill, Lauren Reiser, Allison Hartry, Christon Salinas, Sandra Valerio, Sara Kaplan, Bryan Stone, Derek Oden, Paul Gottemoller, Liz Flores, Renato Ramirez, Bruce Olson, Fernando Rodriguez, Teresa Klein, Mike Nelson, Paul Robbins, Sharon Hauge, Daniel Robbins, Kristi Rutz-Robbins, Brian Robbins, Michael Robbins, Chalyce Reiser, Will Reiser, Mary Reiser, and the staffs of the Brown University and Del Mar College libraries, as well as those of the libraries and archives listed in the endnotes. I would also like to thank Matthew Lassiter and Maris Vinovskis for offering strong guidance when I began studying the post–World War I period while a student at the University of Michigan.

This book would not have been possible without the generous support of grants and fellowships from Brown University, Del Mar College, the Newberry Library, the Herbert Hoover Presidential Library Association, and the Historical Society of Southern California/Haynes Foundation. Parts of the manuscript were previously published as "Transitioning Labor to the 'Lean Years': The Middle Class and Employer Repression of Organized Labor in Post–World War I Chicago," *Labor History* 54, no. 3 (Fall 2013): 321–42. Sections of this article appear in this book with the permission of Taylor and Francis.

I am grateful to Dave and Debbie Sprecher for being there for me every step of the way, always offering kindness, encouragement, and support. Patty and Larry Robbins have been dedicated and loving parents since the day I was born, and, as educators and authors, they also provided mentorship, editorial feedback, and research assistance. Christine Reiser Robbins has shared unwavering love and companionship as my life partner each and every day, bringing out the best in me as a person and as a professional. Her insights and encouragement shaped this work significantly.

# Contents

# List of Abbreviations

| | |
|---|---|
| APL | American Protective League |
| BCEA | Building Construction Employers' Association |
| CCELA | Citizens' Committee to Enforce the Landis Award |
| CFAR | California Food Administration Records, National Archives Division, San Bruno, CA |
| *CT* | *Chicago Daily Tribune* |
| CTPA | Chicago Tenants Protective Association |
| DOJ | Department of Justice |
| DOJ-HCL | Records of the High Cost of Living Division, Department of Justice Records, RG 60, National Archives II, College Park, MD |
| LACCR | Los Angeles City Clerk's Office, Records Management Division, Los Angeles, CA |
| *LAT* | *Los Angeles Times* |
| MCU | Middle Class Union |
| MMC | Minute Men of the Constitution |
| NAWM | National Association of Wool Manufacturers |
| NCL | National Consumers' League |
| NCLR | National Consumers' League Records |
| NL | Newberry Library, Chicago, IL |
| *NYT* | *New York Times* |
| *RIBIC* | *Report of the Illinois Building Investigation Commission Authorized by the 52nd General Assembly* (Springfield: Illinois State Register Printers, 1923) |
| RPTPA | Rogers Park Tenants Protective Association |
| UCSCL | University of Chicago Special Collections Library |
| USFA | United States Food Administration |
| USFAR | United States Food Administration Records, Herbert Hoover Presidential Library, West Branch, IA |

# Introduction

The doctor sat patiently with a revolver in his hand. His seat was familiar, one that he had taken frequently over the past few days. It faced the front door of his apartment, which he had barricaded with chains and a piano. Dr. L. C. Zeigler did not live in a dangerous area, but on May 1, 1921, his neighborhood on Chicago's North End had become filled with tension. Like many of his white-collar neighbors, Zeigler and his landlord had developed a contentious relationship during the previous months. The trouble began when Zeigler's landlord informed him that he would increase his rent by 60 percent at the end of the lease. Infuriated, Zeigler publicly criticized his landlord in the press and through window placards.[1]

The situation only escalated when his landlord responded. To counteract Zeigler's criticism, he placed a poster in his own apartment window reading, "For Rent—Second floor, after April 30. Do not desire present tenant to stay there after, under any conditions." Upon the appearance of this new poster, residents of the neighborhood flocked to the street and sidewalks surrounding Zeigler's home. One account proclaimed, "Passing motorists stopped their machines. Traffic was soon at a standstill. Crowds congregated." A man shouted, "Three rousing cheers for Dr. Zeigler." Another person declared, "We want Doc. Zeigler. Bring him on. Speech! Hurray for Doc. Zeigler." Zeigler came to his window and aired his grievances. Applause followed. A local hero, Zeigler remained steadfast in his refusal to move out. Two weeks later, when Zeigler awoke to find his window broken and his placard missing, he created a new one with a brasher message: "Warning—This sign is hung with hairspring automatic guns, suspended at each corner and can be discharged only by an attempt to steal the sign again."[2]

Zeigler was not alone. Collectively, white-collar tenants who were part of the nearby self-proclaimed "middle class" Rogers Park Tenants Protective

Association displayed placards that referred to their landlords as "rent hogs" and "profiteers." Members of the organization lamented how high rents had threatened their ability to afford a middle-class lifestyle in a middle-class neighborhood. The association declared a "rent strike" for May 1, hoping that their collective refusal to move out would flood the municipal courts with forcible detainer cases, and convince the local and state governments to enact rent reform. On May 1, Zeigler fired a shot at a new tenant attempting to move in to his residence. Unharmed, the new tenant fled and Zeigler continued to wait. Local middle-class consumer activism moved closer and closer to its pinnacle.[3]

The much discussed "high cost of living" of the late 1910s prompted widespread middle-class consumer organizing, of which Zeigler was only one small part. Throughout the decade, Americans encountered substantial price increases for the "necessaries of life." Between 1913 and 1919, retail food prices escalated by 86 percent and average rents rose by 11 percent from 1914 to 1919 with substantial fluctuations occurring in 1919–20. Retail clothing and other dry goods prices exhibited even more drastic trends, climbing by an average of 223 percent from 1915 to 1919. Meanwhile, as the average working-class wage rose by approximately 55 percent between 1913 and 1919, white-collar salaries remained stagnant.[4]

By the immediate postwar period, middle-class Americans were livid. John R. Patterson, a librarian and the president of the Rogers Park Tenants Protective Association, expressed this common frustration. Testifying before a Senate Committee on Reconstruction and Production, Patterson declared that Americans "forget" the hardships of "the so-called middle class, the so-called white collar class . . . the class that is suffering." In his well-publicized book *Return of the Middle Class* (1922), contemporary commentator John Corbin identified the middle class as the "Forgotten Folk." Victims of the postwar political economy, the middle class disproportionately suffered from skyrocketing prices for food, clothing, housing, and other commodities. Corbin characterized the strain that the high cost of living placed on white-collar citizens' growing consumer identity as "the tragedy of the new poor."[5]

In this book, I explore how white-collar Americans responded to this strain by organizing politically as "the middle class," representing their economic interests as those of the public, and even claiming to *be* the public. While their organization efforts eventually faded, a self-interested consumerist politics that cast the middle class as the centerpiece of the nation continued to be a fixture in American society for years to come.

## White-Collar Workers and Consumer Organizing

The composition of the middle class underwent significant change throughout the late nineteenth and early twentieth centuries. A smaller nineteenth-century middle class had consisted mostly of what many scholars have termed the "old middle class." They were primarily owner-operators and skilled artisans, who usually held a producer-centered worldview, in which they identified more through work than consumption. They commonly associated the values of honesty, thrift, manhood, diligence, and democracy with either working the land or creating a product. From 1880 to 1920, the number of white-collar workers swelled by approximately 200 percent relative to the population, counting among their ranks, retail clerks, bookkeepers, stenographers, accountants, lawyers, doctors, and other clerical and professional workers. In contrast to the "old middle class," they largely did not produce goods with their hands, instead working in office buildings, classrooms, and stores. They held a complex, dynamic, and varied relationship to the categories of the producer and consumer.[6]

A number of these white-collar workers maintained a close connection with the priorities and organizing practices of working-class producers. First-generation white-collar teachers often sought to assert the "trade-union values" of their fathers onto their white-collar work, and affiliated with the American Federation of Labor. Yet, as Marjorie Murphy notes, many of them simultaneously grasped "at the values of their new social status, embracing middle-class ideals of respectability."[7] The department store saleswomen discussed in Susan Porter Benson's *Counter Cultures* also experienced contradictions in their class identity. They undertook what society widely considered white-collar work, in which managers asked them to act in accordance with middle-class culture to sell merchandise effectively to middle-class customers, but came from largely working-class environments and received low pay. They related to their customers through a gendered "domestic culture," but diverged from them in their expression of a "worker culture."[8]

However, many white-collar workers more firmly distanced themselves from working-class environments and priorities, as well as from the labor movement. Managers, brokers, and attorneys generally received higher compensation, performed less physically demanding labor, and held more prestigious jobs than blue-collar workers. The nature of professions under the "business clerk" category, including penmen, bookkeepers, and many sales agents often led these workers to identify more with capital than labor. As Michael Zakim notes, they "owed their existence" to "the capitalist transformation of both the countryside and the city."[9] Because their work days consisted of recording and managing financial transactions they were comfortable with selling their labor as a commodity, and broadened their definition of producerism to extend beyond working the land or creating a product. Poorer male clerks and salespersons—what Jerome P. Bjelopera terms "lower-level white-collar workers"—often did not receive higher pay than skilled blue-collar laborers, but in many cases more strongly identified with higher-level white-collar workers. As Bjelopera argues, because they believed that their positions as clerks could provide upward professional mobility, "lower-level white-collar workers tended to identify with those higher on the social and economic scale."[10] Even though a number of male retail clerks came from working-class backgrounds and some affiliated with the American Federation of Labor, many others eschewed the labor movement, instead identifying with those above as fellow members of the middle class.

As the United States became more deeply a consumer society in the late nineteenth and early twentieth centuries, white-collar workers ranging from sales clerks to managers, developed, to a large extent, a common "middle class" identity through their consumer aspirations and behavior. Lower-level white-collar workers (sales clerks and many office workers) and higher-level managers participated in the same consumer-based leisure activities together, which, according to Bjelopera, "indicates the enchantment that middle-class life held for clerks and salespeople." As Carole Srole notes, many male stenographers asserted their middle-class identity and differentiated themselves from the working-class by wearing work clothing that projected a blend of masculinity and respectability, and through their attachment to particular middle-class cultural narratives of independence and professionalism. Consumption habits in the home also marked a middle-class status. As Marina Moskowitz notes, middle-class Americans aspired to a "standard of living" that consisted of owning a variety of consumer goods for display in specific areas of the home as "a measure of the middle class." Advertisements, fiction, magazines, and other cultural media represented and popularized these markers of middle-class identity to construct "a national community with a shared standard of living." Even if a number of white-collar workers and their families came from working-class backgrounds and had varied markers of identity, many of them formed a significant part of their middle class subjectivity based on these common consumer practices.[11]

When the post–World War I high cost of living threatened their ability to consume up to the standards of a middle-class lifestyle, they often blamed the working class. As white-collar workers read daily reports of widespread labor strikes for increased earning power, they reflected on their own struggles to meet rising living costs. Many of these middle-class Americans suggested that each strike or pay raise for manual laborers inflated prices for consumers. To make matters worse, throughout the beginning decades of the twentieth century, cheaper consumer goods increasingly blurred many cultural class distinctions between the white-collar and working classes. Mass-produced clothing, single-family homes with a variety of furnishings, and new forms of entertainment became affordable for a wider range of Americans, leading to middle-class resentment of working-class indulgence. As John Corbin declared, "The war had obliterated untold billions of the world's wealth; yet never in times of fat prosperity were luxuries more eagerly consumed. But not by the salaried brain worker, nor yet the professional man—the educator, the physician, the clergyman." While the rich remained rich and laborers seemingly enjoyed a better lifestyle, Corbin queried, "But what distinction have the Forgotten Folk with which to feed their inward pride?" Or, as one middle-class consumer activist proclaimed, "the members of labor unions receive large incomes," while "the middle class suffers in silence."[12]

Elite "profiteers," who were defined as manufacturers, retailers, and middlemen who made excessive profits, shared an equal part of the blame for high prices in the eyes of many middle-class consumers. A 1920 *New York Times* article noted that both organized labor and the "profiteer" had ground middle-class Americans into a "pulp." The statements of white-collar citizens reflected similar outrage over the exploits of profiteers. Los Angeles real estate broker Newton M. Allen wrote the Los Angeles City Council to demand that the government "send every profiteer to jail," while a New York drama critic and writer, resented high prices for the middle class due to "tyranny and greed," singling out as culprits "oppressive pork packers," "particular landlords . . . [who are] sordid beasts," and "unnecessary middlemen." Across the United States, many white-collar workers commonly associated their grievances as consumers, and their disdain for profiteers, with a cultural sense of themselves as the middle class.[13]

In this climate, middle-class consumers undertook an unprecedented attempt at organization to protect their pocketbooks and assert their vision of a just economy. They formed home garden committees and pressed for municipal markets to combat rising food prices. They founded "wear overalls clubs," in which members agreed to don only the garb of diligent labor, to bring down the cost of clothing. White-collar Americans also organized the first "middle class" tenant associations to protect themselves from rent increases, and even attempted to establish a "middle class union" to unite all middle-class consumer organizing movements. Observing the growing power of the middle class, Vice President Thomas R. Marshall de-

This cartoon, "Keep 'Em in Balance," is a representation of a growing post–World War I discourse that suggested that capital and labor had profited at the expense of the middle class, and that justice would be achieved by paying attention to the concerns of middle-class consumers. (*Corpus Christi Caller*, February 18, 1920.)

clared, "There is a great middle class in America who have had nothing to do with these special privileges [of high wages and profits] otherwise than that they happened to live in the Republic when they were granted." But, "they are rapidly coming together"; they are "The Awakening Middle Class." John Corbin concluded his introductory chapter to *The Return of the Middle Class* by optimistically exclaiming that "in the years since peace began to rage among us, the sheer might of economic pressure has forced 'the public' . . . to a sense of its rights—and its power." Through anti-high-price agitation and "buyers strikes," he indicated, "the Forgotten Folk are remembering themselves."[14]

This moment of white-collar consumer organizing helped to establish popular representations of the middle class as the central class in American politics and society over the course of the twentieth century. During the post–World War I recession, citizens, newspapers, and politicians reflected on the middle class's growing importance in society, and described it as "the public," "the people," and the "middle class majority." C. L. Elliott was just one white-collar citizen to do so claiming, "We, the middle-class, are the chief consumers," "the majority and the backbone and the gray matter of the country." Nearly two decades after that era, *New York Times* journalist Francis Brown proclaimed that "America . . . is a middle class nation" wherein consumption largely shaped people's identities. They had "a desire that [their] children go to college, that a new automobile be parked in front of the house, that homes be furnished in the approved fashion, that clothes, whatever else they are, shall be in style." This book examines the emergence of this political and cultural discourse in the immediate postwar period, exploring how the middle class used consumption to proclaim itself the centerpiece of American economic and political life.[15]

Even as consumption increasingly defined people's belonging in the middle class, they expressed a connection to producerism and producerist values, often with ambivalence and tension. Whether wearing overalls with a collared shirt underneath in 1920, or, decades later, driving pickup trucks from office jobs to the suburbs, twentieth-century white-collar workers continually found the cultural imagery of the working class attractive to their identity. However, while middle-class Americans frequently attached themselves culturally to the worth and ruggedness of the producer image, their actions and attitudes toward working-class producers often undermined rather than supported producers' lives. To protect their ability to comfortably consume, middle-class Americans attacked labor by calling for lower blue-collar wages, harder work, and the open shop. As Rev. Gilbert Wilson declared while advocating the wearing overalls as a symbol of protest at an April 1920 church service in Chicago, the "high cost of living" was to a large extent attributable to "the rise in wages and the failure of producers to produce." According to Wilson, America needed a return to "the old fashioned economy" of its producerist past. The implications of this middle-class pursuit of low prices reached a crisis moment for working-class Americans in the immediate postwar period, and persisted as an ongoing debate for many years to come as Americans discussed and contested what kinds of people and values rightfully belonged in the middle class.[16]

In imagining themselves as members of the "middle class" in the postwar period, many white-collar activists forged a category of "middle class" that simultaneously had a wide rhetorical reach and specifically defined boundaries. On the one hand, they constructed seemingly clear boundaries by positing themselves against labor, as well as against profiteering elites. However, as Patrick Joyce and Dror Wahrman have noted, the culturally constructed language of class often has been intertwined with a variety of unstable and elusive political and cultural meanings. Joyce suggests that by embracing terms like "middle class," historical actors might be embracing "a political or social vocabulary with 'the nation' and 'the people' at its centre." The activists discussed in this book, driven by the historical contexts of the high cost of living, the first red scare, an upsurge of labor unrest, and a growing consumer society, applied a blend of nationalistic, producerist, and consumerist identities to the term "middle class."[17] As a result, their activism, as they and many others imagined it, carried multiple meanings and expressed the broad, but strong, rhetorical power that was associated with each of these cultural identities.

In this book, I analyze the emergence of this organized self-interested middle-class politicization of consumer identity. How did this class—so frequently described as the public and the fabric of America—come to be defined as "the people"? How did they politicize consumption to protect their own economic needs under the guise of it being a neutral defense of the public? According to what justifications did they more firmly establish themselves as arbiters of economic justice on behalf of the public? My consideration of these questions draws not on my own theoretical criteria for how to define the middle class, but, rather, on the basis of how white-collar workers defined themselves as the middle class. This examination of white-collar workers' self-expressions of middle-class identity will draw on analysis of the power and shifting nature of consumer and producer identities, the legacies of Progressive Era reform movements, and the historical possibilities of using government action to assert economic justice.

## Consumer and Producer Identities

Historians have discussed middle-class consumer identity as emerging in the early twentieth century and crystallizing in the post–World War II period. By analyzing the political strategies and cultural symbols invoked in these movements, I argue that the politically conscious consumer identity so critical to middle-class life throughout the twentieth century developed as one selectively infused with the ideals of an older producerism.[18] While middle-class Americans confronted a growing consumer economy, they looked to and idealized the industriousness and thrift of nineteenth-century citizens and appropriated symbols of hard work from the working class. Whether condemning the laziness or spendthrift ways of labor organizations during strikes, the unproductiveness of middlemen, or the greed of elites, they portrayed their sense of economic fairness as universal. Their activism represented a bold endeavor by middle-class citizens to define a consumerist politics as an impartial and righteous defense of "the public" against selfish groups, who demanded, charged, or spent excessive amounts of money. It was through their consumer identity and opportunistic use of "neutral" producerist values that white-collar workers and their families saw themselves as part of a large and powerful middle class and positioned the public interest as their own.

This book builds on previous scholarship examining the relationship between class and consumption in twentieth-century American history. Labor historians have explored how wage earners and their families used consumption as an organizing strategy to achieve better working conditions, higher pay, or lower prices in the early twentieth century. Works analyzing the relationship between consumption and the middle class, however, have given only limited treatment to the role that consumption played in forming an active middle-class political identity as early as the 1910s and 1920s. Rather, historians have focused on the politics of middle-class consumer identity when it became fully entrenched after World War II. Much of the scholarship on the early 1900s eschews politics, instead discussing the development of a "middle class" lifestyle based on a shared culture of consumption of products ranging from clothing to furniture.[19] These works have added significantly to our understandings of middle-class consumer identity, but they have not explored how this identity was politically mobilized. Rather than influencing middle-class Americans to direct their energies inward and disengage from politics, consumption served as the primary means through which they developed an outward middle-class political identity.[20] Works that do analyze outward expressions of middle-class consumer politics in the early twentieth century generally focus on progressives, who used consumerist political strategies, such as boycotts and product labeling, in the name of justice for the working class and the urban poor.

Instead, this book differs from previous interpretations by arguing that middle-class Americans organized on a national scale in defense of their own exclusive interests as early as the immediate post–World War I period. This effort lasted only a few years (primarily 1919–21), but it represented the largest self-identified "middle class" organizing movement then to date, and provides an important window into larger changes in the meaning of middle-class identity over time. During this moment of transition in middle-class identity, white-collar Americans combined consumerist and producerist discourses, symbols, and styles of protest, to shape their class identity in the post–World War I period. While organizing as consumers, middle-class citizens championed the values and symbols of diligent production. They condemned the supposedly indolent working class for lacking proper producerist values even as their primary grievance was the impact that strikes and underproduction had on middle-class *consumer* needs. They accused workers of going on strike for wages that would bring them lives of luxury at the expense of the middle class. Refiguring a nineteenth-century producer-centered worldview that celebrated honest hard work and thrift, they used the seemingly universally neutral language of defending producer values to promote their vision of justice in the growing consumer society. Much like many middle-class citizens in the following decades, they did so while claiming to be the nucleus of American society.[21] As Dr. Otto P. Geier proclaimed of the "the great middle class" in an article examining their struggles to meet the high cost of medical care, they are "the backbone of the nation."[22]

At the same time, middle-class consumer activists appropriated symbols and strategies of productive labor from the working class. They chose overalls, a symbol of hard work, as the centerpiece of their activism against the high cost of clothing. In localities ranging from New York City to Lansing, Michigan, white-collar Americans formed "wear overalls clubs," and paraded in overalls down the streets, vowing to wear them until prices returned to reasonable levels. Overalls club members promoted the value of industriousness as they put on the "uniform of manual labor" to "signal for America to return to work." White-collar Americans also formed the first middle-class tenants' unions and called "rent strikes," a strategy hitherto only used by the working class to fight escalating rents. Perhaps most representative of middle-class attachment to producerism, "tiring of their unenviable role of helpless consumers," they "turned the tables on the food purveyors by turning producers" and planted their own gardens.[23]

## Projecting a Blue-Collar Nemesis and Middle-Class Political Directions in the Postwar Period

Even though middle-class activists appropriated working-class culture, ranging from fashion choices to organizing strategies, an ideology of antipathy toward the working class accompanied these practices. Whereas this book demonstrates how middle-class Americans established themselves as distinct from the working class, recently historians have emphasized the fluidity between the middle and working classes, sometimes united by distaste for rising prices or a mutual opposition to trusts. I explore a different strand of middle-class politics, and argue that because many white-collar Americans believed that wage increases and labor unrest contributed to high prices, they identified labor unions as a distinct enemy, equal to that of corporate trusts. Music teacher Fred Haight, for instance, proclaimed, "Labor is certainly getting its rake off now and we are paying. Always the common people are paying one way or another. Labor unions are very strong and they are playing the game to the limit using every ounce of their gigantic power."[24] Indeed, in the immediate postwar period, Americans witnessed massive labor unrest and a substantial upsurge in the number of strikes. In 1919, 4,160,000 workers, or 22.5 percent of all workers, went on strike, more than triple the percentage of the previous year.[25] In letters to the editor, fraternal lodge bulletins, diaries, and personal correspondence, white-collar citizens pointed to the laziness, underproduction, and greed of the producing class as a reason for high prices. Corbin summed up these feelings, writing, "Labor is organized, class-conscious; it takes its own abundantly" from "the great range of folk between." The solution, according to many middle-class Americans, was to demonstrate their own producer values and strike as consumers until the working class lived up to a middle-class paragon of hard work.[26]

Their antilabor actions took on additional meaning in the context of the first red scare. In the aftermath of the Bolshevik Revolution, when bolshevism spread across much of Russia in less than a year, many Americans worried that radical threats to their own political and cultural institutions could emerge quickly and from a variety of places. Their fears were fed by widespread ideological opposition to socialism, the Bolshevik government's signing of a peace treaty with the Central Powers while American and other Allied soldiers were still fighting, and the U.S. government's repression of alleged domestic radicals through actions ranging from deportations to judicial crackdowns on strikes.

In this climate, antiradical language came to express a number of cultural anxieties relating to race, class, sexuality, and, in the case of middle-class consumer activists and their sympathizers, tensions in the shifting meaning of consumption and producerism.[27] Expressing some of these anxieties in a 1920 editorial, the *Beatrice (NE) Sun* proclaimed that the "great middle class," who "neither gouge the people by profiteering, nor clamor for revolution," and who "go to work," participate in the institutions of "church," "the lodge" and family life, reject "the doctrines of less effort and more enjoyment," and exercise thrift by "sav[ing] enough from the family income," are not "carried away by the soap box philosophy of those who preach the dictatorship of the proletariat." As long as they "hold the reins of power in the long run," the *Sun* continued, "the country will be safe." In fact, some commentators suggested that bolshevism had taken hold in Russia because it lacked an extensive, empowered, or democratically minded middle class. An article in the *Shiner (TX) Gazette* asserted that "Russia's downfall was due primarily to the fact that there was no adequate middle class," while the *Cincinnati Enquirer* declared that the "great middle class" in Russia had been "despised, insulted, robbed and even murdered." Taken together, this popular antiradical discourse suggested that the middle class embodied America's sacred values, and that its existence and power were critical to the defense of these values from radical threats.[28]

Despite having faith in both the moral might of their producerist values and the economic power that they held as consumers, middle-class Americans still expected a great deal of change to come from government. They had seen local, state and federal government power grow during the Progressive Era in the name of creating a fairer economy and political system, whether it meant limiting political corruption or monitoring food safety. They had also experienced the power of state-centered voluntarism during World War I, when they participated in unprecedented government campaigns to conserve food for the war effort. In the postwar period they expected an aggressive government to achieve success in lowering prices and establishing a supposedly impartial middle-class vision of economic justice. Their consumer organizing in this moment represented an important additional step toward the often state-centered middle-class activism of the 1930s and beyond.

With their eyes on the state, the middle-class activists discussed in this book generally expressed neither entirely radical nor entirely conservative political identities. On the one hand, they lobbied for more government intervention into the economy in ways that resembled the regulatory impulses of both progressivism and the later New Deal state. However, their emphasis on returning to a "traditional" America defined by honest hard work, self-reliance, and thrift supported a culturally conservative politics. While disapproving of the unfairness of the existing economy, they did not advocate a radical overhaul of the system. They blamed strikers and profiteers for the high cost of living rather than capitalism itself. The experiences of middle-class Americans in this book contrast with Robert D. Johnston's influential narrative of the early twentieth-century middle class.[29] According to Johnston, middle-class Americans in his case study of Portland, Oregon, allied with laborers and promulgated a "radical" "anti-capitalist" populism through antivaccinationism, single-tax agitation, and the *Portland Labor Press*. Conversely, the organizing middle-class consumers represented in this book were critical of an economy seen to be dominated by *both* striking laborers and elite profiteers, and largely did not criticize the system itself. They sought protection from these groups, but from within the existing economic structure and through existing political institutions and actors. They claimed to be protecting traditional, conservative values, such as thrift, honest hard work, and "middle class" notions of marriage and family life.[30]

In fact, despite also playing to liberal strands of American politics by calling for more state action, middle-class consumer activists empowered the conservative business leaders, politicians, and discourse that came to characterize much of the political history of the 1920s. In the postwar period, the United States largely moved away from Wilsonian progressivism and the strong role of a wartime government to what Warren G. Harding championed as a "return to normalcy," under which many of the nation's political leaders ceased to aggressively regulate business and failed to support many workers' desire for collectively bargaining. Abetting this trend, business conservatives holding political offices ultimately responded to middle-class consumer activists' call for the government to do more to bring about economic justice by proclaiming their faith in the people to independently effect change. Their willingness to expand the government's role in the economy was mostly limited to using it to weaken labor unions. Although conservative business leaders were often denounced by middle-class consumer activists for alleged profiteering, they found common ground with them by criticizing union greed, corruption, and indolence, and used this rhetoric to reduce the power of the labor movement. These politicians and business leaders came from both parties, thus empowering both the business conservatism of Republicans and the conservative wing of the fragmented 1920s Democratic Party.[31]

In the 1930s, middle-class Americans expressed multiple strands of activism that reflected both the immediate context of the Depression and the strategic and cultural forms of the earlier post–World War I activism. Some organizations, like the American Majority, the leader of which the *New Republic* characterized as a "Rabble Rouser of the Right," continued to embrace culturally conservative rhetoric. Others advanced a largely pro-labor solution to the Depression by attempting to join hands with the working class in a call for higher wages to stimulate the economy from the bottom up.[32]

The seemingly contradictory political actions and legacies of postwar middle-class consumer activism illustrate what scholars have characterized as a significant gray area in the political identification and behavior of many middle-class Americans in the early twentieth century. Eschewing the categories of "Left" and "Right," David A. Horowitz notes how historical actors from a variety of backgrounds and a range of organizational and political affiliations have become insurgents in "conflicts over concentrated power and centralized authority," while simultaneously attaching themselves and their activism to traditionalist discourses and producer values.[33] His work builds on the insights of David Thelen, who, as Horowitz observes, has noted "the power of tradition to inspire resistance," and Jackson Lears, who suggests that "the most profound radicalism is often the most profound conservatism."[34] In their activism against the seeming concentrated power of labor unions and elites, the middle class of this book came together in part through a mutual celebration of the cultural value of diligent production and an attachment to overalls, as a romanticized symbol of a producerist past. As Rev. Jesse Halsey, pastor of Cincinnati's Seventh Presbyterian Church, declared in an effort to expand the overall movement, "it represents a return to fundamental American ideals, it is an expression of a willingness to work for what one obtains, a readiness to cast off the finery and to become sensible, industrious citizens."[35] Their activism, tied to flexible and nationalistic cultural symbols and sentiments, and to an ideology of traditionalism, did not reflect only one strand of American politics. Instead, it reflected and empowered multiple political parties and ideologies. Middle-class consumer activists were insurgents, traditionalists, and mainstream members of major political parties, all at the same time. They were capable of advancing each of these historical identities even if in contradiction.

• This book interweaves a local and national approach in chronicling middle-class consumer activism in the postwar period. Because consumer organizing often occurred at the grassroots level—in city parks, meeting halls, school auditoriums, and backyards—I formulated much of this work around local case studies in cities, such as Los Angeles, Chicago, and St. Petersburg, Florida. By studying the history of social movements at the local level, we gain not only a better understanding of the local and spatial contexts that made them meaningful but also a more detailed sense of their potential.

Local middle-class consumer activism both drew on and fueled a national discursive space of middle-class consumer activism. As Lawrence Glickman has aptly pointed out, modern consumer activism has been "defined by efforts to coordinate the consumption of like-minded but not necessarily proximate people."[36] The consumerist discursive space that fed postwar middle-class activism drew on a long-developing expression of nationalism predicated on shared consumption, which, as early as the pre-Revolutionary era, had provided a means for people to "become" American and forge a common language and mode of protest. As Benedict Anderson notes, nationalistic expressions of community have depended on shared literary media that allow community to transcend physical space, and which have tacitly or directly defined an "imagined community" against an oppositional other.[37] Writers in national magazines and other purveyors of popular culture in the post–World War I period forged this middle-class consumerist space through expressions in print media, music, film, and theater, which collectively cast the United States as a middle-class nation, and reified labor unions and elite profiteers as threats to the middle class's common consumer identity and its values. Woven into this discursive space was also a symbolic space of whiteness, wherein the "middle class" and its consumer behavior were represented as both white and white collar. Depictions of the supposed threats to their consumer identity often took shape through racialized language and images, from "cunning" Japanese food merchants to nonproducing European immigrant workers.[38]

In this book, the discursive space of middle-class protest and the local activists who organized in geographically defined spaces are both important; they were mutually reinforcing. Writers, commentators, politicians, musicians, and actors all popularized middle-class consumers as victims of the postwar economy, thereby building a national discursive space of middle-class consumer activism. They actively and tacitly encouraged middle-class Americans to form overalls clubs, join tenant associations, plant home gardens, and condemn labor unions and profiteers. Concurrently, overalls club members, municipal market patrons, home gardeners, rent strikers, and sympathetic politicians in localities ranging from Birmingham to Detroit spoke of the plight of the middle class and denounced profiteers and laborers. In doing so, they contributed to the national discursive space of middle-class consumer activism, which covered their activities and tied them together as part of a common narrative. For instance, a *Literary Digest* article titled "A Nation in Overalls" synthesized examples of the actions and statements of specific overall clubs, as well as coverage of the movement in local newspapers. Similarly, an article in *Chicago Daily Tribune* interwove under the headline "A New Dawn for the Middle Classes" a politician's advocacy of a middle class union, tenant activism in New York, New Jersey, and Chicago, and public opposition to the 1919 steel strike. The popular writings and art forms that made up this discursive space, the physical acts of consumption that represented the pursuit of a middle-class consumer lifestyle, and the organizing that occurred in local places are best understood not in isolation, but intertextually, as connected narratives, practices, and experiences. As Nan Enstad reminds us through her analysis of working women and popular culture in turn-of-the century America, this kind of interpretive framework provides a more complete understanding of the meaning of each text, experience, or act of consumption than does disconnected analysis.[39]

A symbiotic relationship between local movements and a broader discursive space of middle-class protest provided an important foundation for self-righteous middle-class consumer activism on a national level. Local forms of activism made national discussion meaningful to individual communities, and yet local activists and commentators also depended on a national discussion that normalized and legitimized their assertion that their consumer identity made them "the people" (or at least righteous protectors of them). In the post–World War I period, as white-collar Americans increasingly realized their shared place in society as consumers of the same types of goods, they politicized this consumer identity, and drew on the local and national spaces of protest that empowered them to proclaim themselves both impartial defenders of the public, and *the* public.

Participants in each movement believed that they were part of a broader movement to make the economy meet the ideals of middle-class consumers as "the people." Local overall club members, tenant activists, home gardeners, and municipal market supporters made reference to a general rise in middle-class organization, and cast their efforts as part of this trend. Middle-class Americans also took part in multiple consumer campaigns simultaneously. John R. Patterson, for example, was the president of the Chicago Tenants Protective Association, wore overalls, and discussed how middle-class consumers struggled to pay high prices in general. Nevertheless, in each campaign, participants centered their activism on individual commodities, particularly with reference to food, clothing, and housing. Accordingly, this book focuses on consumer movements relating to these three commodities, and will show how the personal choices of what to eat, what to wear, and where to live carried significant political implications for how many Americans developed conceptions of national and local community through class. I have chosen to discuss each of these movements separately and often in specific localities, because unique stories highlight why individuals ranging from Baptist ministers to city mayors found overalls a useful symbol of protest against rising clothing prices; why middle-class Chicagoans chose both typical and specific culprits for rent increases; or why the strategy of state-sponsored home gardening resonated especially with the Los Angeles middle class. Yet, whether attending a tenants' meeting, digging up a backyard, or wearing overalls, they understood themselves to be part of the same story.

It is a story of the political, cultural, and social identities of many middle-class Americans in their greatest moment of class consciousness then to date. In the following pages, I argue that, even though this book focuses largely on a relatively short period of time (chiefly 1919–21), the immediate postwar period was a pivotal moment in the development of middle-class consumer politics. I contend that in the postwar period, middle-class Americans developed and organized around a shared identity that simultaneously reflected their acceptance of their roles as consumers and their ambivalence toward the actual characteristics of the consumer society. Middle-class Americans sought to impose a set of "universal" producerist values on a consumer economy that seemingly favored the working and elite classes. They drew on the Progressive Era organizing strategy of state-centered voluntarism, and called for an even more direct state intervention into the market, while simultaneously using culturally conservative rhetoric. Rather than embracing progressive goals, they separated themselves from the working class, and organized on behalf of their own self-interested values. These values, they asserted, were the moral values not only of consumers, but those of "the people."

# 1 • Politicizing Consumption in the Community

## Middle-Class Consumer Organizing during the Progressive Era and World War I

On September 20, 1918, Helen R. Kenealy, the wife of an accountant, and volunteer for the Los Angeles branch of the U.S. Food Administration, reported a "flagrant evasion of the rules of the Food Administration." According to Kenealy, a woman entered her office and requested a permit for 50 to 60 pounds of sugar "for the purpose of making grape juice for use as communion" in the services of the "Little Church of Christ." Kenealy refused to issue the permit, citing insufficient reason given the necessity of wartime restrictions on consumption of sugar. When, four days later, Dr. W. B. Thompson, head of the church, requested a permit for 25 pounds of sugar for "canning purposes," Kenealy's "suspicions were aroused." She asked Thompson how he intended to use the sugar and he responded that he had a family of four to feed. Suspecting that Thompson had no family at all, Kenealy notified the head of the U.S. Food Administration for Los Angeles, Louis Cole. Inundated with other cases and administrative work, Cole sent the case to the L.A. American Protective League (APL), a federally sponsored group of mostly white-collar volunteers who investigated individuals suspected of subverting the war effort through food hoarding, profiteering, or other actions. After further inquiry, Los Angeles APL agents determined that Thompson had, indeed, lied about having a family and intended to use the sugar for his church. Found to be holding an excessive amount of sugar, Thompson was reprimanded under the Lever Food Control Act, which had made hoarding and profiteering federal crimes.[1]

As a volunteer organization with official power, the newly formed United States Food Administration (USFA) helped to mold and legitimize white-collar consumer organizing during the war. The Wilson administration had created the USFA during the summer and fall of 1917 to address rapidly advancing food prices and to conserve food for American troops and allies abroad. It used volunteers to aid in the supply, distribution, and conservation of food, and to prevent hoarding and profiteering. The USFA requested observance of many guidelines, ranging from "Wheatless Wednesdays" to "Meatless Tuesdays," and mandated sugar and flour conservation. USFA volunteers like Helen Kenealy or those working under their auspices coordinated with each other to police USFA measures in the own communities.

Many USFA volunteers organized not just to help win the war but also to assert a vision of economic justice shaped by producer values. They claimed to be diligent, honest, and thrifty consumers, and defined themselves against hoarders, labor agitators, and profiteers. They cast these producer values as simultaneously their own and those of a model American past, and argued that they should be adhered to universally in the present. As Jean Roberts Albert, a Chicago magazine publisher, suggested, "We need to curb our extravagant tastes" and "get back to the simple ways of living. . . . The time is ripe for teaching a sense of fitness and thrift, habits of living such as prevailed in the pioneer days, habits that built the strength of this nation. . . . The old time integrity of the nation is rapidly disappearing." Albert and many other USFA participants believed that the producer values of the past needed to define behavior in the emerging consumer society.[2]

Through USFA activities, Americans holding white-collar jobs and their families developed the makings of a middle-class *political* identity as consumers. Throughout the late nineteenth and early twentieth centuries, white-collar families had consumed in similar ways. They had lived in single family homes in many of the same neighborhoods, and had frequently bought the same styles of furniture, shopped at the same types of stores, ate similar foods, wore comparable clothing styles, and read many of the same magazines. Participation in the USFA encouraged many white-collar Americans to politicize their already shared consumption practices, and use producer values to define what was just or unjust in the economy. What they and their neighbors purchased and how much they paid increasingly became political issues. As a result of their engagement with the USFA, they developed a greater political consciousness as middle-class consumers in the postwar period, when continually increasing prices threatened their consumer-driven class identity and the producer values they had incorporated into it. Building on their wartime experiences, middle-class Americans in the postwar period would organize to demand economic justice on the basis of their version of seemingly neutral and nationalistic principles.

## Consumer Organizing on the Eve of World War I

The formation of the USFA came on the heels of a period of rapid economic and demographic change, reform-minded public activism, and expanded government power. Between 1870 and 1900, the growth of industries, such as bituminous coal, petroleum, steel, and manufacturing, helped to cause a simultaneous increase in the urban population from 9.9 million to 30.1 million. Accompanying these changes were a number of growing problems, including poverty, unsanitary neighborhoods, and labor unrest. Progressive Era organizations, many led by the country's growing middle class, aimed to help the working class by lobbying federal, state, and local governments to address injustices brought on by industrial America. Progressives successfully convinced these governments to play an increasingly active role in the economy, introducing new regulations on the market ranging from milk and meat inspection to antitrust legislation. Coinciding with these efforts at economic regulation, as one scholar notes, a number of progressives (often on a bipartisan basis) focused on employing the initiative and referendum to "circumvent" corrupt political bosses and "reinvigorate a responsible middle-class citizenry."[3]

As part of the progressive movement, some middle-class Americans altered their consumption habits to pressure the state to help usher in a more just economy for the working class.[4] Most notably, members of the predominantly white, middle-class National Consumers' League (NCL) led boycotts of products that were made under unfair labor practices. Along with consumer activism, the NCL lobbied for protective labor legislation and published books on the subject, such as *A New Province for Law and Order: Industrial Peace through Minimum Wage and Arbitration* and *The Waste of Industry, Overworked Women and Girls, Ill Health, Danger, Low Wages. Some Reasons Why Protective Laws for Women in Industry are Necessary*. The NCL and other progressive organizations that used consumption as a political weapon generally sought to join hands with the working class to improve society as they saw fit, though often neglecting to follow the lead of the labor unions formed by workers themselves.[5]

Even as progressives aimed to work on behalf of producers, Americans increasingly saw the consumer as having legitimate and defensible interests. Nineteenth-century classical liberal ideology had placed the producer at the forefront of the political economy. Consumption often had represented a sign of moral laxity and lack of commitment to hard work and discipline, so much so that the "consumer" was largely a pejorative term. However, by the 1910s and '20s popular liberal writers began to consider how to construct the political economy to meet the consumer's needs. According to this view, prices, as much as wages, shaped considerations of what was economically fair. Representing this sentiment, a number of newspaper editorials printed headlines such as "Where Does the Consumer Come In?," "How to Lighten the Burden to the Consumer," and "Robbing the Consumer," each focusing on the impact of unfair prices on consumers.[6]

The price increases that came with the outbreak of World War I in Europe particularly jeopardized the interests of both working- and middle-class consumers. From January 1913 to October 1916, wholesale prices of all commodities rose by 34 percent, while retail food prices escalated by 23 percent. A glance at the streets of a few American cities would have spoken to the implications and urgency of the situation for working-class Americans. In Providence, Rhode Island, for example, during August and September of 1914, working-class residents of the city's Italian district responded to a "sudden rise in food prices" by attacking a local wholesaler. The incident expanded into a large-scale neighborhood protest led by socialists and the radical Industrial Workers of the World. After the riot, the underlying problem of high food prices remained.[7]

On the eve of U.S. entry into the war, food prices continued to climb, and additional working-class protests erupted throughout the country. Reports from Philadelphia chronicled "a crowd of women" who "rushed a fish store and upset a tank of live carp." Thousands participated, and an elderly woman was trampled. The *Chicago Daily Tribune* sarcastically declared, "If things are a bit slow in Chicago, why not import Sweet Marie and Mother Jones to start food riots of our own." Just months later, part of the paper's wish materialized, when hundreds of residents attacked "food grafters" and profiteers on the West Side, pouring kerosene on displays and throwing bricks at police officers. In New York City nearly 10,000 people stormed the streets and overturned pushcarts in response to rising food prices. A number of participants advocated socialism and blamed capitalism for their woes during a time in which some commentators suggested that American business was making excess profits off the war. These protests, deemed radical by politicians, newspapers, and many participants themselves, shaped the political and public discussion of the landmark federal food control legislation that would follow.[8]

Alarmed by the growing wave of unrest, Congress empowered the Federal Trade Commission to investigate "alleged manipulation of food prices" and debated legislation intending to stabilize food prices and discourage the continued growth of radical unrest: the Lever Food Control bill. Recalling the political urgency of the moment, one USFA booklet stated, "If there had been no prospect of lower food prices, no curb on speculation, 'upheaval' may well have ensued."[9]

## Targeting Hoarders, Profiteers, and Labor: The Development of the Lever Act

As working-class protests reached American streets, white-collar citizens looked to multiple levels of government for solutions to rising prices. The Consumers' League of Los Angeles requested that the L.A. City Council "pass a law to the effect that the City government shall control all food products and sell same to the public at moderate prices." Similarly, the white-collar East Jefferson Improvement Association and the "Los Angeles Housewives" asked that the city attorney "be instructed" to make foodstuffs a public utility "for relief against the high cost of living." A Chicago resident was one of many white-collar workers who expected action from the federal government. "In these urgent times there are many demands made on the average salaried man of family," the resident proclaimed. "But living expenses are mounting steadily and much faster than salaries. Several score millions of American citizens are looking to their government to regulate the price of food. . . . Let the government do its duty and at once." Using language that would become more common in the immediate postwar period, some white-collar Americans began to associate their concern over high food prices with a "middle class" identity. In support of a boycott by Tampa housewives and other residents who were protesting the high cost of potatoes and onions and calling for government price regulation, Reverend Paul B. Blanshard proclaimed, "The movement against the high cost of living demands the passion and sympathy of the women. . . . If once they are aroused to the meaning of the struggle of the middle classes they will make victory certain."[10]

The government at the highest level was prompted to act to address food prices. On April 11, 1917, Rep. Asbury Lever (D-South Carolina), chairman of the House Committee on Agriculture, met with President Wilson to consider introducing legislation that would become known as the "Lever bill" to discourage further unrest and help to control the cost of food.[11] Introduced in the House on June 11, 1917, the Lever bill provided the legal framework to set up the U.S. Food Administration, which would enlist volunteers among the American public to promote food conservation. It also contained key provisions seeking to prevent profiteering and speculation on foodstuffs through a licensing system and by criminalizing hoarding or destruction of food. The licensing system required that dealers of food whose annual sales exceeded $100,000 obtain licenses to conduct business. If a dealer proceeded to charge excessive prices or neglected to "keep all food commodities moving in as direct a line, as with as little delay as far as possible," it risked losing its license. In some cases, accused profiteers could even face jail time. According to one USFA document, these rules "aimed to eliminate various trade practices which tend to raise the price to the consumer." In effect, the Lever bill also fueled Americans' expectations during and after the war that the government could and should lower prices by prosecuting profiteers.[12]

Wilson and many congressmen and federal officials, concerned about speeding up war mobilization and alarmed by the recent wave of radical protests against high food prices, hoped to "rush" the Lever bill through Congress. With reporters present, George W. Anderson, a U.S. attorney and special assistant to the attorney general "in connection with the administration food control," declared to the House Agricultural Committee, "Something must be done. That social and political upheaval is threatened cannot be denied or disregarded. I see signs of it. Anyone with his ears to the ground knows it."[13] During House debates of the Lever bill, Rep. Sydney Anderson (R-Minnesota) worried about "social disturbances," while Rep. Lever warned of the "wrath" of the people if the legislation were to die in Congress. Rep. Harold Knutson (R-Minnesota) declared, "This congress must take immediate steps to effectively stop all sorts of speculation in all the necessaries of life or the American people will arise in their righteous indignation and repeat the performance of the Russian people." Applause followed his remarks. Heightening matters were reports of unrest abroad, such as the discontent occurring in Norway, of which an American newspaper wrote, "one of the gains [in socialist activity] has been the high cost of living, and many of the middle-class people whose wages have not increased proportionately have gone over to the socialist platform." Many congressional leaders believed that without the Lever bill high prices might radicalize the country and cause irreparable and widespread disorder.[14]

Nevertheless, the Lever bill faced strong opposition. Opponents of the bill admonished the country not to go down the path of "autocracy," and preferred to call Herbert Hoover, the prospective head food administrator, "the food dictator," a label Hoover despised. Chief among the bill's opponents was Senator James Reed (D-Missouri), who called the bill "despotic and unconstitutional," and claimed Hoover's power would exceed that of "a king, a potentate, a Czar, a Caesar, or a Kaiser." Unsurprisingly, Woodrow Wilson characterized the process to Hoover as "tedious and vexatious."[15]

In response, the proponents of the bill justified the measure not just by referencing the potential for domestic unrest, but also by reifying hoarders and profiteers as villains that caused high prices. During a House debate, Rep. Lever declared, "Milk, the food of the babies of America, in April, 1914, sold at 9 cents per can. In April, 1917, it sold at 15 cents per can, or a 67 per cent increase. . . . there is no reason on earth except that manipulators are controlling it." Lever proceeded to reference the "hysteria" in hoarding necessities and "wild speculation." Rep. Anderson spoke of the "manipulation of the speculator" and Rep. Knutson exceeded the intensity of either Lever or Anderson's rhetoric. In a passionate speech on the House floor, Knutson exclaimed that the proposed Lever bill did not even go far enough to prevent the profiteering of "food speculators and pirates."[16]

Congressional supporters of the Lever bill also connected antiprofiteering sentiment to patriotism. Rep. Anderson called profiteers "unpatriotic" and "vicious." But his words did not match the extreme statements made by other members of the House and Senate, including Rep. W. Frank James (R-Michigan). James proclaimed, "The man who to-day charges an exorbitant price on the necessaries of life puts himself into the class of Benedict Arnold." He concluded that "[t]here is only one way to stop these vultures in human form from preying on our people, and that is to place the control of food in the Government, the same as the Lever bill will do." Supportive newspapers were equally blunt. For example, underscoring the threat of high prices to American democracy, the *Chicago Daily Tribune* stated, "The revolution in Russia began with the food riots. . . . we certainly must guard against promoting any such condition in this country."[17]

In congressional debates on the Lever bill, federal lawmakers associated patriotism with the producer values of hard work and thrift. Senator Frank Kellogg (R- Minnesota), for instance, discussed the need for the government to "encourage industry and thrift" and "control material resources." Those opposed to the bill also spoke of conservation in producerist language, even if disagreeing on how to use the federal government to facilitate it. Senator Reed declared that "every man must be encouraged to produce" as he emphasized the need to "rigidly punish" people who exhibited unfair consumer behavior such as "hoarding" and "gambling." Whether in favor of or against the Lever bill, federal politicians tended to portray consumption as a political act, which could either affirm or deny one's patriotism and producer values.[18]

Congressmen debating the Lever bill also underscored the need to stabilize prices by curbing the wartime opportunism of blue-collar laborers, who allegedly strayed from American producer values. In addition to labor turnover, in 1917 the United States witnessed a 17 percent increase in the number of strikes from the previous year. Politicians and the press often portrayed workers as greedy and unproductive. During a debate in the House of Representatives, Rep. Simeon D. Fess (R-Ohio) expressed concern over the scarcity of farm labor, claiming that agricultural workers were chasing high wages and moving to cities to obtain them. Because of this, Fess declared, the country was experiencing heightened underproduction and high prices. Others, both politicians and private citizens, expressed similar feelings about workers, whether industrial or agricultural. As the Piqua, Ohio, *Daily Call* declared, "There is a pernicious feeling among many people that the war should enable them to get their bit rather than do their bit."[19]

Sensing a growing rhetoric against unions, labor leaders worried that the Lever bill would allow the U.S. government to prosecute laborers, not just profiteers, middlemen, or hoarders. In a June 27, 1917, letter to President Wilson, American Federation of Labor president Samuel Gompers wrote that while organized labor supported the "fundamental principles of the Lever Bill," under it "the ordinary organized activities of the workers engaged in an effort to maintain standards of work and life could be construed and stigmatized as conspiracies" to halt the production and distribution of food. Gompers was not alone. A letter from Herbert Hoover to Rep. Lever stated, "The labor representatives are very much exercised over the possible reading of the food-control bill to stretch to control wages." In fact, union leaders were concerned enough that a collection of labor-friendly representatives supported an amendment to the Lever bill to prevent its use against unions. The amendment failed by a vote of 152 to 45 and organized labor would suffer the consequences in the postwar period, when the increasingly politically conscious "middle class" "public" demanded that striking workers be brought to justice.[20] Fueled in part by an antilabor brand of producerist rhetoric, the Lever bill was signed into law on August 11, 1917. Shortly afterward, the newly created U.S. Food Administration began to officially solicit volunteers to disseminate and enforce its guidelines.

## Conservation and Consumer Organizing: The U.S. Food Administration

In passing the Lever Act, congressional supporters, along with the Wilson administration, suggested to Americans that high prices could be most effectively addressed through a combination of bringing hoarders and profiteers to justice and organizing consumers to practice and promote food conservation. In contrast to the working-class food protests that had permeated the nation, scores of middle-class Americans took part in what was a government-centered approach to stabilizing prices. The U.S. Food Administration, created by the Lever Act, consisted entirely of volunteers who were charged with the task of implementing the Lever Act's conservation provisions and with keeping an eye on the prices charged by retailers. As participants in the USFA and as consumers, middle-class Americans had high expectations for themselves, their neighbors, and their government to adhere to and enforce the consumer behavior that they and USFA leaders believed would reduce the cost of food. Reiterating this goal, W. F. Priebe, a USFA official, wrote in a publicly reported letter, "It is a fixed principle with the Food Administration that, taking the Nation as a whole, prices should be kept within reason, so that the middle classes may [be able to] purchase food stuffs."[21]

The USFA devised a variety of suggestions and rules to promote food conservation. Through pamphlets, display cards, letters, and other media, the USFA asked consumers to observe "Meatless Tuesdays" and "Wheatless Wednesdays," and to avoid using sugar as much as possible. Additionally, the USFA promoted the "abundant" consumption of fruits and vegetables, which, as perishables, were more difficult to send overseas without spoiling. Consumers were encouraged to have at least one meal per day without wheat and two days without pork, and to make every day a "fat-saving day." The USFA tailored many suggestions to each targeted group. For example, a pamphlet titled "United States Food Administration Suggestions for Enlisting the Active Support of Religious Organizations" asked churches and synagogues "to teach conservation as a matter of self-sacrifice." Many ministers followed this advice and continued to do so in postwar anti-high cost of living movements.[22]

Herbert Hoover, President Wilson's choice to direct the U.S. Food Administration, envisioned it as a grassroots movement of active consumers that would operate under government management to conserve food and keep prices at reasonable levels. Even before the passage of the Lever Act, Hoover wrote to President Wilson, "a sense of volunteer service . . . is absolutely critical in order to amass the devotion of the people." The USFA put these words into practice. One USFA press release asserted that "this is being done without compulsion of the law; but by spontaneous effort and self-denial of the people." The document elaborated, "There have sprung up over night throughout the United States, in every city, county, village and state, definite and positive organizations, practical in their ends and unflagging in their efforts, which have the will to solve [the] food question." Yet, these efforts did not "spring up" without direction—"the first requirement of the situation was to arouse this great force, which was to a large degree dormant

An example of the USFA's efforts to promote sugar substitutes for consumers. The USFA circulated this image to public libraries as a suggestion for a "food float" in a parade. (Food News Notes for Public Librarians, July 1918. Folder: Food News Notes for Public Librarians vol. 1–12, Box 8, USFAR.)

and only potential, and then to direct it toward the elimination of waste in all the economic processes."[23]

The federal government awakened this "great force" by calling for the formation of new organizations and by encouraging existing groups to focus their efforts on proper consumption habits, as outlined in government instructions. This included primarily middle-class fraternal lodges and women's clubs, as well as general merchant, wholesale, retail, and labor organizations. L. D. Sale, president of the Los Angeles Chamber of Commerce, reflected, "Our organization during these twelve months, has gone through a period of transition that has brought it from a body devoted almost exclusively to our community development, to an auxiliary organization of the national government."[24]

Significantly, USFA volunteers observed and disseminated USFA regulations largely within the context of their own social and economic classes. The volunteer groups that undertook the work of the USFA were often stratified by class, and the USFA appealed to them through these divisions. The USFA circulated pamphlets directed specially at women's clubs, public librarians, organized labor, churches, banking groups, farmers, and fraternal lodges. In many cases, these and other organizations drew their membership from a specific class, community, or line of work. For instance, leaders of the Women's Committee of the Illinois State Council of National Defense, who "got behind Hoover" and signed a public pledge for food conservation, consisted of wives of white-collar workers.[25] Correspondingly, most of the chairpersons of the Women's Committee of the Kentucky Council on National Defense, which asserted that "the emphasis was [placed] on *FOOD*," were members of families whose breadwinners held white-collar professions. A list of the town chairpersons for the Los Angeles County State Council of Defense Women's Committee reflects a similar statistical breakdown (see data in the pie chart graphs). Some residents who reported apparent USFA violations or expressed frustration over the persistence of unfair business practices in their community also wrote in class-laden language. For instance, Ursuline Hartley, the wife of a railroad brakeman, wrote to the Food Administration that a local retailer who sold diluted sugar was profiting off "the wage earner [who] pays his all to maintain his family." She asked, "Who will stand for our rights[?]" While the USFA received a significant level of support from a range of Americans, some did express ambivalence toward the agency and its practices. In a letter to the USFA, one working-class Los Angeles resident embraced the shared goal of lower prices, but criticized the administration for asking people to conserve wheat while failing to keep wheat substitute prices at reasonable levels. "If you want to conserve wheat flour," he asserted, "put the price of substitutes down."[26]

In their appeals for cooperation in the conservation of food and the prevention of profiteering, USFA officials and collaborating citizens often invoked the producer values of a model American past. Volunteers in the USFA distributed cards displaying an American flag emblem and a quote from Herbert Hoover stating, "Go back to the simple life, be contented with simple food, simple pleasures, simple clothes. Work hard . . . Do it all courageously."[27] Summarizing the principles put forth in a government conservation bulletin, *Home and Garden Magazine* asserted that the "extensive middle class," or "just folks," should continue to work hard, be earnest, and

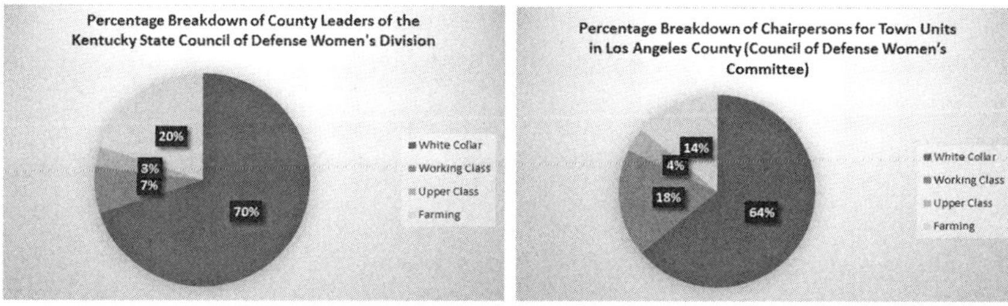


The professional class breakdown for two volunteer organizations supporting USFA efforts, one in Kentucky and the other in Los Angeles County, is representative of groups across America

exercise thrift as they had since the beginning of the war. They needed to remain committed to the ideals of their forefathers and continue to take up "the 'unfinished work' to which Lincoln so nobly dedicated this nation in his speech at Gettysburg." The American people, the magazine proclaimed, "are going to be richer in wisdom when this war is over. They will have regained an appreciation for thrift, and thrift, remember was what made these 'just folks' possible, made them worthy citizens, gave them a solid foundation for the future."[28] Proudly connecting the vigilance of patriotic authorities and thrifty consumers against hoarding and profiteering in the founding era to similar efforts in the current day, historian Frank Willing Leach published an article in the *Washington Post* titled "How Our Forefathers Checkmated the Food Profiteers during the Revolution."[29] According to these and similar appeals, a patriotic consumer identity should be based on a recommitment to the producerist values that defined an idealized American past.

While the USFA could only encourage consumers to follow some of its guidelines, hoarding and profiteering were punishable by law. In many cases, no longer could an individual store extra food in a cellar or buy as much as he or she pleased. To prevent retailers from profiteering, the USFA helped to form "fair price" committees, which included representatives from merchants, labor, and "the public," for the purpose of investigating and publishing "fair" retail prices in newspapers. "A system of checking prices charged by retailers" was undertaken by "Housewives Committees." If accused of profiteering, retailers not only could lose customers because of negative publicity, they also faced the prospect of forfeiting their licenses, which would force them to go out of business.[30]

Whether organized in existing or new class-stratified groups, USFA volunteers dedicated themselves to abiding by and promoting the agency's guidelines. They did so voluntarily in the name of patriotic sacrifice and producer values, and for their pocketbooks. However, the USFA not only relied on its volunteers to spread its messages, it also depended on them to *enforce* its most crucial rules.

## Government and Citizens in Cooperation: The USFA and the American Protective League

The reach of the USFA extended even beyond its conservation programs to the practice of coordinating community vigilante justice against hoarders and profiteers. Over the course of the war, the USFA and participating organizations worked with the American Protective League, a semisecret vigilante justice group consisting disproportionately of white-collar citizens. Food administrators provided APL "agents" with information on suspected hoarders and profiteers and allowed them to carry out investigations as quasi-federal investigators. Feeding off World War I superpatriotism, APL agents and the citizens who accused their neighbors of hoarding and profiteering, tied their consumer activism to a host of unrelated community matters, ranging from a couple's marital problems to the standoffishness of a neighbor.[31]

Throughout the war, Food Administration officials received a number of letters from citizens reporting hoarding or profiteering in their local communities. In fact, the USFA had asked Americans to report violations as part of their voluntary cooperation. Many of these letters came from citizens holding white-collar professions, reporting a variety of instances of alleged profiteering or hoarding. Myron McNeal, an office worker, wrote the USFA merely on suspicion of a neighbor. "Their actions are rather peculiar in that they will not associate with any of their neighbors," McNeal wrote. "They have large orders of groceries of all kinds delivered. . . . no one is permitted to come nearer [to] the house than the sidewalk."[32] Many other letters simply reflected a general distaste for rising prices and profiteering. One writer declared, "It is a damnable outrage the way the Cafeterias of this city are allowed to gouge the people in prices. . . . to see a damn bunch like the Boos Bros and the B&M take advantage of the situation and charge several hundred per cent profit just because they can is very discouraging to anyone who has to patronize such places."[33] Consumers flooded the Food Administration with such letters and the agency could not possibly investigate all of them. As a result, they turned to a recently formed, loosely federally sponsored vigilante justice group called the American Protective League.

Established by Albert M. Briggs in the early months of 1917, the American Protective League defined itself as a "volunteer organization to aid the Bureau of Investigation of the Department of Justice." Its official history characterized the "A.P.L." as "a silent, unknown army of more than a quarter million of the most loyal and intelligent citizens of America, who indeed did spring to arms over night." The Bureau of Investigations (the early FBI) empowered the APL as a secret organization of private citizens to investigate cases of alleged food hoarding, as well as pro-German subversion and draft dodging. Displaying "secret service" badges, purchased for 75 cents, APL agents investigated complaints of profiteering and food hoarding with the encouragement of the U.S. Food Administration and the Department of Justice. They followed persons of interest, interrogated them, searched their property, peered into their lives, and even assisted in arrests or detentions.[34]

Drawn from the ranks of "business and professional men," a substantial percentage of APL agents held white-collar professions. While APL administrators ensured that virtually all occupations were represented among agents in order to address espionage and hoarding in all sectors of society, white-collar professions were most prevalent. Because APL documents rarely listed the actual names of agents, it is difficult to obtain extensive data on their backgrounds. However, a list of agents for precinct 1 of the Washington Minutemen division of the APL and their occupations is available (a statistical breakdown of their professions is displayed in the nearby graph). Moreover, APL agents were prone to undertake their consumer activism within the spatial contexts of their own class. Like many Americans, APL "agents" were encouraged to snoop on people they worked with and those in their residential communities.[35]

Cases often involved a detailed level of collaboration between the APL, the USFA, and its cooperating organizations. One case originating from Grace C. Simons, the wife of an attorney and member of the Women's Division of the California State Council of Defense, serves as a compelling example. Simons was an active supporter of woman's suffrage and the Republican Party and member of local women's clubs, which would later take part in an "anti-extravagance campaign" during the postwar period in conjunction with a massive Department of Justice–led "Women's Division" campaign to bring down the postwar cost of living (discussed at length in chapter 3). Before the war, she was politically active, but not centrally through her consumer identity.[36]

Throughout May and early June of 1918, Simons took periodic walks down La Brea Avenue and noticed a man on top of a garage tossing pieces of bread, rolls, and cakes to the birds. The man, Chris Paul, reportedly said "it

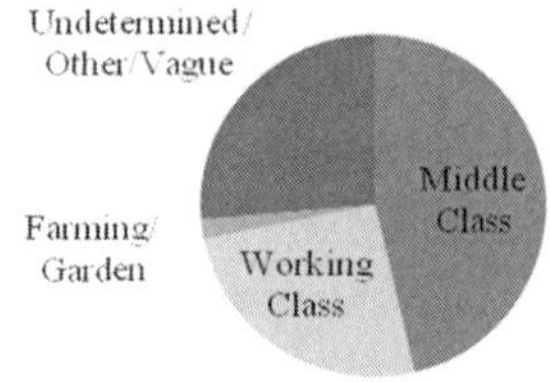


Professional classifications for the Washington Minutemen division (precinct 1) of the American Protective League

was for God's birds" as he discarded the baked goods. As a member of the Women's Division of the State Council of Defense, Simons was dismayed to observe such a "deliberate motive in the waste." After witnessing this behavior, Simons drafted a letter to the Food Administration, describing the violation and signing her name on State Council of Defense letterhead. On June 6, the Los Angeles USFA received the letter. Already burdened with countless reports of food hoarding, waste, and profiteering, the office forwarded the information to the American Protective League branch in Los Angeles, with whom they had been working for many months.[37]

During the next two weeks, Operative #895 snooped around Paul's neighborhood. Investigating the case "thoroughly," the operative found that the suspect's odd behavior was actually normal. An interview with one of Paul's neighbors and tenants had convinced him of the conclusion. According to the neighbor, Paul was born in Germany and moved to the United States when he was nine years old. "His attitudes and remarks were always patriotic," he subscribed to Liberty Bonds and the Red Cross Fund, and "his daughter is now practically devoting all her time to the Red Cross work at the Los Angeles Station." The neighbor proceeded to tell Operative #895 that "it was his custom" to survey nearby garbage cans and pick out "scraps of bread, etc." to feed the birds. The operative concluded that he had not wasted any food. The APL subsequently informed the USFA that "nothing of importance developed in this case."[38]

As Simons's inquiry suggests, APL and USFA activities encouraged many citizens to not only politicize people's consumption practices but also connect them to their senses of community. A growing number of Americans no longer considered consumption of food to be primarily only an individual or even familial matter. Indeed, some believed that it was their duty to their country and community to inform the authorities of a neighbor that might be hoarding food, a restaurant that might be using excessive amounts of flour, or a corner market with prices a little too high. Americans had periodically associated their consumption practices with organized communities since the colonial period. However, the Food Administration, through the language of patriotism and the desire of Americans to stabilize prices, made consumption a paramount concern for individuals in largely class-stratified neighborhoods and organizations that had hitherto usually focused on other issues.

Even though food prices increased by approximately 17 percent from 1917 to 1918, by most documented accounts government-sponsored consumer organizing was a success. Whereas many hoarding and profiteering allegations ended up being as benign as Chris Paul's bird feeding, others, with the help of USFA or APL volunteers, or both, led to successful convictions. A number of these cases received substantial publicity, including the conviction of Pasadena millionaire Hulett Merritt for hoarding sugar for private use. Punishing men like Merritt for hoarding while less wealthy Americans sacrificed for the war effort seemed to represent the epitome of economic justice.[39] USFA conservation efforts also received positive publicity—a *New York Times* editorial, for instance, declared, "We showed that we were willing to make sacrifices, that we could save." Some even penned poems about USFA accomplishments. One, entitled "the imperishables," stated, "On profits false they waged war / And business ways that were not clean / Were quickly banished from the scene."[40]

Participants in the USFA sent its leaders letters of praise, commending the USFA's achievements. One letter to Harold Powell, head of the perishables division, expressed thanks for "the wonderful gift of leadership that my superior officers possessed, particularly our chief, Mr. Hoover." Another reflected on the "success achieved in the work of the Perishables Division." Many Americans departed from the war with high hopes that the combination of state action, voluntarism, and the conservative rhetoric of returning to "traditional" producer ethics in a consumer society would be effective in addressing consumers' concerns.[41]

## Conclusion

Despite the fact that prices had steadily increased during the war, many Americans viewed the U.S. Food Administration as a success. Under federal government control, organized USFA volunteers politicized and policed their consumption habits and those of their fellow citizens. Similar to some organized middle-class consumers of the pre–World War I decades of the Progressive Era, who decried monopolies and unfair labor practices amid rapid industrialization and urbanization, the USFA focused on the concept of fairness in a transitioning economy.

However, the rhetoric surrounding the passage of the Lever Act and the language of a variety of USFA documents in many ways differed from the progressive-minded consumer activism of the prewar years. In addition to heightening their rhetoric against "manipulators" and "profiteers"—now calling them unpatriotic as well as greedy—politicians, the press, and USFA volunteers took an increasingly antilabor tone, which condemned strikes and the controversial anti-high-food-price protests of the working class. By the end of the war, Americans, including many who had worked with the Food Administration, grew more upset with working-class radicalism and their supposed greed—attributes that they argued contrasted with the celebrated values of industriousness and thrift. A synopsis of a National Council of Defense Report summarized this feeling by suggesting that the middle class had suffered the most from "profiteering among capitalists and profiteering among labor," citing underproduction and high wages as primary culprits. One of Senator Hiram Johnson's (P-California) campaign advisors, who had worked with USFA volunteers during the war, mirrored the sentiment of the Council of Defense report, stating "a very crying issue of the times is the lack of stability in the price of labor and commodities, both of which are of course at the bottom of the evil known as the 'high cost of living.'" He elaborated that while laborers enjoyed higher wages, "the great majority of the people and especially those who work for regular salaries . . . have an exceedingly hard time to make ends meet." Having been mobilized during the war, these middle-class consumers connected their own and their neighbors' consumer behavior to their national identity. In due time, they would increasingly define themselves not just as the nation's primary consumers, but as "the people."[42]

# 2 • Becoming Producers and Avoiding the Middleman

## Home Garden and Municipal Market Campaigns

In the summer of 1919, an individual only identifying himself as F. G. B. called on the government to take action against "rank profiteering" of food throughout Los Angeles. Writing to the editors of the *Los Angeles Times*, he lamented, "Last year we 'middle class' could buy a pound of fine cherries for fifteen or twenty cents, two pounds of grapes or almost any other fruit for fifteen cents. . . . Why are we now asked thirty-five cents for the same cherries and fifteen or twenty cents for a single pound of the same grapes?" F. G. B. considered himself "one of that 'middle class'" who had trouble making ends meet. He would support any politician, regardless of party affiliation, who would embrace the slogan "Down With Profiteering" and "seriously consider the subject at once ere matters become more complicated and revolt inciting." Among the central "profiteers" of postwar Los Angeles to individuals like F. G. B. were middlemen that stood between "honest" and hard-working food producers and consumers. Middle-class consumers protested middlemen's stranglehold over food production, distribution, and retail, and supported new and existing methods to curb their influence.[1]

Middle-class Los Angeles residents embraced two primary solutions to weaken the power of the middleman. First, during the war middle-class consumers participated in the "home garden" movement. Consumers, private organizations, the city government, and the United States Food Administration collectively organized the movement in order to both aid the war effort and lower rising food prices. As backyard and vacant lot farmers, home gardeners circumvented food profiteers by becoming producers. As the war came to a close, middle-class residents attempted to continue the movement.[2] Second, throughout the war and postwar periods, citizens petitioned the local and state governments to maintain municipal markets, at which small producers sold directly to consumers. In these endeavors, middle-class consumers claimed to be promoting producerist values and protecting the "public" interest from profiteers and greedy nonproducing middlemen.

Whether criticizing the greed of food trusts, wholesalers, or profiteering merchants, middle-class consumers self-righteously portrayed their values as those of the public. They believed that all sectors of society should operate in accordance with the values of honesty, industriousness, self-reliance, and thrift—as they, middle-class consumers, defined them. Even as white-collar activists organized to defend their own pocketbooks, they depicted a variety of middlemen as self-interested. They claimed to be undertaking a neutral defense of the public against selfish groups.

Drawing on their experiences during the war, these middle-class activists continued to connect their consumption practices to their senses of local community. They called for gardens in both backyards and unused community lots, and for neighborhood municipal markets that they hoped would give consumers the ability to buy from a subset of hardworking and honest producers. By creating alternative places for food production and purchasing, middle-class consumers sought to police the honesty of the major groups engaging in the local economy. Because the municipal market and home garden movements largely occurred at the local level, this analysis focuses on these movements in one city, Los Angeles, with regular mention of national voices and trends. A spatially large city with a warm climate that was conducive to backyard gardening, and an early twentieth century destination for middle-class midwesterners, Los Angeles provides an ideal setting to chronicle white-collar anti-high-food-price activism. The city became an important local space in a national story of rising middle-class consumer activism.[3]

## Food Prices, Growing Middle-Class Discontent, and the Vilification of the Middleman

Throughout the 1910s, food prices had increased rapidly. From 1913 to 1919, prices for all articles of food rose by 86 percent, with a 27 percent increase occurring between 1917 and 1919. People everywhere took notice. One Chicago resident lamented in a letter to the *Tribune* that "[b]utter, already high for this time of year, has been suddenly increased . . . just when it should be steadily on the decline. A comparatively small head of lettuce at 15 cents seems exorbitant, while yeast has risen 300 percent." In suburban Boston, one woman complained of the struggle to feed her family properly. "How long are these prices to continue?," she wondered. "Thousands of housewives are on the verge of a nervous breakdown trying to feed their families. . . . Wives especially of clerks and men whose salaries have not increased while prices of foods daily soar higher." Stating that "[l]iving has become a struggle these days," a Washington, DC, resident wrote to the *Post* that she buys stewing meat once a week and "never get[s] it for less than 30 cents per pound." Unsurprisingly, the *Post* called the high cost of food a "universal problem."[4]

The media began to report on the particular struggles of middle-class Americans to pay high food prices. Many articles in newspapers, bulletins, and magazines noted that as income had remained stagnant for salaried workers during the war, prices had increased. One *New York Times* article argued that whereas farmers and the working class had the power to demand higher compensation to meet rising costs, the middle class had not enjoyed this privilege. "Farmers and workmen have seen to it that they do not suffer," the article asserted. Although farmers and industrial workers also encountered high prices, "middle-class homes everywhere are suffering as deeply; and for them no remedy is at hand or proposed. The grievance of the mother who sees her children skimped and often hungry is more serious than that of the farmer and the workman." "There is an inequity here," the article concluded, "and a deep one; it will test the full virtue of republican institutions to correct it."[5]

The Los Angeles media reported on the same anxieties. "Never has the country been confronted with such economic chaos," a *Los Angeles Times* editorial declared, adding that"[i]t is the middle classes that are hardest hit by the chaotic conditions and soaring prices; the men and women with moderate incomes." An editorial in the *Daily Courier* of neighboring Oxnard entitled "middle class woes" noted that "the American middle class [man] is full of indignation as he considered its wrongs and misfortunes." His salary "has known no increase" and he is one "whose living expenses have mounted higher and higher each year." More pointedly, another *Los Angeles Times* editorial declared that "the middle classes are suffering a gradual but certain impoverishment."[6]

Middle-class citizens themselves expressed outrage as victims of food price increases. One Boston woman wrote, "I think there are several agencies at root of high prices of food," and "[i]t is the middle-class, like myself, who are suffering. The rich don't, nor do the men in Washington actually feel the privation that I and my family are experiencing." B. F. Gray, a Los Angeles insurance agent, referenced "many complaints" about the prices charged by cafeterias in the city. Offering a specific example, he wrote, "Thought this morning as I looked at my breakfast and figured the cost of the articles . . . I had 5 prunes in my dish for which I paid seven cents a little shameful sized dish of oatmeal—6¢ . . . it's ridiculous as well as criminal." In Medford, Oregon, Fred Dalton Haight, a music teacher, wrote in his diary of his frustration over elevated food prices. According to Haight, "sugar and flour are way up and spuds [potatoes] nine dollars a hundred. Hell! Where is the end of this H.C.L. anyway. No relief is in sight." Fittingly, the *Los Angeles Times* proclaimed, "In this country that wail of the middle classes is already heard," through few solutions to their troubles had been enacted.[7]

Many Americans focused on eliminating or limiting the influence of the middleman to bring down the cost of food. These popular villains included farmers' cooperative marketing associations, storage plants, wholesalers, meat packers, the railroad system, greedy retailers, and undefined "speculators." Embodying this popular villainization of the middleman, Edmund Vance Cooke's poem, "The Middleman," proclaimed, "'Reduce! reduce, my cost of living!' / I cry to butcher, baker, grocer. / They all politely answer, 'No, sir!' / They all smile at me, without misgiving, / And claim they're doing all they can, / But can't cast out the middle-man." In Georgia, the state government responded to such frustrations by enlarging its role in the marketplace, offering to sell consumers one to five dozen eggs and one to five pounds of butter at the lowest farm produce price in the country. The purpose of the plan was "to establish as quickly as possible a regular weekly interchange of orders and deliveries between the farmers and the people in the cities, thereby eliminating the middle man."[8]

Middle-class Los Angeles consumers and their sympathizers suggested that multiple levels of the government should take action to eliminate or circumvent middlemen and reduce food prices. They looked to a variety of public officials to accomplish these objectives. A July 1919 *Los Angeles Times* editorial called on the federal government to help middle-class victims of high food prices. "Second only in importance to the ratification of the peace treaty" the editorial asserted, "is Federal legislation to . . . reduce the untenably high cost of living." Other editorials looked to governors or other state officials to facilitate lower prices. Norton F. W. Hazeldine, a chemist living near Hollywood, believed that the L.A. City Council could provide relief from food price increases by circumventing the middleman. In a letter to the city council, Hazeldine proposed a multipart plan to make food more affordable. He asked the city council to facilitate the erection of a building in which farmers could slaughter their cattle and sell the meat "at cost to the people," and build a public kitchen with a frying tank "where fish can be brought direct from the boats," cleaned, cooked, and "sold direct to the public at cost."[9]

While Hazeldine's plan did not come to fruition, middle-class Los Angeles residents did focus on two primary strategies that they hoped would eliminate the middleman and lower food prices. Looking to local, state, and, in some cases, federal politicians for support, Los Angeles residents proposed the continuance and expansion of the home gardens and municipal markets that had appeared to flourish throughout the war.

## The Home Garden Movement

On the eve of American entry into World War I in April 1917, middle-class Los Angeles residents had already started planting wintertime home gardens to fight the high cost of food. Los Angeles offered two features that were typically unavailable to urban dwellers. First, the warm, ocean-side climate allowed for year-round growing seasons. Secondly, because Los Angeles was a spatially large city, many residents had relatively large backyards, or lived near vacant lands. Fittingly, a February 1917 *Los Angeles Times* article declared, "Every backyard in Los Angeles is a Potential Producer." According to the *Times*, residents increasingly seized upon these advantages, as "the home garden has assumed somewhat important proportions for the present season in view of the advanced food prices in all lines." By planting gardens, residents used Los Angeles's unique urban environment to protect their pocketbooks from profiteers.[10]

As the United States moved toward entry into the war and prices continued to increase, participation in the "home garden movement" soared. Citizens throughout the United States dug up their backyards, planted gardens, and attended home garden meetings to publicize the efforts and to coordinate resources. One gardener spoke happily that "[t]his vegetable raising is sure cutting down the high cost of living for us."[11]

While the impetus to plant gardens often came from individuals, local communities, or city governments, a national organization called the National Emergency War Garden Commission also facilitated home gardening. In March 1917, Charles Lathrop Pack of the American Forestry Association organized the National Emergency War Garden Commission to respond to anticipated food shortages and to coordinate citizens' latent and active eagerness to plant gardens. The commission worked in conjunction with federal officials from the Department of Agriculture and the U.S. Food Administration, and circulated numerous leaflets instructing citizens on what could be gained by planting a garden. In addition to patriotic motives, the commission emphasized how gardens would fight the high cost of living. In particular, the commission specified that "we must make a big drive to produce food in this country as near the point of consumption as possible, rout the middleman and cold storage man." Whether responding to the Commission's specific statements or on their own initiative, many Americans were eager to take on these enemies.[12]

In Los Angeles, William Randolph Hearst's *Los Angeles Examiner* played a central role in encouraging urban consumers to become producers. In February 1917, the paper offered ten cash prizes totaling $210 for "best results in growing vegetables on lots in [the] city and county." The prizes applied to both small backyard gardens and large vacant lots, and the *Examiner* created a special prize for gardens maintained by schoolchildren. Publishing numerous announcements and articles on the contest and the necessity of home gardens, the *Examiner* printed sensational headlines such as "Home Garden Idea Spreads Like Wildfire." The *Examiner* asked Mayor Frederick Woodman to name a garden contest judging committee and encouraged the city government to lend its further support for home gardens. Reporting that the contest was "given the impetus of enthusiasm," the mayor complied, appointing a group of judges, ranging from the director of the Housewives League to the superintendent of schools. One member of the committee, Mrs. Josiah Evans Cowles, who was also president of the National Federation of Women's Clubs, expressed optimism for the plan. "Certainly, as one sees the vast spaces which are available to the people of Southern California, and of Los Angeles County for the purpose of growing things," Cowles stated, "one cannot help but wonder why there should be the problem of the high cost of living." Mayor Woodman sensed that the contest and the nascent gardeners represented only the beginning of a larger movement, declaring, "I believe that we may start a movement which will grow to much greater proportions than we foresee, as we become familiar with the problems to be met." Woodman would be correct. Thousands of residents attended home garden meetings and even more planted gardens.[13]

Widespread support for home gardening from Mayor Woodman, a Republican, to the *Examiner*, a pro-Democratic newspaper, to Cowles, who was characterized by one newspaper as a "strong Republican," indicates that the movement defies easy political categorization. This diverse participation further speaks to the insights of David A. Horowitz, who, in the context of his analysis of political insurgency, showed that many citizens of multiple political affiliations have centered their politics on pursuing "traditional needs, interests, and values," often with "strong nationalist sentiments."[14] Indeed, the home garden movement, which took shape during a moment of budding wartime nationalism, appealed to traditional producerist values against the concentrated economic power wielded by profiteers. Nevertheless, despite the movement's seeming ability to bring together politically diverse historical actors around these values, key proponents like Woodman and the editors of the *Examiner* joined hands on this issue as they continued to advance their own personal and political parties' standard agendas.[15]

In response to advocacy from citizens and the *Examiner*, the Los Angeles City Council also offered official support for the movement. The council voted to make the home garden committee official, giving it an initial appropriation of $500 with $1,000 more to come. Second, in June 1917, the city council instructed the city purchasing agent to loan to the home garden committee approximately 700 feet of secondhand fire hose for use in the gardens. Each of these initial measures of encouragement of home gardening received a unanimous vote by the council (which included former or current Democrats and Republicans, as well as a Socialist), indicating multipartisan support. In addition to these initial actions from the council, the Public Service Commission worked with the home garden committee to offer water at a reduced rate for vacant lot gardeners. Praising the home garden movement in his annual message to the city council in July 1917, Mayor Woodman asserted that the Home Garden Committee "is performing a very important work in this city, and is attracting the attention of the country at large." "Many people are now engaged in the cultivation of small tracts," Woodman continued, and "this work should be encouraged, and carried forward during the next year with increased vigor."[16]

Newspaper reports and promotional literature from the USFA, the National Emergency War Garden Commission, and other sources suggested that white-collar Americans should be at the forefront of home garden campaigns. One USFA press release praised the North Carolina food administrator for encouraging employers to allow clerks to play a critical role in the movement by rescheduling work days to allow them to garden in daylight hours. The *Los Angeles Times* reported on a number of white-collar men and women who took special initiative in leading the movement. Theater operator J. A. Quinn, for instance, received publicity for putting on productions of *The Garden of Allah* to benefit the Home Garden Committee. The *Times* also lauded office men who planed gardens on the rooftops of Los Angeles office buildings. In addition, the Los Angeles media and the USFA published a number of pictures and cartoons of white-collar families, wearing collared-shirts and ties, working diligently on home gardens.[17]

White-collar Americans generally did, in fact, lead these home garden campaigns. The presidents of both large and small home garden committees and associations typically came from the ranks of the white-collar class. For example, an attorney was initially at the helm of the Los Angeles Home Garden Committee, while the presidents of committees in cities ranging from

Chicago to Winona, Minnesota, were managers. A USFA "Organization Plan for City War Gardens" mentioned Rotary Clubs, parent-teacher associations, and women's clubs as key groups from which to solicit involvement. Other USFA documents chronicled the successes of middle-class participants in the movement. A San Francisco man who raised six hens, Belgian hares, and vegetables represented just one white-collar worker "who worked all day in an office and devoted his after hours to such a splendid act of thrift and valuation."[18]

At almost the onset of the home garden movement, newspapers, magazines, and a variety of politicians cast the movement in patriotic terms and suggested that fighting the high cost of living and aiding the war effort were intertwined. In Los Angeles, newspapers printed headlines, such as "Garden Brigades, Attention, Report for Back Yard Duty, Time for Combined Assault on Redoubts of High Cost of Living Is at Hand," "City's Idle Land Means Nearly Five Million Dollars This Year: Great Army of Gardeners Ordered Swiftly Mobilized in Los Angeles," and "Get Busy in Your Back Yard So That Our Army May Eat and Win," for articles that discussed how home gardeners could combat high food prices and do their patriotic duty simultaneously. Similarly, U.S. Food Administration press releases applied militaristic language to the home garden movement, with one declaring that "[t]he hoe has become a weapon of war." Taken together, these words reinforced the idea that white-collar home garden participants acted in the name of, or as, the patriotic public.[19]

Participants and supporters of the movement also emphasized how home gardening promoted the value of diligent production. The *Los Angeles Examiner* "issued a striking call to every man, woman and child to get to work to make our soil productive" through the home garden campaign. A circular of the National War Garden Commission also equated those who did not produce in home gardens with lazy draft-dodging "slackers." Even criticizing unused vacant land itself, the issue stated, "More than 5,000,000 people in the United States are this year cultivating back yards, vacant lots and other city and town tracts which hitherto have been 'slacker' land." Fitting the movement's emphasis on the value of diligent production, when Los Angeles theater operator J. A. Quinn showed *The Garden of Allah* to raise funds for the movement, his ticket-takers wore overalls—a symbol of hard work. Similarly, in Venice, California, the mayor and a city trustee supported the movement by posing in overalls, and holding a hand-plow while transforming the soil of the front lawn of city hall into a garden.[20]

In the postwar period, a blossoming discursive space of middle-class consumer protest in newspapers, magazines, and other sources encouraged white-collar Americans to associate the home garden movement with a middle-class consumer identity. Calling on the "intermediate millions" or the "middle class" to combat "heartless profiteering," the popular cultural sources that made up this discursive space grew during the late Progressive Era and World War I and peaked after the war.[21] Letters to the editor, works of art and music, politicians seeking to appeal to white-collar workers, and middle-class citizens parading in overalls or participating in rent strikes celebrated thrift and hard work and praised home gardens as one of many solutions to their consumer woes.[22] In some cases, home garden advocates implored middle-class citizens to take part in gardening. Calling the "unorganized middle class" "the poor," the *Jackson (MI) Citizen Patriot* declared to middle-class citizens that the "war garden . . . was never more in need that it is right now."[23] It was in this environment that citizens like Mary Anderson continued to build the movement.

Throughout the closing months of the war and in the postwar period, Mary Anderson (Mrs. J. T.), a member of the local upper middle class, led the home garden movement in Los Angeles. Similar to many middle-class Los Angeles residents, Mary Anderson was part of substantial migration of white middle-class midwesterners to the city in the late nineteenth and early twentieth centuries. Born in Missouri, Anderson moved to Los Angeles sometime between 1885 and 1910, when approximately 41 percent of the city's American-born population consisted of midwestern migrants. While it is unknown why Anderson and her family moved to Los Angeles, in many cases migrants from her socioeconomic background moved for the climate or a middle-class suburban-style environment, or both.[24]

Anderson became a primary leader in the Los Angeles Progressive Era middle class. A social worker and wife of a civil service worker, Anderson served as president of the Council of Community Service of California, which "include[d] representatives from all active and progressive organizations of the city and county" and was involved in the Society of American Music Optimists of Los Angeles and the Wa-Wan Club. During the war, Anderson served as the president of the Liberty Loan drive for Los Angeles, which helped to finance the war, and was a key member of the Los Angeles Council of Defense. In the latter capacity, Anderson worked directly with the U.S. Food Administration. Within the first two days of their efforts, Anderson helped to secure pledges from 40,000 local residents to observe USFA guidelines. According to another USFA volunteer, "To Mrs. J.T. Anderson . . . goes the entire credit for working up such a wonderful and efficient organization."[25]

During the war, Anderson also worked with the government to police the consumption practices of people in her community and throughout Los Angeles. Not only did Anderson serve on the "consumers' branch" of the Los Angeles Fair Price Committee, she also reported cases of food hoarding and profiteering. On one occasion, Anderson instructed the Los Angeles USFA's office to "please investigate" a Mrs. L. H. Multer, who allegedly possessed 200 pounds of sugar. On other occasions, Anderson forwarded complaints ranging from one of a women burning bread and rolls in her backyard to another alleging that a wedding party had wasted rice by throwing it at the bride and groom as part of a ceremonial tradition. Anderson acted with the direct encouragement of federal officials. A deputy Los Angeles food administrator, for example, even asked Anderson herself to investigate a case of potential hoarding that had been sent to his office. Through her wartime activities, Anderson had gained experience working with the government to stabilize food prices by policing consumption practices in her community. Given her previous activism and leadership, it comes as no surprise that press reports from the postwar period would describe Anderson as leading the charge to "tackle [the postwar] H.C.L. problem."[26]

Mary Anderson and other participants in the postwar home garden movement focused much of their attention on persuading the city government to assist the movement. During the war, the mayor and city council felt pressure both from below and above to use the resources of the local government to encourage home gardening. The U.S. Food Administration was in regular contact with city governments regarding measures that would conserve food, and national politicians had issued statements and made speeches that encouraged local governments to take on a central supportive role. After the war, the U.S. Food Administration disbanded and participating organizations in USFA programs were left to their own devices to maintain city support for voluntary programs like home gardening to fight the high cost of food.[27]

The fact that many government officials themselves remained critical participants in the movement helped organizers like Anderson garner city assistance for it. Anderson's husband was a civil service worker, and both newspaper accounts and city council records chronicle the participation of numerous government employees. In May 1920, 500 city workers petitioned the city council "to do some local daylight saving" by beginning the official city work day at 7:00 a.m. instead of 8:00 a.m. to enable municipal employees to garden after work at 4:00 p.m. Their efforts coincided with urban residents in many other communities advocating daylight saving times, which on occasion drew the objections of farmers, who saw it as privileging urban needs over those of actual producers. One writer to *Indiana Farmer's*

This drawing depicts white-collar workers using daylight savings time to work on home gardens. Charles Lathrop Pack, *The War Garden Victorious* (Philadelphia: J.P. Lippincott Company, 1919), 168.

This January 1920 cartoon is one of many depictions of white-collar workers' and families' attachment to the home garden movement as a strategy to fight the high cost of food in the postwar period. *Corpus Christi Caller*, January 26, 1920.

*Guide* responded even more pointedly, suggesting that any manipulation of the clock could not affect farmers' superior work ethic and productivity. He proclaimed that "most farmers work as a rule on the eight-hour system—eight hours before dinner and eight more afterwards—so no matter how the clock may read it cannot squeeze out of the twenty-four hours any more daylight than these naturally contain."[28]

Despite these criticisms, many urban governments, including Los Angeles, remained in favor of home gardening. As the mayor of Los Angeles reported to the city council at the end of 1918, "This work has been conducted during the past year with a wonderful degree of efficiency, and deserves our highest commendation. The fact that there were 98,537 gardens conducted under the direction of Mrs. J.T. Anderson and her associates speaks volumes for their work." According to the mayor, "The Home Garden idea . . . should be continued."[29]

Maintaining financial support for the movement was easier said than done. It required the persistent efforts of Anderson and other participants. At first, support came at Anderson's request, backed by substantial community participation. In February 1919, Anderson wrote to the city council, "If the Home Gardens work is to be continued, we must have an appropriation of at least $2000 at this time to continue the work." Anderson continued, "There is a most incessant demand for assistance in a way of seeds and plants by the citizens located in all parts of the city who have the soil prepared." She explained that 15 community centers for distribution of seeds and plants had been established, and "the seed supply is exhausted. . . . We must provide them at once or immediately notify the public that the work will be discontinued." Anderson concluded by asserting, "In view of the fact that the accompanying report shows such enormous interest on the investment made by the city in the return of seeds for her people, I trust the allowance will be granted at once." The council voted unanimously in support of the funds and "commend[ed] the efficient work done by the Committee."[30]

Participants and supporters of the postwar movement continued to speak of their activities in producerist language, and suggested that they were reasserting the revered values of American past. A *Los Angeles Times* editorial explained of the postwar movement, "countless thousands of householders in Los Angeles, tiring of their unenviable role of helpless consumers, have turned the tables on the food purveyors by turning producers." Taking up where the "American pioneers" left off, they refused "to believe the fiction that it is as cheap to buy vegetables as to grow them" and "cleared the trash out of their back yards, routed out the pansy bed and spaded up the last square foot available for gardens." The *Times* considered a bed of pansies to be unacceptable to the producerist values of the Los Angeles consumer. The value of production would be instrumental in "beating the H.C.L." Similarly, one Chicago woman looked to the past and suggested that people get back to "simple ways . . . make gardens everywhere" and exercise thrift. With these actions, "prices would fall."[31]

White-collar home gardeners maintained that these traditional producerist values, upon which the home garden movement was based, were the proper values of the people. Charles Lathrop Pack declared that "the home food producer" was widely thought to be the best citizen, elaborating, "Don't forget that the garden produces something besides food. It produces thrift, so important to the nation at this time."[32] Stella Richmond Hill, the wife of a clerk in Grand Rapids, Michigan, noted that publicly minded citizens supported home gardening, because it promoted law and order instead of criminal behavior, and teaches "a desire for the clean and orderly, increases the productiveness . . . of the world and helps to acquire the thrift habit."[33] Thomas B. Buckner, a Kansas City judge, similarly noted that practicing economy in purchasing and raising "a garden [and] chickens" exemplified "real independent self-respecting citizenship."[34]

Anderson and other Los Angeles home gardeners also used the movement to teach children the values of production, patriotism, and economic fairness. As one home garden leader put it, "the purpose" is "to train our boys and girls in thrift, industry, service, responsibility and patriotism."[35] National garden bulletins reflected similar themes, one noting that "children engaged in [the home garden] work will be benefited physically, mentally, and morally." A national school garden pamphlet published in 1919 suggested that gardening had taught children to be enthusiastic about hard work. They made "pupils eager for the real work of outdoor gardens."[36]

Mirroring the rhetoric of many Progressive Era reformers, middle-class home garden leaders also underscored how enlisting the participation of the working class in the movement would assist and uplift them. A number of home garden proponents emphasized the need to teach the value of production to the working class for their future and immediate economic, social, and moral well-being. According to one city document, working-class Los Angeles residents would benefit from being taught "to become interested" in producing. The city council and the Social Service Commission offered its support partially on this basis of helping the less fortunate. Many other home garden leaders throughout the United States expressed their attachment to producerist values by purporting to be teaching them to the working class. National Garden Commission president Charles Lathrop Pack summarized this understanding of the larger role of gardening for the working class. Pack declared that home gardening "means contented workers everywhere" and an "antidote for Bolshevik doctrine." To leaders like Pack, gardening taught the working class values that would curb labor unrest during a year in which more than 20 percent of workers went on strike, amid the first red scare.[37]

## Food Prices and Working-Class Spaces of Activism

These appeals to "teach" working-class families made no reference to the fact that many of them, in Los Angeles and elsewhere, already raised their own food. The home and the neighborhood were focal points of working-class Los Angeles residents' identities, both for their recreational purposes and for their productive capacities. After World War I, working-class residents, particularly in suburbs such as South Gate, continued to, as Becky Nicolaides notes, "[turn] their domestic property into sites of production."[38] As a "semiproletariat," working-class gardeners supported themselves through wage work, and through the cultivation of the Southern California land.[39] Many families bartered produce, or raised rabbits and chickens, and similar to the *Los Angeles Times* and *Los Angeles Examiner*, the newspapers of working-class suburbs like Torrance and South Gate, as well as union periodicals throughout the nation, offered advice on home gardening practices.[40]

These efforts at working-class gardening took place in the often class-segmented spatial context of their residential neighborhoods, or at the workplace. At the workplace, for instance, Los Angeles railroad workers on the Southern Pacific planted "bumper crops" along the tracks to help feed their families.[41] These efforts complemented protests at blue-collar work sites over the inability of low wages to keep up with the high cost of living. As just one example, in April 1920 members of the Brotherhood of Railway Trainmen in Los Angeles, Fresno, and other California cities walked off their jobs, because, in the words of one witness, they "had been waiting now indefinitely for relief from the high cost of living . . . and they were not going to wait any longer."[42] When blue-collar workers planted gardens at home they often did so as part of neighborhoods made up of largely working-class residents.[43] In South Gate, residents raised food in working-class neighborhoods for their own consumption or to barter or sell.[44] In the San Pedro section of Los Angeles, James Spillane, a railroad laborer, articulated the need to support gardening through the lens of class by juxtaposing the troubles of the urban/suburban blue-collar workers to afford high prices with the supposed greed of farmers. According to Spillane, farmers "first clamored for the guarantee of $2.20 a bushel for their wheat; then the price of pork must be sustained for their good. As another mark of favor, the price of farm machinery must come down, even if the wages of men who make it are reduced, although the men who work in the machine shops must still pay a fancy price for their pork and beef."[45] Celebrating home gardens as a means to counteract this situation, he noted that many people "have been able almost entirely to live from those gardens."

Even through a number of working-class Americans used home gardening as a means to support themselves, at least some expressed resentment of the white-collar discursive space that expected them to fight the high cost of living by gardening instead of receiving higher wages. The *Railway Trainman*, the official bulletin of the Brotherhood of Railroad Trainmen, criticized a white-collar educator's "little lesson in thrift," which was published in several newspapers and which juxtaposed a hypothetical example of a railroad worker named "Mr. Smith," who beat the high cost of living by working hard and planting a home garden, with lazy workers who expected a big paycheck.[46] According to the *Trainman*'s critique,

> [t]his section hand in the "lesson" received approximately $2.75 a day for section handing and about $5.00 a day for track walking. He must take some time to get home to the job both week days and Sundays. He also must have some time to get home to the station, from the station to the postoffice and to his job, or his home, as the case may be, which naturally, would bring his big garden work along pretty late at night or very early in the morning.

While noting that the lesson was emblematic of both educators' self-righteous complaints that they are "not paid as much as workmen," and the type of "propaganda used by railway employers to set the public against railway employees," the *Trainman* concluded that the lesson intended to promote the "belief that certain railroad employees are a lazy, careless, wasteful lot." Ultimately, the *Trainman* proclaimed, "it is not only unfair, it is downright dishonest to play on the prejudices of any class of our citizenship under cover of lessons in thrift." As the *Trainman* saw it, any working-class efforts at gardening by no means required the guidance and support of the middle class. Rather, when white-collar Americans sought to teach the working class home gardening, it served as yet another means of performing their own version of producer values. Instead of acting as a unifying force, the language of producerism served as a class-laden discourse used by both white-collar professionals and elites to claim righteousness and exert power over the working class.

Nevertheless, despite having contrasting priorities and differing visions of producerism, white and blue-collar workers drew on a common language of race, which demonstrated how cultural lines of protest flowed between some forms of middle and working-class consumer activism. As the price of potatoes continued to increase alongside other foodstuffs in the immediate postwar period, both blue and white-collar activists took action through a consumer boycott against the "Japanese monopoly of the Southern California potato crop."[47]

In identifying Japanese Americans as culprits of the unfair postwar economy, white consumers appealed to popular ethnic categorizations and fears of an era marked by rapid immigration, the red scare, and post–World War I culture war. Only a few years before the National Origins Act, which severely limited immigration to the United States from "undesirable" locations and "undesirable" "races," many people of the 1910s and early twenties differentiated themselves from scores of immigrants that had traveled to American soil in the preceding decades from southern and eastern Europe, and, on the West Coast, particularly from Mexico and Asia.[48] This period featured an extensive milieu of unstable racial categories that reflected immigration patterns. A variety of racial categorizations, such as Celt, Slav, or Hebrew, defied a black-white dichotomy, and the character and extent of racism and racial classification were often relative to factors such as geography.[49] As such, Mexican, Chinese, and Japanese Americans became popular racialized villains in California, while residents in other localities often preferred different malevolent ethnicities. The antiethnic tendencies of first red scare of 1919–20 intensified fears of how foreigners and nonwhite Americans could adversely impact American society. In this context, an image of a Japanese American profiteer conveyed cultural meanings that were tied to a host of political, economic, and social anxieties of both a national and local scale.

The boycott against the "Japanese potato monopoly" began in January 1920 with a meeting of Southern Pacific railroad workers. Soon after, they circulated boycott petitions at the workplace, first at the Southern Pacific, then at the Santa Fe and Salt Lake shops.[50] Though originating in predominately working-class spaces, the boycott was soon taken up by a number of middle-class women's clubs, beginning with the Ebell Club, and followed by a resolution for a boycott by the Los Angeles District Federation Convention of Women's Clubs, which consisted of a purported 16,000 members.[51] As the *Los Angeles Evening Herald* noted, "The potato boycott movement started among employees of the railroad shops in the city. It is spreading to all classes. Only a sharp cut in potato prices will kill it."[52]

The focus of the boycotts was George Shima, the so-called Potato King of

Southern California. Alleged to have controlled 85 percent of the potato supply, Shima was characterized as the "Japanese potato magnate," and allegedly also worked only through Japanese American middlemen.[53] The mayor, county attorney, a state senator, and several others also accused Shima of hoarding, by one estimate storing 3,160,000 pounds of potatoes, for the purpose of driving up prices.[54] With Shima serving as the villainous figurehead, white merchants and white- and blue-collar consumers all claimed to be victims of Japanese greed. As Donald and Nadine Hata note, Shima and other wealthy Japanese immigrants, "although few in numbers, were perceived as being too successful, and therefore became 'indispensable enemies' for their alleged threat to Anglo socio-economic supremacy in California and the West Coast."[55] On a cultural level, Shima also had made headlines for favoring interracial marriage between white and Japanese individuals, a position that the *Los Angeles Times* called "horrifying," "morally repugnant," "biologically impossible," and threatening to the "sacred" character of "American womanhood."[56] The boycotts against Shima helped to forge a cross-class political and discursive space of whiteness, ultimately bound through the cultural connections of sexuality, race, and consumption. Much like with home gardening, this consumer activism was about much more than prices.

Despite the wide appeal of this racial discourse, the boycotts still illustrated tensions within Los Angeles anti-high-food-price activism. In addition to most organizing taking place in the class-segmented spaces of workplaces or women's club meetings, local activism continued to travel between multiple strategies of consumer protest. Upper-middle-class home garden leader Mary Anderson implored residents to return their focus to becoming producers through home gardening: "I have always been of the opinion that the boycott would not help. The only solution to the problem is to produce potatoes, and that we are trying to accomplish through the Home Gardens Association."[57] Della M. Corwin, the widow of a railroad engine watchman, a leader of the potato boycott, and also a proponent of home gardening, disagreed. Claiming that the boycott and home gardening had a symbiotic relationship, Corwin stated, "We want everybody in Los Angeles to plant a garden the same as when the war was raging, and we want everybody in Los Angeles to refrain from buying potatoes until the price comes down."[58] While the boycotts reportedly did temporarily reduce potato prices, the cost of food generally remained high, and this continued to be a point of focus for both working- and middle-class consumers. As a result, though drawn together through a common racial discourse, white working and middle-class Los Angeles residents continued to express their own forms of consumer activism. While it was increasingly on the decline as an organized movement, this included gardening, where they typically cultivated the land in separate spaces and through differing visions of producerism.

## The Decline of the Home Gardening Movement

Despite its growth during and immediately after the war, the home garden movement suffered from waning support from the city council by the middle of 1920. The council continued to be in favor of gardening in principle, but no evidence suggests that it maintained its financial commitment to the movement. It received correspondence protesting the decision, with one resident asserting, "The city should encourage everyone to cut down the H.C.L. and home gardens are the means of doing that."[59]

Municipal government support for the movement fissured for a number of reasons. First, already facing a limited budget, the city no longer received substantial pressure from above to support the movement. Absent was the massive wartime bureaucracy of the United States Food Administration. Second, even at the onset of the movement, the city attorney had informed the council that providing financial support for the movement was of questionable legality. At least one seed dealer, upset that the city was undercutting his profits by distributing free seeds, opposed the movement in its current form and claimed that the city government had no legal authority to lend its support financially. He brought the case before a judge and rested his argument on the idea that "there is no authority in the law" to appropriate money for home gardening. While the outcome of the case is unknown, L.A. City Council records include another protest "against the distribution of free garden seeds" before the council. Without the urgency of aiding the war effort, the council may have been less willing to take the legal risk of supporting the movement. Most of all, middle-class residents exerted less pressure on the council, because food prices had dramatically decreased. By December 1921, food prices in Los Angeles fell to early 1917 levels and some consumers began to express optimism that the trend would continue.[60]

Middle-class home gardening persisted into the 1920s, but it lacked the coordination and publicity of the period from 1917 to 1921. Los Angeles newspapers continued to publish gardening advice that promised to reduce living costs and included stories of middle-class residents, such as James G. Owen, an attorney, whose garden "produc[ed] . . . part of [his] living." Yet, these stories were not part of an organized and extensive movement.[61]

During the war and immediate postwar years, the home garden campaign represented a popular movement inspired by the potent combination of the high cost of food, wartime/postwar patriotism, and a projection of whiteness on the heels of a period of substantial immigration to the United States. The movement also showcased the desire among middle-class consumers to work in conjunction with multiple levels of government to fight what they defined as an unjust economy. In this endeavor, middle-class residents embraced the value of diligent production and gardened to strengthen their own pocketbooks against profiteering middlemen. They also continued to draw on the Progressive Era impulse to protect and teach children and educate and uplift the working class. White-collar home garden leaders provided them with resources and claimed to instill in them producerist values. By organizing as consumers against a seemingly unfair economy, but also by becoming producers, middle-class home gardeners made producerism an important part of their consumer identity. They flexed their economic muscles as consumers and drew on producer rhetoric to represent their values as those of the nation.

## Building Municipal Markets

Even before the start of the home garden movement, in the mid-1910s many Los Angeles residents embraced municipal markets as a means by which consumers could circumvent high food prices.[62] In Los Angeles and other communities throughout the United States, city governments established municipal markets to assert local control over urban economies that were increasingly supplied by widening food production, distribution, and retail systems. These expanded economic networks had increased the influence of so-called middlemen, such as wholesalers, cold storage facilities, and railroad companies. Municipal markets aimed to bring food producers directly to consumers in public spaces where the increasingly vilified "middleman" would be unwelcome. With this goal in mind, on April 15, 1913, the city council passed an ordinance for the establishment of four "experimental" municipal markets "as a possible means for reducing the cost of living." Each would be monitored by a municipal market inspector.[63]

On May 4, 1913, the markets opened to "a high degree of popularity among consumers." Approximately 30,000 residents visited the markets. Scores of automobiles lined up, and the supply of farmers' goods could not keep up with demand. The director of the Hollywood market, Mrs. Ingle Carpenter, explained, "it was disappointing not to be able to accommodate them. But we are going to make this municipal market a success and the people of Hollywood are determined to stand by us." Encouraged by the demand, residents were optimistic for their future growth.[64]

While municipal markets throughout the United States attracted a variety of patrons, white-collar consumers constituted a major customer base. Municipal markets in the early twentieth century reflected the needs and desires of middle-class shoppers. Architects crafted aesthetically pleasing buildings for middle-class consumers, who had developed heightened expectations for their shopping experiences with the emergence of department stores. In Los Angeles, among the chief patrons of the markets were women's clubs, including the Los Angeles Housewives' League.[65]

Despite their support, throughout the war and postwar periods Los Angeles municipal markets encountered a number of problems that threatened their existence. First, the markets brought significant operating costs, including a market director's salary and the upkeep needed to maintain their safety and aesthetics. Second, some press accounts treated the markets as merely a "fad" that offered little real value to the public. Official reports and investigations into the prices charged at markets provided conflicting evidence for this contention. Third, the markets suffered from a scam by a local private merchant to capitalize on the name "municipal market." The "Municipal Market Co." opened 23 locations throughout Los Angeles featuring signs stating "municipal market" that drew customers who mistakenly thought that they were shopping at city-operated markets. The city council instructed the city attorney to prepare an ordinance to outlaw such deception. However, two months later the city attorney concluded that the city lacked the legal authority to prevent it.[66]

The fact that middlemen found their way into municipal market stalls represented a greater blow to the aims of the market. For instance, in July 1918 the superintendent of the municipal markets defended a decision to move a "Mr. Cohen" from a front stall to a back stall in a municipal market. What to do with Cohen represented a difficult decision. Cohen was a producer, but "does not produce all of the stuff he brings to the market," while the new occupant of the stall "does and it has always been the policy to discriminate in favor of the producer." On other occasions, occupants of municipal market stalls sold "groceries and other commodities" instead of selling only self-produced goods. A December 1918 report by the "Special Committee with reference to the workings of the Municipal Market" stated that the municipal markets were failing to keep "the peddler" from selling goods at the markets, which prevented the "citizens at large" from "reap[ing] the benefit." Exasperated by these circumstances, members of the city council first attempted to close the markets in December 1918/January 1919.[67]

Throughout the postwar period, white-collar residents made repeated attempts to keep the municipal markets open. Both middle-class organizations and private individuals pressed the city council to sustain its support of the markets. The Ebell Club of Los Angeles wrote the finance committee to speak "on behalf of the continuation of City Markets." According to the City Council Public Welfare Committee, the Friday Morning Club had shown itself to be "strongly in favor of maintaining the public markets." The Friday Morning Club consisted of largely middle-class members and participated in an "anti-extravagance campaign" in conjunction with a widespread Department of Justice–led "Women's Division" campaign to reduce the postwar cost of living (discussed at length in chapter 3). The Public Welfare Committee also reported that the Hollywood Women's Club was opposed to closing the markets. Summarizing citizens' support for keeping the markets open, Councilman Frank Lincoln Cleveland stated that "only one or two persons appeared to advocate the closing of the markets, while several persons, as individuals and representatives of Women's Clubs, were strongly insistent for their continuance." In response to the overwhelming support for the markets, the Council voted to continue them, in spite of the markets' failure to sufficiently bar middlemen and the fact that they were "run at a loss of approximately $3000 per year."[68]

Like home gardens, municipal markets became a physical space of middle-class consumer activism throughout the war and postwar periods. They represented a symbol of economic fairness and a means to combat the economic injustices levied by middlemen and other profiteers. The Reverend G. D., one of Washington, DC's "salaried employees," believed that municipal markets provided literal spaces for residents to enjoy a just economy. Bringing the producer and consumer "into direct contact through the intervention of the government," city markets gave consumers relief from "soaring prices" and held the potential to create a "social center" where patrons could interact and enjoy "an end to the middle man." Similarly, one newspaper noted how Baltimore municipal market consumers "were of the great middle class—most of them well dressed." According to the paper, these middle-class shoppers represented "the public" taking "a swat at the H.C.L."[69]

These physical spaces of middle-class consumer activism took shape alongside of a mutually reinforcing discursive space in magazines, newspapers, and other media, which encouraged middle-class consumers to protest a political economy that seemed to favor everyone but the middle class. In this discursive space, which developed in the 1910s and flourished in the immediate postwar period, newspapers, magazines, academic journals, books, advertisements, and popular art forms fanned the flames of frustration for middle-class Americans. As just one example, an *Outlook* article declared, "The middle class finds that it is being crushed between its fixed income and rising prices. If need and merit ever gave the right to strike, the middle class has the right on its side." A significant presence of this discursive space was evident in Los Angeles. Newspaper articles and political cartoons juxtaposed the victimhood of white-collar workers with the high wages and underproduction of blue-collar laborers and the greed of elites, while suggesting that the physical action of consumer protest would help to even the playing field (see examples from the *Los Angeles Evening Herald*). These or similar examples of this discursive space either tacitly encouraged middle-class consumer protest or directly suggested that salaried employees form home garden associations, petition municipalities for city markets, or engage in other forms of consumer organizing. The ubiquity of articles, books, or artistic expressions describing the plight of the middle class fueled a desire among "salaried" white-collar citizens to create physical spaces of protest. These spaces, in turn, heightened interest in middle-class discontent and provided real examples for popular periodicals and other media discussing middle-class consumer grievances and activism. The physical and discursive spaces of middle-class consumer protest held a symbiotic relationship that represented the confluence of both physical, spatially constituted groups, and a nationally "imagined" community of like-minded middle-class consumers.[70] Altogether, these spaces reinforced the narrative that victimized white-collar middle class consumers were standing up for producer values against selfish groups, including *nonwhite* profiteers.

## Fighting Produce "Combinations," and the Whiteness of Food Activism in Los Angeles

Contributors to this discursive space of middle-class consumer organizing contrasted the honesty and whiteness of middle-class consumers with nonwhite, dishonest, and un-American speculators and profiteers. While white middle-class consumers organizing against the high cost of living (through a variety of methods including the formation of municipal markets) only occasionally spoke of themselves in ethnic terms, their nemeses took on nearly all shapes and forms. Stereotypes of profiteers, hoarders, and speculators ranged from gluttonous white millionaires or money-hoarding Jews

An example of a visual depiction in the Los Angeles media of profiteers and a white-collar victim. Editorial cartoon, *Los Angeles Evening Herald*, June 12, 1920.

Editorial cartoons in the Los Angeles media portraying the greed of the working class and profiteers, and the righteousness of white-collar consumer protest. Editorial cartoons, *Los Angeles Evening Herald*, May 25, 1920 and June 14, 1920.

to socialist workers or "cunning" Japanese food peddlers. Visual depictions of profiteers in popular magazines and newspapers displayed primarily images of obese, white millionaires, but also portrayed nonwhite profiteers. The victims of profiteering in these depictions, however, were almost uniformly white, middle-class-looking Americans.

White Los Angeles consumers, the politicians seeking their support, and the merchants aiming to deflect blame for high prices mainly placed responsibility on immigrant groups with significant regional populations in Southern California.[71] This focus on regionally significant immigrant populations reflected the tendencies of early twentieth-century nativism, wherein notions of whiteness and Americanism were regionally and temporally constituted as part of an unstable set of racial and cultural categories. In a letter to the Los Angeles City Council, George S. Blackstad focused on deceitful and dangerous Mexican and Asian restaurateurs while defending the honesty and worth of white lunch wagon operators. According to Blackstad, "The majority of our lunch wagons are operated by white men. It is the Oriental who most requires privacy in the preparation of mysterious foods served. Our better and cleaner restaurants do not fear the competition of the lunch wagons; and it is my belief that the most bitter opponents of the lunch wagons

Visual depictions of profiteers: while the image of the fat rich man was more common in national popular newspapers and magazines, such as *Life* and the *Chicago Daily Tribune*, portrayals of non-white profiteers, such as the Mexican stereotype and the devil with stereotypical African American features, were also printed. *CT*, August 27, 1919; *Life*, January 30, 1919, February 23, 1919, and January 22, 1920.

are the Mexicans, the Japanese and the Chinese," whereas "a number of our lunch wagons are operated by returned soldiers." Blackstad's words are emblematic of prevalent fears of nonwhite vendors endangering the health of white consumers and threatening American values. According to Natalia Molina, this era in Los Angeles saw an "official marking of [nonwhite] vendors as unscrupulous and unclean" while "health and hygiene norms increas-

IF THE PROFITEER COULD BE COMPELLED TO REIMBURSE HIS VICTIMS

Editorial cartoons, *CT*, May 21, 1920, and September 20, 1920; *Life*, February 20, 1920.

ingly became standards for 'Americanness.'"[72] Having questioned the whiteness, honesty, cleanliness, and patriotism of some of Los Angeles's most prominent immigrant groups, Blackstad asserted that the true defenders of economic justice were white men, who kept prices low for those living on "stationary" salaries as "the high cost of living climbs."[73]

In particular, white consumers, politicians, and retailers in Los Angeles identified "un-American" Japanese speculators as profiteers.[74] According to this narrative, Japanese growers and retailers, who were allegedly controlling a significant part of the California produce market, combined to deliberately hold back their crops to extract higher prices from white consumers. As Los Angeles resident Dr. George P. Clements noted to the *Times*, "The Jap combines in his selling, and in his buying. . . . The Jap pushes the small man out, excludes him from the market places and the consumer pays what a smiling Nipponese gentleman requires."[75] Neal Olsen, a conservative city councilman, member of the Los Angeles Anti-Asiatic Association, and supporter of the boycott against George Shima (the "potato king"), registered an even greater complaint against Japanese combinations of dishonest farmers and sellers.[76] Olsen supported the expansion of the Municipal Market Department and voiced frustration that the markets had hitherto inadequately eliminated the middleman. He also, however, was the former president of the Southern California Retail Grocers' Association, which represented white retailers and had been accused of profiteering.[77] In spite of his background in food retailing, Olsen skillfully appealed to the masses by speaking in popular antiprofiteering language and combining it with antiethnic rhetoric. At a June 2, 1919, city council meeting, Councilman Olsen declared, "the war is over and the food profiteers must be stopped from continuing to make their raids." "After making a complete investigation of the matter of the strawberry situation," Olsen continued, "I find, upon irrefutable proof that an ironbound combination exists and that this trust or combination has been organized by Japanese fruit and vegetable growers." Drawing on stereotypes of the Japanese, Olsen asserted that Japanese growers' and sellers' "cunning" "schemes" were operated with "arrogant authority." According to Olsen, Japanese growers sold goods at an agreed-upon price to only the "Japanese Association" each night, and sent excess crops to Japanese canneries. Independent packers and buyers had to pay exorbitant prices to receive goods from the association. By identifying Japanese growers and retailers as major profiteers, Olsen may have been attempting to shift blame for high prices away from white grocers to a popular ethnic culprit. In any case, his words resonated with the widespread nativist fears of the immediate postwar period.[78]

Olsen described these speculators and middlemen in nativist antiethnic terms that held the potential to appeal to whites across classes. To Olsen, they were distinctly nonwhite and un-American—categories that were antithetical to both white retailers and white middle-class consumers. Olsen called the Japanese food trust "our Japanese food profiteering menace" and further racialized Japanese Americans by identifying them as "a rapacious cunning, selfish race . . . which can never become assimilated with true Americanism." Juxtaposing Japanese growers with the honesty, care, productiveness, and empathy of whites, Olsen declared that Japanese farmers "Japped" the productiveness out of American soil by having it "sucked of all richness by the intensive farming."[79]

In an additional attempt at political theater, Olsen followed his rhetoric by proposing to expand the powers of the municipal market department to shut down the Japanese Association altogether. During the 1919 session, Olsen introduced a resolution to give the municipal market inspector czar-like power beyond the inspection of municipal markets. The resolution, which had little chance at passing, sought to give the inspector "complete and arbitrary power over the entire food distribution system" to prevent profiteering by all persons. The resolution predictably failed, but Olsen and others making similar accusations, including the claim that Japanese Californians willfully destroyed crops, had the attention of the Japanese Association of Southern California. The association issued a statement that blamed high prices on railroad congestion and offered to provide examples of white farmers who had allowed crops to spoil because they could not reach the public. Most important, the association asserted, "there is no organization among" Japanese farmers in Los Angeles, and that they "are powerless in the regulation of prices." Despite these statements, Japanese farmers and sellers remained a popular culprit of high prices. Months later, the *Los Angeles Times* accused Japanese growers of destroying melons to inflate prices.[80]

## Shifting to a State Government Solution

Even though Olsen's unsuccessful resolution appealed to nativist consumers, it was just one sign of the supposed failure of municipal markets to solve the city's food problems. Not only could alleged food "combinations" like the Japanese Association ignore them, middlemen continued to find their way into market stalls. To make matters worse, the buildings and facilities of the municipal markets were deteriorating, which may have discouraged as frequent attendance from middle-class consumers. For some middle-class Americans "cash and carry" shopping was a relatively new experience. According to the *Ladies' Home Journal*, middle-class consumers, who had abstained from having groceries delivered because of the high cost of living, had only recently stopped shopping at food stores with somewhat elegant-looking décor in favor of a "middle class market." Dilapidating buildings at the municipal markets might well have dissuaded these middle-class consumers from frequently patronizing them. Middle-class shoppers extolled the value of thrift, but ultimately sought to maintain an aesthetic standard for their purchasing. After all, it was their consumer identity that they aimed to protect.[81]

Municipal markets also suffered from underwhelming support from farmers. Nationally, farmers expressed only mixed opinions of municipal markets. One Indiana farmer asserted that city-sponsored markets had brought benefits to producers and consumers, but "farmers can not afford to go to the city market and sell their products for the same price that dealers would pay for them." Another farmer from Michigan exclaimed that the markets had not been completely successful, because some farmers would only charge retail prices and many city residents "refus[ed] to pay a fair price for the farmer's products." City council records suggest that farmers in and around Los Angeles also had misgivings about city markets. In an August 17, 1920, report on the municipal markets, Sterling Boothe, superintendent of the Municipal Market Department, argued that "the present system of Public Markets in this City . . . does not serve its intended purpose." The markets intended to bring producers and consumers together, but there was a "difficulty in keeping producers on the market" because of license fees and the inability to sell a large amount of crops at once. Boothe favored municipal markets in principle and, as just a few examples of successful ones, cited those in St. Louis; Dubuque and Des Moines, Iowa; Reading and Philadelphia, Pennsylvania; Portland; and Seattle. Since the Los Angeles Municipal Markets struggled to achieve similar results, Boothe offered his resignation and suggested that the council close the markets.[82]

White-collar Los Angeles consumers fought to keep the markets open. In particular, residents "living in the vicinity of the Vermont Avenue and Forty-Eighth Street Municipal Market," an area that consisted of mostly white-collar workers and their families, requested that the mayor visit the market and amassed over one thousand signatures for a petition urging its continuance. The mayor visited the market and "found it very active." "It seems that this particular market has been of great benefit to a large number of people living in the city," the mayor observed. After hearing that the council would attempt to close the municipal markets, John G. Brophy, who worked under the Municipal Market superintendent, wrote the city council to request that the council allow him to continue to operate the market on 48th Street and Vermont Avenue.[83]

Despite these appeals, the city council voted to close the markets. Frustrated by the substantial costs to the city and the markets' divergence from their intended purposes, the council overruled the mayor's support for keeping the Vermont and 48th Street market open. Unceremoniously, the council sold the remaining market equipment and building materials.[84]

With the city-operated markets closing, many citizens and local city officials shifted their attention to a proposed California initiative to open state-run city markets as a last effort for relief from high food prices. Championed by State Senator William Brown, the state market initiative aimed to create new and stronger city markets in Los Angeles and San Francisco where, according to Brown, "the farmer . . . can consign his products with confidence," receive a reasonable profit, and help to "reduce the high cost of living" for consumers.[85] To achieve this end, consumers and supportive politicians faced the formidable task of compiling the 80,000 signatures needed to place the initiative on the ballot.[86]

The proposed 1920 market initiative represented a rebirth of a previous effort undertaken by consumers and state politicians to establish state-run markets during the late Progressive Era and World War I. In 1915, Assemblyman H. E. McPherson and Senator William Brown successfully advanced legislation to enable a new director of state markets to procure fruits and vegetables directly from farmers and sell them to consumers through public markets. Yet the governor's appointee as state market director, Harris Weinstock, a longtime supporter of farming interests, neglected to undertake this role. Claiming that whether or not to actually open public markets was a discretionary power of the market director, he opted to instead focus his efforts on obtaining higher prices for farmers. Weinstock raised crop prices by expanding distribution networks and by strengthening cooperative marketing associations, which allowed farmers to collectively influence prices. Seeking to validate his undertakings, Weinstock asked Senator E. A. Luce to propose a bill during the 1917 session to absolve him of any duty to open public markets and to confirm his authorization to organize cooperative marketing associations. Furious with Weinstock's departure from his supposed duties, Senator Brown and consumer organizations throughout California fought the proposed legislation. They were unsuccessful, as farmers provided a key bloc of support for Luce and Weinstock's measure. In a last legislative effort, Brown proposed a bill in the 1919 session that mandated that the state market director open public markets and prohibiting him from organizing cooperative marketing associations. The bill failed, and Brown decided to take his quest to open state-run public markets to the people.[87]

Middle-class consumers organized the Producers' and Consumers' League to advocate on behalf of Brown's plan to amass enough signatures to place state-run markets on the ballot. Katherine James, the wife of a photographer, served as secretary of the League, while A. G. Bartlett, former president of the Los Angeles City Club, and L. B. Phelps, a doctor, were among the League's other organizers. Attorney Fred Spring also presided over at least one meeting. Collectively, they sought to "put [the] State Market Act on the Initiative Ballot."[88]

The League's motives for action reflected the same impulse for middle-class support of municipal markets—to protect consumers from profiteering middlemen. One *Los Angeles Times* headline asserted that the organization sought to "Start War on Middlemen." The League employed the slogan "Swat the Profiteer." In an open letter to California governor William Stephens on the topic of the need for better legislation to protect consumers, Katherine James asserted that during the war the state market director organized food producers to "a greater degree than ever before," which "was fine for the producer but the consumer suffered and the middle man did most of the actual profiteering." James continued, "In nearly all cases the producers were benefitted by the organization and were able to demand thru their organization fair prices for their products. But then what happened? The middle man paid the increased price because he had to and then tacked on enough more to his price to make sure that he had not lost anything by the producers' increase." By serving as a competitor to the middleman, the state of California, James hoped, would bring lower food prices for consumers.[89]

Creatively placing the word "Producers" in the title of the Producers' and Consumers' League, the League misleadingly portrayed themselves as an alliance of farmers and consumers. Among the primary middlemen targeted by a number of Los Angeles consumers were cooperative marketing associations, of which many farmers supported. For the Producers' and Consumers' League, it was only certain producers—those who were willing to market their crops directly to the consumer—who needed protection. This farmer represented, for the most part, a paragon of organizing consumers. It comes as no surprise that available sources documenting the League's activities provide no evidence of support from farmers, nor a presence of farmers among the League's organizers. Farmers by and large were on record opposing measures to shift the state market director's role from aiding cooperative marketing associations to establishing and maintaining state-supported city markets.[90]

The Producers' and Consumers' League represented a collaborative effort between middle-class citizens and members of local and state governments. Both politicians like Brown and middle-class consumers served as figureheads of the effort. Alongside white-collar residents, Mayor Meredith Snyder, former congressman William Kent (R/I-California), State Senator William E. Brown, the author of the plan, and Judge Fred Taft, who made headlines for wearing overalls at the Los Angeles County Courthouse as part of the "middle class" anti–high cost of living "wear overalls movement" (see chapter 4) and had called the middle class "the backbone of the nation," spearheaded a campaign committee to gain enough signatures to place the state market bill on the initiative ballot. At a public meeting, consumers and politicians collectively expressed their support for the petition. They reiterated that the markets would fight a common enemy in the profiteer. The markets, in Brown's words, "will prevent profiteers from squeezing the market, causing the destruction of foodstuffs and keeping prices up."[91]

Existing organizations consisting mostly of middle- or upper-class residents also lent their support for the plan. In particular, members of the City Club and the Women's City Club helped to collect signatures for the petition. Brown continued his antiprofiteering rhetoric at one City Club meeting by exclaiming that "the public markets will hurt only the profiteer, not the honest merchant, and will reduce the high cost of living." Despite the formidable task of securing the necessary 80,000 signatures for the petition, supporters of the state-run city markets appeared to be optimistic.[92]

## Conclusion

The petition for state-run municipal markets in Los Angeles and San Francisco failed to appear on the November 1920 California ballot. The initiative received a mere 7,294 signatures. Of these, 6,883 signatures came from Los Angeles, San Bernardino accounted for 367, and Ventura supplied the remaining 44. According to Senator Brown, "owing to a misunderstanding, San Francisco failed to make proper filing of her names in the prescribed time." The last hope for public markets in Los Angeles had vanished.[93]

By 1922 the impetus for middle-class consumer organizing for lower food prices had diminished. In Los Angeles, after food prices had increased by 56 percent from January 1917 to July 1920, prices began to slowly decline in August 1920. By December 1921, prices had returned to early 1917 levels. Nationally, food price levels exhibited a similar trend. As food prices dropped approximately 3 percent below 1917 prices, home garden organizations disbanded and municipal markets in localities ranging from Oshkosh, Wisconsin, to Hartford, Connecticut, closed or reduced capacity. The national discursive space of middle-class consumer organizing against high food prices that had reinforced Los Angeles middle-class protests shrank, as politicians, the press, and organizing citizens elsewhere in the country began to abandon their anti-high-food-price activism.[94]

For the duration of these movements, middle-class Americans expressed and performed producerist values as part of their growing consumer identity. Middle-class citizens romanticized the "traditional" values of industriousness, honesty, and thrift as a means of protecting their consumer identity from greedy middlemen and profiteers. They took on the role of actual producers and embraced consumption practices that would avoid the supposedly greedy and nonproducing middleman, with a particular vilification of those deemed nonwhite. Middle-class residents and sympathetic or opportunistic politicians championed these culturally conservative producerist values and condemned alleged speculators, such as the Japanese Association, which supposedly counted its profits as white middle-class consumers suffered from high prices. In attempting to teach producerist values to children and the working class, activists and supporters were further able to project their own understandings of honest hard work as selfless, neutral, and representative of the public interest. Even though these movements declined, popular discourse that cast middle-class values as the public's values persisted for years to come.

For white-collar citizens like Mary Anderson, food prices had not been their only concern. The price of wearing apparel had advanced rapidly, leading to an unprecedented federal peacetime program to prevent clothing profiteering and encourage conservation. It too became a space of middle-class consumer activism—an opportunity to impose onto the consumer economy the values of diligence and thrift. Mary Anderson was one of many volunteers to participate in the work of the U.S. Department of Justice's High Cost of Living Division, which faced the formidable task of reducing the cost of clothing. I turn to this story in the next chapter.

# 3 • The "Flying Squadron" Declares War on the Profiteers

## The High Cost of Living Division and Federally Sponsored Middle-Class Consumer Organizing

In the summer of 1919, journalist Frederic Haskin proclaimed that without immediate action from the federal government to lower the price of wearing apparel, "the buying public" would stage a "revolt" and the country would undergo a "panic." One cloak and suit manufacturer, who was interviewed for Haskin's article, predicted that "the public will stand just so much and then it will rebel." Citizens would cease to buy clothing, "the balance of trade will be upset, firms will be driven out of business and huge numbers of people will be thrown out of work." Haskin wondered "[h]ow any man can afford to have a family." A few years ago, "The mother who went downtown with a ten-spot could buy three complete outfits for her child, and still have enough left over to buy a boy a bag of peanuts and a game of dominoes. Today she is fortunate if she is able to obtain one lone outfit for $10" and pay "$15 for anything with real wool." Many white-collar Americans, who expressed their grievances in newspapers, popular magazines, and letters to politicians, shared Haskin's sentiments. They demanded swift and decisive action from the U.S. government and increasingly associated their dissatisfaction over the rising cost of wearing apparel with a middle-class identity.[1]

By the end of the war, it became clear to federal lawmakers that they could no longer ignore public outcry over high clothing prices. Working with Congress and the Department of Justice, the Wilson administration devised a two-pronged approach to tackle the high cost of clothing. First, after gaining the legal machinery from Congress, the Department of Justice prosecuted the "profiteers" in the clothing industry to set an example for any who chose to "gouge" the American public. Second, they drew on existing women's organizations to build a movement that aimed to educate American women, whom they estimated made 90 percent of all clothing purchases, about how to be thrifty consumers. Congress and the Wilson administration hoped to meet preexisting and rising expectations from the public that the government had the ability to eliminate the high cost of living.[2]

This two-pronged approach drew on an organizing tradition of middle-class state-centered voluntarism. During the Progressive Era, groups such as the National Consumers' League had attempted to tackle social and economic injustices through voluntary political action. In conjunction with their private efforts, they had also called on local, state, and federal governments to institute new laws, programs, and agencies to address prices, wages, and working and living conditions. The federal government and middle-class Americans had continued and enlarged this tradition through wartime U.S. Food Administration programs, in which middle-class citizens organized conservation campaigns and policed the consumption habits of their neighbors. As the persistence of the home garden and municipal market movements into the postwar period suggests, white-collar participation in the USFA had far-reaching effects beyond assisting the war effort. Many white-collar Americans had brought new political meanings to their consumption practices and to those of their neighbors. Selectively blending producerism and consumerism, they mobilized to defend their ability to affordably consume, and positioned themselves as champions of producer values against greedy and dishonest middlemen and elites.

With high expectations from middle-class citizens, the Wilson administration pinned its hopes on government-directed voluntarism as a strategy for reducing clothing prices in the postwar period. The federal government made clothing profiteering punishable by law and relied on middle-class Americans to report violations. The Department of Justice (DOJ) also enlisted middle-class female volunteers to teach other women in their communities how to be diligent and thrifty consumers in accordance with specific DOJ guidelines. Ironically protesting an economy that had limited their ability to afford to easily consume, middle-class Americans expected the government to impose on the clothing market the producerist values of hard work, thrift, and honesty. The Wilson administration faced a formidable task, and realized that failing to meet these lofty expectations would lead to the eruption of independently organized middle-class grassroots activism.

## Rising Expectations: Discourses on Clothing Prices before and during World War I

During the 1910s, the Wilson administration fueled public expectations that the federal government could and should control rising prices. On the eve of the presidential election of 1912, Wilson sought to make the high cost of living a central aspect of his campaign. Upon accepting the Democratic nomination, Wilson declared to a crowd in Sea Girt, New Jersey, "the majority of us have been disturbed to find us growing poorer, even though our earnings were slowly increasing. . . . prices are fixed by private arrangement." Underscoring the power of the federal government to influence prices, Wilson asserted that reasonable prices and business competition "can be revived by changing the laws and forbidding the practices that killed it, and by enacting laws that will give it heart and occasion again." By repeating this message throughout the campaign, Wilson and his supporters asserted that legislative and executive action could solve the high cost of living and promised the American public that the Wilson administration would be up to the task. Of the rising costs for "the necessaries of life," clothing prices, which had increased by 85 percent from 1900 to 1912, became a particularly hotly debated issue.[3]

Throughout the war, middle-class discontent over rising clothing prices surfaced steadily in the popular press. Stuart Chase, identifying himself as a member of the middle class, told the readers of the *Independent* of his inability to maintain a white-collar standard of living with wartime increases in the necessaries of life, even after using an itemized household budget. Chase noted, "Our clothing item has advanced 36 percent over last year," further informing his readers that his family "allowed only $150 for 'advancements,'" such as "recreation, education, books, periodicals, gifts, charity, club dues, etc." Yet, "we did not have the grit to sacrifice the moderate extras that our middle-class standard of living had accustomed to us." An article in *Life* magazine presented a more pointed portrayal of wartime middle-class consumer grievances: "The laboring classes will benefit extremely [from the war] because while they have to pay more for the necessities they can get all the work they want at double the old wages. The rich people pay a few thousands down now and then, which is a small price for the excitement of having a war," but "the middle-class people contribute about everything." Or as an article in the *Forum* asserted, "the salaried man" has "not enjoyed the increase in earnings that have come to the laboring classes . . . however, [he is] not striking or sending out ultimatums."[4]

When clothing prices reached unprecedented levels shortly after the armistice, middle-class disgruntlement in the popular press over clothing prices came closer to the point of "sending out ultimatums."[5] An increasing number of people publicly complained of profiteering and reiterated its disproportionate effect on the white-collar class. One Chicago woman explained that because her husband could no longer afford the nice clothes expected of an office worker, he had "decided to drop the pen and get a hoe," quitting his job in favor of higher paying blue-collar employment. Suggesting cause for "middle class protest," the *New York Times* complained that the office of the U.S. Commissioner of Labor Statistics overestimated the necessary amount of funds to clothe a working-class family. Middle-class Americans, they asserted, clothed their families on less money even though they worked just as diligently and also had to pay the exorbitant prices charged by profiteers. The *Riverside Independent Enterprise* stated that price increases have "hit the so-called 'middle class' or 'salaried people' so hard that their affairs are in far worse shape than those of 'wage earners.'"[6] A comparison of changes in the incomes of a selection of white versus blue-collar professions next to price changes from 1912 to 1919 suggests that blue-collar wages had risen at a rate closer to price increases, while white-collar earnings remained stagnant.[7]

According to many of these commentators, the problem resided not just in the greed of organized labor or capital but also in the inactivity of the federal government. While Congress had enabled the Department of Justice to prosecute food profiteers and hoarders through the Lever Food Control Act of 1917, the law did not apply to clothing. The Wilson administration was left only with antitrust legislation, as well as influence over federal economic policies and labor relations, to fight the high cost of clothing. As a result, throughout the war the Department of Justice arrested no hoarders or profiteers of wearing apparel, and the price of clothing continued to soar.

Writers also complained about the federal government's active role in encouraging high labor costs. Under the Wilson administration, the U.S. government had officially recognized the right of labor to collectively bargain as a wartime measure. Unsympathetic to the aims of organized labor, many white-collar workers and like-minded writers understood high wages to mean higher prices and criticized an "unproductive" or "unconstructive" working class. In the context of a national wave of strikes in 1919, individuals ranging from the president of the Illinois Freemasons to Oliver M. W. Sprague, a Harvard banking professor, viewed recent governmental support for collective bargaining and the current inability of the U.S. government to prevent strikes as central causes of high prices. According to this understanding, inflated union wages and underproduction engendered by strikes formed a deadly combination in causing price increases. One "member of the middle class" summed up such sentiment in his poetry: "When workers win a shorter day / The cost is passed along to me /. . . . And so it goes down the line / From shoes and clothes to light and heat / No old-time luxuries for mine— / I'm thankful now if I eat. . . . / When someone wins, I always lose."[8]

Despite these critiques, many in the working class did suffer from high prices. Blue-collar workers and sympathizers communicated examples of working-class struggles to meet the high cost of living to a number of government officials. One letter to the federal government referred to "profiteers who take the last drop of blood from the working classes." Charles Bowles, who operated a drilling machine for the American Body Company in Buffalo, stated in federal testimony that he had to buy on credit or "I would have had to go without clothes for the children. . . . [I] had to have them because it was getting cold." In addition to needing clothing to stay warm, working-class Americans emphasized the importance of consumption to their cultural identities or aspirations. Anna Dobmeier, who "was working for weekly wages" at the Monarch Knitting Mills in Buffalo, spoke of struggling to afford the cost of a dress that she wanted for a party. A Los Angeles working-class housewife who reported an unscrupulous retailer to federal authorities, told of how a wage earner pays all of his earnings to support his family, "his faithful housewife," and to live "to the law of God and the land." Disregarding the economic difficulties of working-class consumers, a number of white-collar Americans and commentators saw the middle class as the real victims of high prices, and the working class as perpetrators of high prices.[9]

But, as many in the popular press noted, the middle class lacked the necessary independent organizations to undertake any formal or collective action to achieve economic justice. It only needed to take this crucial step, popular writers asserted, before the country would see its true power. Charles Henry Meltzer's polemic of the middle class as "the intermediate millions" reflects the feeling of the latent organizing potential of the middle class. To Meltzer the salaried class was becoming "restless" in large part because "the cost of shoes and suits and gloves has gone up by leaps and bounds." Much like the sentiments of other social and cultural critics, Meltzer's assessment emphasized how these price increases "meant little to the rich," and had minimal impact on wage laborers, "but to the helpless and unorganized intermediates it may be calamitous." Although the outlets for organization were few, Meltzer suggested that, unless prices declined, the intermediate millions would take action.[10]

In this atmosphere of rising discontent, the Wilson administration received particularly pointed criticism from opponents in Congress for allowing profiteering to flourish and failing to lower prices. Perhaps attempting to redirect to the president any blame on Congress, critics such as Senator Robert La Follette (R-Wisconsin) argued that Wilson should have found a way through existing laws to make good on what they interpreted as the most central promise of his first presidential campaign. To a divided and discontented Senate, La Follette declared,

> I say if you study the Democratic platform of 1912, that there never was a clearer-cut issue made than that platform . . . there never was a campaign in which all other platform pledges were so ignored and the whole contest narrowed to one single issue as was the case in Mr. Wilson's campaign of 1912.[11]

Believing that an empowered government had simply failed to act, many politicians and citizens alike remembered the promises of 1912. Such a situation demanded an immediate response from the highest levels of government.

## The Department of Justice's Strategy

The Wilson administration devised a two-part federal strategy to reduce the cost of clothing. While it would be a couple of months before they would implement the second half of the strategy, the first received immediate attention from Congress. Claiming that high prices were "created by vicious practices" and "ought immediately to be checked by law," Wilson made the first part of the plan to prosecute profiteers. Since Attorney General A. Mitchell Palmer asserted to Wilson that the DOJ did not have the legal means to prosecute clothing profiteers and that the 1917 Food Control Act lacked a *specific* penalty for any kind of profiteering, Wilson wasted no time in bringing their strategy before Congress. Mandating that Congress postpone its upcoming recess, Wilson exclaimed to the Republican floor leader in the House, "I feel that it is my duty at the earliest possible moment to present certain recommendations now ready for submission to Congress," and called for special joint session of Congress on August 8, 1919.[12]

Before a packed chamber, Wilson proclaimed that the federal government had the ability to control prices. Wilson implored Congress to add a specific penalty for price gouging and to amend the Lever Act to include wearing apparel.[13] He admitted that authorities could not prosecute every opportunistic person or organization that drove up prices. Nevertheless, by setting examples, Wilson argued, other profiteers would refrain from charging exorbitant prices "of their own motion." Wilson contended that with swift action people "will not then have looked to us for leadership in vain."[14]

While Wilson's Republican opponents wasted little time in criticizing the tardiness of his attention to rising clothing prices, most intended to provide him with the legal machinery to prosecute profiteers. Even though a number of Republicans insisted that further legislation was unnecessary, they did not want to give Wilson an excuse to avoid taking responsibility.

Other congressmen just reiterated the urgency of the situation and fed public outrage over the issue. For instance, Sen. Pat Harrison (D-Mississippi) asserted, "the country is expecting the U.S. Senate to act because the man who to-day works upon a fixed income, with a family to support, can not do it with the profiteers running mad in the country." House and Senate committees reported the Lever Act amendments quickly and with few additions. It was only up to Congress, united in the desire to prevent price gouging, but divided by different understandings of the identity of the true culprits, to empower the DOJ with powerful and clear legislation.[15]

In particular, representatives from cotton-producing regions opposed an effort to use the proposed anti-clothing-profiteering legislation against cotton farmers. When Rep. Walter Newton (R-Minnesota) offered an amendment to include not just wearing apparel under the profiteering provisions of the Lever Act but also the materials and crops that make clothing, Rep. Thomas Blanton (D-Texas) retorted, "Raw Cotton is not wearing apparel, Mr. Chairman." According to Blanton, cotton farmers were not profiteers and needed a fair monetary incentive to produce. To strip more income from farmers would hurt innocent producers, decrease production, and cause further clothing price increases for consumers.[16]

But, it was this consumer, not cotton farmers, that many congressmen sought to protect. In their remarks before Congress, these supporters used emotional appeals to enlarge the implications of high prices for consumers. For example, Rep. John Summers (R-Washington) exclaimed that he wanted to "punish the profiteer, be he great or small, who fattens his bank account on the blood of little children." And specifically in response to Blanton's charge of victimization of the cotton farmer, Rep. Philip Campbell (R-Kansas) retorted, "There is not a child in the United States to-day whose necessities do not require cotton every day, just as they require food." Rep. James Young (D-Texas) fired back by inquiring, "Do children wear *cotton* or cotton clothes?"[17]

Campbell then pointed out a flaw in the design of the legislation that held the potential to doom future prosecutions of clothing profiteers under the proposed Lever Act amendment. "Children do not use fertilizer," Campbell declared," "yet it is included in this bill. This bill is to insure an adequate supply of clothing. Clothing is made of raw cotton." By including food and the materials that produced food and not those that went into clothing, Congress would only enable the DOJ to prosecute profiteers selling the finished clothing product. Judges could point to the inclusion of fertilizer as an indication that the act only intended to target retailers of wearing apparel, narrowly defined. The legal ability to prosecute organized textile workers, businessmen involved in the production process, or various middlemen, would be uncertain.[18]

Ultimately, Campbell's reasoning failed to change the bill. The intention of the legislation seemed clear: to bring the clothing profiteers to justice and to clothe American families at a reasonable price. Yet, when congressmen inquired into the true identity of profiteers, and the true identity of the victims, these categories overlapped. Was the cotton farmer a profiteer, or another exploited member of the public at the hands of this nefarious threat? The ambiguity of this situation led Congress to silence Campbell's complaints.

When, on October 22, Congress presented the amendments for Wilson's signature, most congressmen had high hopes. Only a few recognized the impossible task of meeting the expectations that their rhetoric, along with Wilson's, had collectively helped to enlarge. Reps. William Venable (D-Mississippi) and Anthony Griffin (D-New York) were among the few who sensed the full extent of the public's hopes and assumptions. Venable declared, "the people are restless and I fear the results if they be disappointed in their expectations." But perhaps Griffin said it best: "you are only sowing the seeds of discord; planting mistrust in the hearts of the people who have their eyes centered, with longing gaze, upon this Congress to give them a modicum of relief."[19]

## Prosecutions and "The Flying Squadron"

Even before Wilson signed the Lever Act amendments, the DOJ began to mobilize its forces. Since Palmer sought to make "conspicuous examples of profiteers," time was of the essence.[20] As early as August 1919, DOJ officials wrote to former USFA fair price committees and commissioners, as well as to state and local politicians, to organize new city and state fair price committees. These committees were entirely voluntary and constructed from "members of the general public," local businessmen, housewives, who represented primary agents of consumption, and some organized labor officials. Middle-class citizens, who in their wartime experiences as U.S. Food Administration volunteers had organized as consumers and had developed new political meanings for their own and their neighbors' consumption practices, were eager to participate. As one DOJ letter stated of a fair price committee, they "[are] mostly professional men." By 1920, fair price committees existed in all but six states. These committees conducted investigations into local economic conditions, published fair price lists in local newspapers, and reported violations to federal prosecutors. Upon receiving a complaint, the DOJ sent a "flying squadron" of investigators to compile information on the alleged violation before making the decision whether to prosecute.[21]

This strategy was costly, time-consuming, and ambitious. Local, state, and federal governments did not officially set prices and one form of clothing differed in cost and material from another, often with greater variation than fair price committees were able to investigate. As a result, many merchants argued that, in its functional context, the law was too vague. To what degree could a merchant charge above a price recommendation without facing prosecution? Would the DOJ leave room for variation in prices relative to a price recommendation? And for the DOJ, investigations might take too long relative to public expectations. Although Attorney General Palmer declared that "it is now possible to deal vigorously with all cases of profiteering," he recognized that "in every campaign of this character time is required to perfect an organization."[22] In sending investigators, preparing indictments, compiling witnesses, and having to coordinate between various localities and Washington, the DOJ would also incur significant costs.[23]

As perhaps the largest obstacle, investigators and prosecutors struggled to enforce a clear standard for what fit under the category "wearing apparel" and constantly had to fight over the constitutionality of the Lever Act. This question led every case to become a test case: it controlled the legal discourse of the prosecutions, making discussion of cases often focus primarily not on whether defendants were profiteers, but on whether the federal government possessed the constitutional power to reach this decision. Such a constraint on the prosecutions' speed and efficacy did not mesh well with public impatience with the high cost of clothing.

One of the first of these test cases concerned allegations of price-gouging for women's shoes in Providence, Rhode Island. Broadly speaking, the Attorney General's Office reasoned that since many shoe dealers only sold shoes, "it would seem less difficult to show that the profit of a particular sale was unreasonable" and establish a consistent pattern of profiteering, because the data would not be clouded by shifting conditions in other areas of the wearing apparel market.[24] As Assistant Attorney General Howard Figg told a price commissioner in Pensacola, Florida, we "suggest action on most flagrant cases first."[25] Before other local price commissioners and federal prosecutors acted, they observed as the DOJ prosecuted a crucial initial case.

A flagrant case is what Palmer and Figg thought they had found in Providence. On October 30, 1919, Henrietta Sharpe of North Providence traveled into the city to buy a new pair of shoes. She walked into a store owned by F.G. Collins Shoe Company on Westminster Street. After deciding on a pair, she asked the salesman about the cost of the shoes. He informed her that the price was six dollars. Unbeknownst to Sharpe, the company had already set the price for that type of shoe at $3.98. The company, it seems, had offered a commission of 50 percent of the difference between the actual sale price and the set price to any salesman who could convince a customer to pay above the original set price. Later realizing that she had overpaid for the shoes, Sharpe reported her case to the authorities.[26]

By late November, with the help of the DOJ in Washington, DC, Providence federal prosecutor Harvey Baker had compiled enough evidence to prosecute. In response to Sharpe's complaint, Baker and his staff interviewed F.G. Collins' employees and inspected the company's financial records. They found multiple violations, with percentages of the discrepancies between sale prices and set prices seemingly paid to salesmen. All in all, the company had charged up to 800 percent of what it had cost them to purchase the original product.[27] "Gratified with the extent of the evidence," Figg provided funds for Baker to hire an additional accountant and stenographer for the case.[28]

After the U.S. Attorney's office filed the indictment on December 8, 1919, the four members of the firm entered a plea of not guilty. The government alleged that the company and its four agents "did unlawfully, knowingly and willfully engage in a discriminatory, unfair, deceptive practice and device." The *Providence Evening Bulletin* added the words "feloniously conspire" and "combine" for sensationalized emphasis in their reporting on the case. From the standpoints of whether the company had charged inconsistent prices for shoes and that some of these prices surpassed what was commonly considered fair, the defendants had a weak case. Rather, they denied being profiteers for two reasons. First, operating sales on a commission system did not differ from the practices of other shoe dealers. Second, the company reported a modest 6 percent total profit for 1919. Nevertheless, F.G. Collins Co. faced charges for profiteering in individual sales, not for profiteering on total profit margin. Sensing the merits of the government's case, Judge Arthur Brown held each defendant on a bond of $3,000.[29]

The DOJ's strategy centered on using the company's account books as evidence and offering testimony from a Federal Trade Commission shoe price investigator as an expert on "reasonable" shoe prices.[30] Between travel and coordination expenses and funds for the investigator, Baker, and his staff, the case became costly, but the prospects for conviction looked promising.[31] When Michael Lynch, counsel for the defendants, filed a motion to quash, declaring the Lever Act amendments unconstitutional, the eventual outcome seemed less certain.

Lynch argued on multiple grounds that the Lever Act amendments were unconstitutional. First, since what constituted a fair price varied based on location, the size of the business, the quality of material used in wearing apparel, labor conditions, and other factors, Lynch claimed that the profiteering provisions violated the Sixth Amendment, which entitles the accused "to be informed of the nature and cause of the accusation." In essence, the price of one item could vary from another item for legitimate reasons, thereby preventing the government from using "language with such certainty to inform a person of the nature and cause of the accusations." The government could only claim that a defendant charged "unfair" prices; they could not tell a merchant precisely what was "fair." A fair price committee published suggested price levels, but, as volunteers, they had no authority to actually set prices. Even their lists could not be so specific as to cover every exact shoe. Without set prices, dealers of wearing apparel had no way of knowing how much would be considered too much.[32]

Lynch also argued that in singling out certain kinds of alleged profiteers, the government discriminated between different persons, "in violation of the Constitution," which indicates "that all persons are entitled to equal protection and subject to the same penalties" for the same type of crime. Lastly, Lynch asserted that the Lever Act amendments infringed on the Tenth Amendment, because it "attempts to interfere, control and regulate purely internal and intrastate matters concerning the business relations of persons which are reserved to the states." If a level of government did have the authority to regulate prices in commerce within rather than between states, the Constitution mandated that this power belonged to the states.[33]

On January 23, 1919, Judge Brown overruled the motion to quash with no written opinion.[34] At this point Lynch and his clients understood the outcome of the case to be a foregone conclusion. As a result, the defendants each issued a plea of nolo contendere, in which they did not admit to guilt, but accepted the punishment of a guilty plea. Characterizing their behavior as "reprehensible and unfair," Brown sentenced three of the defendants to pay a fine of $1,000 and instructed the fourth to pay $500. While victorious, the time, effort, and funds expended to convict just one company engaging in profiteering of wearing apparel perhaps outweighed the $3,500 penalty with no jail time.[35]

*U.S. v. F.G. Collins Shoe Company* also alerted the DOJ and fair price committees all over the country to the substantial burden that conflicting interpretations of the Constitution could place on future prosecutions. Nevertheless, the verdict and penalties far from signaled the end of the DOJ's strategy. The outcome was significant symbolically. The federal government had publicly recognized the greed of the four profiteers and forced them to pay the consequences in a case that received newspaper coverage within and outside of New England.[36] As a *New York Times* reaction stated, Judge Brown's upholding of the Lever Act might "furnish the Department of Justice with a strong lever—no pun intended—to dislodge a very mean way of extorting undue profit."[37]

Over the next few months, the DOJ prosecuted numerous defendants who objected to the Lever Act on similar grounds. On the whole, the DOJ encountered mixed results. While judges in district courts in Missouri, Michigan, and Colorado found the Lever Act amendments to be constitutional, courts in eastern North Carolina, southern West Virginia, and northern Washington declared the act to be in violation of numerous constitutional amendments.[38] Even with victory, not only did the DOJ face future appeals, but prosecutions rarely met public demand that the DOJ target all profiteers, or at least, the right offenders. For every story of a profiteer being brought to justice, countless other anecdotes of price gouging surfaced in the popular press, private organization newsletters, and in correspondence to local, state, and federal officials.

## The Other Villain: Labor and the Case of Antwerp Diamond Clothing Company

A number of citizens also complained of the failure of governments at multiple levels to address the role of the working class and organized labor in inflating prices. Responding to one such letter from L. A. Sarrow of New York City, Figg explained, "I quite fully agree with you that the continually increasing demands of workers are largely responsible for the high prices in the clothing industry."[39] Seeing success against merchants or wholesalers in Providence or elsewhere did not satisfy members of the public seeking more aggressive action against the "profiteering" and indolence of workers. As one Boston resident, who identified as "one of the great middle class who is getting it both ways by the present profiteering of both labor and capital," proclaimed, "before the war the working day was longer and men gained more because they were willing to work to get it. . . . they have [now] sought the very time when the world is in upheaval and unstable to demand less and less" out of themselves in "a working day or week."[40]

In the midst of a national upsurge of work stoppages, striking workers had become a popular villain for middle-class consumers. The number of strikes in 1919 increased roughly 300 percent in comparison with the previous year. Throughout the United States, railroad workers went on strike, paralyzing transportation; coal miners walked off their jobs; steelworkers went on strike; and a broad cross section of Seattle workers left work in sympathy with the demands of dockworkers. Not the least significant, textile workers struck for higher wages and better working conditions. The connection between labor activism and the high cost of living was not lost on those identifying as "middle class." Reflecting on his conversations with many other salaried workers, Ernest R. Groves, a dean at the University of New Hampshire, stated that many in the salaried "middle class" felt "mercilessly exploited," not only by capital but also by "union labor." They were losing confidence in government and advocating "an organization of the salaried man to protect . . . the interests of the consumer." Attempting to appease both businessmen and the middle class, the U.S. government obstructed labor activism in the postwar period using methods ranging from issuing injunctions against strikes to raiding the offices of radical labor organizations. But, to many, this did not do enough to solve the problem.[41]

The Antwerp Diamond Clothing Company of Buffalo, New York, represented one example of a merchant under indictment for profiteering that attempted to shift blame and exonerate itself by appealing to this antilabor sentiment. In latter half of 1919, the "brothers," Ira and Samuel Cohen, sold items of clothing to 61 patrons with an alleged average profit of 150 percent. After receiving complaints accusing the company of profiteering, the DOJ sent investigators from the "flying squadron" to the store to examine account books in the early months of 1920. The Cohen brothers fully cooperated with federal investigators. Because account books showed that the Cohen brothers had charged significantly above their costs in obtaining inventory, the DOJ decided to prosecute.[42]

Attorneys for the Cohen brothers immediately objected on constitutional grounds. They filed a demurrer in the Erie County Federal District Court, citing violations of the Fifth and Sixth Amendments that mirrored the reasoning of the F.G. Collins Shoe Company defense. The motion was denied, forcing the Cohen brothers' attorneys to abandon constitutional objections, at least for the time being.[43]

The defendants readily admitted to the disparity between their costs in purchasing inventory and sale prices, but asserted that such a stark comparison of numbers failed to account for the particulars of their business. The Cohen brothers ran a credit-retail clothing firm. From the nature of this operation, they incurred additional costs due to not receiving money up front, and more important, because of delinquent accounts. The Antwerp Diamond Company argued that the DOJ should have considered these special costs before filing charges. The makeup of their customer base, they asserted, led to large and inconsistent operating costs for the firm. In Buffalo, this customer base was blue-collar workers, in the midst of frequent strikes.[44]

The defense's strategy centered on how an irresponsible, volatile, and undiligent organized labor force caused the company to charge allegedly "excessive" prices. James Moore, Cohen's attorney, called to the witness stand Joseph Goldstein, a Rochester clothing manufacturer and wholesaler, as an expert on the clothing market to testify on organized labor's relationship to clothing prices. Goldstein explained that, given the high prevalence of strikes in postwar period, employers contended with an inconsistent labor force, which engendered high prices for consumers. If textile laborers would work harder and steadily, prices would decline.

This sentiment was shared even by the man who had reported local price violations to the DOJ. Buffalo fair price commissioner James B. Stafford, a real estate agent, deplored profiteering in clothing retail, but had publicly affirmed laborers' role in causing high prices. At the onset of the investigation, Stafford explained, "union workers in the clothing factories of Rochester and Buffalo were largely responsible [for high prices]. They loitered on the job and demanded a higher wage than ever. Production has been cut and this forced up wages."[45]

On the witness stand, Goldstein also emphasized how workers' dishonesty and capriciousness as consumers played an equally substantial role in increasing the cost of wearing apparel. "There is a large fluctuation amongst industrial workers," Goldstein testified. "That class of people constitutes a large portion of the customers of credit clothing business in places like Buffalo." He elaborated by pointing to "the foreign element" as a central reason why credit clothing merchants increased prices. These laborers, even more than other workers, Goldstein claimed, often skipped town or outright refused to pay. And, because of their tendency to go on strike, foreign workers sometimes simply lacked the wages to make good on their credit. Goldstein testified that in an industrial city—"a place like Buffalo"—it was customary for clothing merchants dealing on credit to have a markup of anywhere between 150 to 200 percent on the cost price to mitigate the losses of a largely inconsistent and transient customer base. By implication, the non-working-class consumer stood as the victim of labor's irresponsibility in driving up prices. The defense sought to blame organized labor for the high cost of clothing, a strategy that had the potential to resonate with an increasingly un-labor-friendly middle-class public. Labor's supposed lack of diligence on the job and as consumers stood in direct contrast to the self-proclaimed middle-class values of industriousness and thrift.[46]

Moore called other witnesses who echoed Goldstein's emphasis on labor's influence on clothing prices, most notably Samuel Cohen. Cohen testified that a great strike at Lackawanna Works, as well as a Buffalo switchmen's strike, led him to increase prices. As Cohen explained, among the clothing business's hazards, in addition or related to strikes, were "people moving away or changing addresses and [in] a great many cases changing the[ir] names and giving us the wrong name or they may buy their clothes in the name of another person." The switchmen's strike had a special impact on the volatility of the labor force, as it caused "other plants to close up on account of not being able to get material, coal, etc." The resultant unproductive workers and unreliable consumers were not named "Jake, Pete or John," as one witness stated in an appeal to the supposed whiteness of proper and legitimate consumers. By implication, the only way to make up for the difference was to raise prices.[47]

Despite the defense's arguments, the jury returned with a guilty verdict. However, perhaps sympathizing with the Cohens' predicament in needing to set prices that would counteract the unpaid accounts that were typical among working-class customers, they "recommended that the punishment be as lenient as possible." Judge John R. Hazel fined the company $18,000 but ordered no jail time.[48]

By mid-1920, another DOJ victory seemed to represent only partial success. Once again, the DOJ had to defend the very law that allegedly had been broken. Equally significant, the battle was not over. Moore appealed to the Supreme Court, and the case would not be resolved until February 28, 1921, when the Supreme Court ultimately found the Lever Act to be unconstitutional on the account of its vagueness. *U.S. vs. Antwerp Diamond Clothing Company*, as much as any Lever Act case, demonstrated that using the legal system to stop profiteering was a slow process, perhaps too slow to meet public expectations.[49]

Additionally, the main issue discussed in the trial, the relationship between the indolence or inconsistency of organized labor and high clothing prices, pertained to a group that the DOJ had not targeted in clothing profiteering prosecutions. While still not concentrating on textile workers, the DOJ was in the process of pursuing clothing profiteering cases based on a wider interpretation of the Lever Act, by building a case against America's most prominent woolen manufacturer: William Wood.

## "Is Cloth Apparel?" Prosecuting the "Most Notorious Profiteer in America"[50]

William Wood, arguably the most famous businessman in the textile industry, offered a target that would generate substantial publicity and might even satisfy public demand. Described by one newspaper as "the most notorious profiteer in America," Wood had been in the public limelight for quite some time. He owned the Lawrence/Andover, Massachusetts–based American Woolen Company, the largest company of its kind in the United States. It was responsible for 21 percent of the country's output of woolen cloth.[51] Wood had also made headlines when his company, local police, and the state militia violently repressed striking workers during the famous 1912 Lawrence "bread and roses" strike. During the strike, one woman was killed, allegedly by police gunfire, and a number of other workers were beaten while attempting to send their children out of town for the duration of the strike.

In many respects, William Wood was a larger-than-life figure. One contemporary described him as a "generalissimo . . . he had a round face and sleek hair, was short, fat, brusque to the point of impoliteness; wore spats and fancy clothes; surrounded himself with yes-men and therefore had few intimates."[52] His loyal office manager called him "a friendly, sympathetic man, possessed of a great driving force," and his son referred to Wood as "generous," "brilliant," "broad minded," "far sighted," "industrious," and "kindly." Rather than an oppressor of the working class, Wood presented himself as a paternal figure.[53] He ran Andover and Lawrence as company towns, either owning or influential over everything from the newspapers to the mayor's office. Wood claimed to care deeply about his workers, wishing to protect them from outside influences, including radical labor organizations.[54]

Wood had made a killing as a result of the war. Due to increased U.S. government demand for textiles, he "landed the largest single textile order that had ever been allocated," amounting to $50 million for the one order with another $52 million to come through separate orders from the government. "The financial position of the company at the end of World War I was impregnable," Wood's son recalled. "The price of its stock had tripled on the New York Stock Exchange. It was a rich plumb for vultures to pluck." Wood decided to take advantage of the situation. "Now that the war was over, the impetus of government orders ceased," his son noted. "Dad thought it wise to cash in on a large part of his holdings in the company at then all-time peak prices." For the year 1919, Wood "cashed in" on a total profit of $15,513,415.[55]

Wood had no intention of sacrificing his wealth for his workforce. In spite of his profits, in the early months of 1919 Wood angered his workers by denying them a 12.5 percent increase in pay. In response, a large contingent of the workforce went on strike for 107 days. Wood conceded raises to avoid continued activism, and played to antilabor consumer sentiment by stating that "the public" would endure higher prices because of the workers' demands.[56]

Yet, just as Wood fought against wage increases and took enormous profits, he simultaneously cast himself as the protector of his workers' interests against profiteering retailers. Perhaps sensing future public outcry over his own profits, Wood blamed local merchants for the high cost of living, portraying himself as a caring paternal figure against opportunistic Lawrence businessmen. On December 17, 1919, Wood let employees off work in the morning to allow them to attend a public gathering, in which he publicly attacked Lawrence merchants for profiteering after the recent wage increases. Calling his company "a great humane institution," Wood exclaimed to the crowd, "You live in Lawrence, you work in Lawrence. It is in Lawrence that you must buy your clothes and your food, I want to see that the workers of the American Woolen Company get all of the advantages that I can give them." Wood's remarks received national attention in the press, as did his threat to open a department store in Lawrence that would sell merchandise at cost, a measure that a local labor leader called an attempt to drive workers into "slavery" by making them dependent on "a company store." Regardless of Wood's intentions, one magazine proceeded to describe him as the "apostle of lower living costs."[57]

Though not representing all types of profiteers, William Wood was precisely the kind of figure the public hoped the DOJ would bring to justice. Already known for his greed and substantial power, the disclosure of his wartime profits led many to consider him the largest robber baron of the clothing industry. One newspaper inquiring as to "where the consumer comes in," declared Wood's practices to be "bold profiteering, nothing else."[58] In a letter to the *Duluth News-Tribune*, Robert Drayton, a Duluth resident, expressed a similar point of view. Identifying as "one of the middle class, which has felt the awful squeeze of high prices more than capital or labor," Drayton criticized Wood's "immense profits," excessive prices, and deceptive "propaganda."[59]

With these sentiments in the foreground, the DOJ launched an investigation that would ultimately lead to perhaps the most noteworthy Lever Act prosecution then to date. To the DOJ, pursuing charges against Wood provided a grand, but risky, opportunity to demonstrate the efficacy of the Wilson administration's approach. Wood would be well prepared, choosing Charles Evans Hughes, a well-known 1916 presidential candidate, as his attorney. A DOJ defeat would draw national attention to its ineffectiveness in bringing down the cost of clothing. A victory, however, could work toward building public confidence.[60]

According to the District Attorney's office, Wood's profits amounted to 300–400 percent. Wood claimed them to be only 12.5 percent and cast himself as a victim. News of the indictment was ubiquitous in newspapers and newsletters throughout the country, many of which hoped for a DOJ victory. On the surface, local sentiment differed. Immediately after the indictment, Wood's "loyal" workers held a parade in his honor against the DOJ. A 40-piece brass band led the procession and the *Andover Townsman* described the sound of "ringing cheers." The mayor and a few employees made speeches to the crowd. One employee exclaimed that "there are people who are anxious to make a victim of some man who stands high in the eyes of his fellow men." Like a grateful father figure, Wood expressed gratitude for their loyalty. "You can never know how fully I appreciate this expression of your loyalty," Wood exclaimed. "I cannot find the words adequately to thank you." Wood's employees seemingly stood united behind him against the wrongful accusations of the DOJ.[61]

Or at least this is the story Wood wanted his contemporaries to believe. In scattered sources, we find the real sentiments of many of his workers, the same workers who, less than a year before, had gone on strike because of Wood's labor practices. George Soule interviewed Wood's employees and found that "the workers are tired of pretending Mr. Wood is popular. On several occasions they have been taken out of the mills on full pay during working hours, and mobilized with brass bands for demonstrations of welcome, or what not, for Mr. Wood, who has entered the city . . . like a little king greeting his loyal subjects."[62] The socialist *New York Call* similarly reported, "When news came that Wood had been indicted for profiteering his agents staged a demonstration in his favor marching out to his residence a body of his workers who expressed their confidence in him."[63] Whether for Wood's own campaign against the alleged profiteering of Lawrence merchants or for a protest against Wood's indictment, Wood expected his workers to respond to his directives: work hard, for low pay, and rally by his side when so commanded. Fed up, some workers staged a one-day strike in protest.

The defense strategy was simple. In addition to questioning the constitutionality of the Lever Act, defense attorney Charles Evans Hughes filed a demurer stating that cloth is not wearing apparel and therefore falls outside of the intent of the law. Judge Julian Mack agreed. Reasoning that Congress had included not just fertilizer in the bill but also the ingredients needed to make fertilizer, Mack declared that if Congress had intended the DOJ to prosecute profiteers in the woolen mills, it would have included cloth in the language of the act. Mack was at least partially correct. Congress had voted down an amendment to include gasoline and oil as part of what constitutes "fuel," and Rep. Blanton had also plainly stated that cotton was not and should not be included in the bill. In any case, Congress had inhibited the DOJ by not using explicit language. As a result, Wood was a free man and he fittingly celebrated by having his workers stage another parade featuring a band concert and bonfire.[64]

Newspaper editorials expressed outrage. The *Modesto Evening News* exclaimed that a profiteer of cloth buttons, linens, silk, and cotton "may gouge all he pleases." According to the *Atlanta Constitution*, "the dismissal of the case upon a flimsy technicality cannot but leave upon the public mind an impression that the court has not 'played fair' with the people." The *Buffalo News* described "the technicalities of the law" as an "abomination to the public." And the *Chicago Daily Tribune* stated that ultimately both Wood and his workers were profiteers: "Its employees naturally took advantage of this prosperity to force up their own wages." The public that was neither capital nor labor seemingly stood as innocent bystanders while Wood and his laborers enjoyed a celebratory concert, parade, and bonfire.[65]

In fact, the public outcry was reportedly so intense that many of Wood's buyers cancelled orders, prompting him to temporarily close a number of the mills. As a result, many of his workers became unemployed. According to Wood, "The only reasonable course was to suspend operations of the mills until a new demand for cloth warranted our opening again."[66] Representatives of labor disagreed, arguing that closing the mills in the wake of the outcome of the case merely served as an excuse to slash labor costs. Sidney Hillman, president of the Amalgamated Clothing Workers, pointedly stated that the shutdown "will permit continued profiteering." Samuel Gompers, president of the American Federation of Labor, queried, "For months we have heard the cry 'increased production.' How can a policy of increased production be accomplished under a policy of laying off thousands of workers?" The United Textile Workers passed a resolution condemning the closings.[67]

Ultimately, Wood's employees ended up in worse shape than before the strikes of 1919–20. Not long after the mills reopened a few months later, they were forced to accept significant wage cuts. William Wood's employees felt the effects of the move toward what historians have defined "the lean years" for organized labor. In the wake of an upsurge of labor activism in the immediate postwar period, workers soon found themselves again under the direct control of the American Woolen Company. The public, eager to blame both labor and capital for the high cost of clothing, would not come to the rescue.[68] While far from sympathizing with the aims of organized labor, they also were largely disgruntled with the Wilson administration's approach to tackling rising clothing costs through Lever Act prosecutions. Of the decision in *U.S. vs. American Woolen Company*, the

*Sandusky Star Journal*, for example, called the Lever Act "a joke" and referred to "a great public outcry since the decision was announced." Another publication perhaps best summed up public sentiment expressed in the press: "In their blissful ignorance Palmer and his satellites rushed into battle; they won a few, a very few cases."[69]

## "So Finally It's Up to the Women!" Organizing the Women's Division

Months before the failure of the Lever Act prosecutions, on October 17, 1919, Attorney General Palmer outlined the second part of the DOJ strategy to lower the cost of wearing apparel.[70] According to DOJ estimates, women constituted 90 percent of the buyers of wearing apparel. Prosecuting profiteers, Palmer reasoned, would address rising clothing prices by curbing greed among clothing dealers, but would do little to prevent women from purchasing items of clothing from merchants who managed to slip through the cracks, or from developing extravagant fashion habits. Thus, the DOJ decided to use a portion of its Lever Act congressional appropriation to educate women on how to be judicious and thrifty consumers.[71]

Mirroring the statements of many politically active middle-class women themselves, the DOJ asserted that women needed to exhibit economy in dress and be diligent consumers for the household. To accomplish this goal, Palmer sought to create a movement that would use existing women's organizations to discourage "extravagance" in dress among American housewives. Women would develop new habits, Palmer reasoned, by building on previous experience in World War I conservation campaigns. Palmer placed the duty of organizing the movement on the newly created Division of Women's Activities, headed by Edith Strauss, a former member of the women's motor corps and the future wife of Figg. Brimming with confidence, Strauss stated "if we all actively unite and put our best effort [in] back of this movement, normal conditions will be restored before we know it."[72]

Before publicizing their strategy, Palmer and his assistants conferred with the National Consumers' League, the League of Women Voters, the General Federation of Women's Clubs, and other women's groups to enlist their support. Though in many ways differing in their political outlooks and aspirations, these organizations largely consisted of middle-class women. In October, the DOJ sent letters to prominent middle-class women in these and other civically active organizations asking for both their support and for their input on how to encourage thrift in clothing consumption. Palmer and

Strauss solicited participation by alluding to women's past efforts during World War I. In a letter to Edna White of the American Home Economics Association, for example, Palmer asked, "May I count on your organization to unite and actively help win the war of reconstruction?" Similarly, in a form letter to leaders of women's organizations, invoking the language of battle, Strauss stated, "Women who occupy responsible positions in a community can put the power of their influence and position behind the movements designed to kill the cost of living." Strauss asserted that women, who made the majority of clothing purchases, "stirred by patriotic enthusiasm" "can to a large extent control prices."[73]

According to the Division of Women's Activities' plans, women would undertake this task within a hierarchy. Each level would be responsible for educating those below on which clothes and fabrics to purchase and how to rework them to make them last longer. Palmer and Strauss stood at the top of the hierarchy. Below them were state chairmen, followed by state advisory boards, county or district chairmen, and then local women's organizations. Local Women's Division officials often were individuals who had previously served on wartime fair price committees. Local clubs participating varied from the Monday Afternoon Club of Kentucky to the Housewives League of Rhode Island. The DOJ circulated educational literature through this hierarchy to each participating club, which would then instruct the women in their local communities on how to fight the high cost of living through proper consumption of wearing apparel.[74]

For the most part, the Women's Division's campaign was strictly educational. Although participants reported cases of profiteering to the DOJ, they mainly sought to spread the message of thrift—through word of mouth, panels, roundtable discussions, speakers, pledge cards, pamphlets, slides in motion pictures, and the local and national press. As Strauss told many participants, "I do not think you can put into the hands of the public a stronger weapon than knowledge." The Women's Division spelled out this knowledge in instructions to women's organizations. One memorandum outlined 10 points that each organization should follow, beginning with spreading interest in the Women's Division among other local women's clubs and ending with a directive to install bulletin boards in club meeting halls that would display information on combating high clothing prices. Other instructions were more specific. A manual titled "Information of Value in Choosing Material for Blouse" provided recommendations on 22 different kinds of material in regards to weight, weaving, and ability to be laundered relative to price. Such manuals aimed to help middle-class women make their clothes last longer without making them look old or ragged. The paragon for middle-class women's fashion under the Women's Division campaign emphasized quality (rather than cheap) fabric, infrequently purchased, and of a plain, unostentatious style.[75]

Such an emphasis on plain but quality clothing fit within a developing tension between a middle-class desire to differentiate itself from the working class in fashion style and the working class's increasing ability to afford more styles of dress. In the late nineteenth and early twentieth centuries, a variety of new consumer goods, including cheap mass-produced clothing, became available to working-class Americans. Middle-class women in particular responded to the "democratization of fashion" not by embracing the extravagant styles increasingly worn by the working class, but by placing a premium on quality grades of clothing and looking down on cheaply constructed clothing increasingly worn by working women. While this trend was in place before World War I, the high cost of living alongside of working-class wage increases versus stagnant white-collar salaries heightened a middle-class desire to culturally define the boundaries dividing them from the working class. Greater relative purchasing power for the working class and the democratization of fashion blurred the lines of class distinction. It was a distinction that many middle-class families were steadfast to defend by self-righteously claiming that their class was uniquely true to the values of hard work and thrift, and by reworking their fashion choices. Yet emphasizing quality clothing over cheap fabric placed limits on how and to what extent middle-class consumers could exercise thrift.[76]

Thus, in instructions telling women how to exercise thrift, the Women's Division had to mitigate the idea of practicing economy in dress with the need to maintain middle-class standards of fashion. A "pledge" for the Women's Division of Texas epitomized the tension between class differentiation and thrift in requiring adherents to adopt the slogan "PLAIN LIVING and HIGH THINKING." While nearly the entire pledge stressed paying low prices, one section resolved, "we will be guided by quality and not by price." A "Do's" and "Don'ts" of clothing consumption circulated by the central office of the Women's Division similarly told women that they should avoid looking cheap by paying attention to fabric quality and by refraining from wearing extravagant styles, or "clothes extreme in style or color." While the guidelines directed women to "Judge by quality," they also told them to "Wear clothes as long as possible." Doing so involved extensive instructions on how to rework clothing. Spreading this kind of detail to all middle-class homes represented an onerous task. Moreover, it wasn't clear whether the DOJ intended to spread its message beyond the middle class. Though never stated in DOJ documents, working-class adoption of the DOJ instructions might further obscure the class boundaries that many middle-class consumers seemed to desire.[77]

DOJ instructions brought significant challenges to even those who adhered to them strictly. Susan Williams, a student at Duvall High School in Jacksonville, Florida, described the substantial amount of time required to acquire "knowledge of textiles, their properties and the rules governing" their alterations necessary to "make up the pretty garments that the young girl naturally craves." Gertrude Sheppard of the *Ladies' Home Journal* instructed her readers to practice on "dummy dresses" and "gradually" work toward real articles to "beat the H.C.L," while declaring "always buy good material." Mothers of students at the Hibbard School in Chicago used Women's Division guidelines to produce "made over" clothes from quality cloth in "big sister's serge dress that was too small, or from dad's coat." But the supply of quality cloth or clothing was not endless. Many women wanted new quality cloth to supplement recycled clothing. This was a problem since, as the chairman of the local Women's Department of the Chicago Fair Price Committee noted, they "refuse to buy articles offered at lower prices because they are afraid that they might be of inferior quality." As a result, they continued to pay high prices.[78]

Because quality clothing was more expensive than cheaply made "extravagant" working-class attire, major women's organizations focused not exclusively on spreading all Women's Division messages, but rather on preventing profiteering in quality cloth and clothing sales. Leading this campaign, the National Consumers' League attempted to mobilize consumers to pressure the U.S. government to pass legislation that would prevent merchants and manufactures from profiteering by misleading consumers on the quality of fabric in their products. The NCL and other supportive middle-class consumers pressed for the enactment of the French-Capper "Truth in Fabric" bill, which aimed "to prevent deceit and profiteering." Modeled on the 1905 Pure Food and Drug Act, the French-Capper bill required manufactures and dealers of cloth and clothing to list the percentage of "shoddy" versus "virgin" material in the end product. Palmer and Strauss had not intended to build a movement for the enactment of more legislation. Nevertheless, the Women's Division's focus on cloth quality unintentionally encouraged women's organizations to focus on the need for more government action.[79]

The NCL used many of the same methods practiced by the state Women's Divisions to advocate for the French-Capper bill. Leaders of the NCL delivered speeches all over the country, asked newspapers to include information on the "honest cloth" movement, wrote editorials, held mass meetings, wrote philanthropic organizations for support, handed out "truth in fabric" stickers to be placed on envelopes, and created pamphlets and posters. The NCL even set up a hierarchy with national, state, county, and city directors that resembled the organization of the DOJ's Women's Division. Ultimately, the NCL sought to build a movement around the honest cloth bill. A pamphlet outlining the campaign summed up their aims:

> The fate of truth in fabric can not be settled in legislative or congressional committee rooms, unless the need and justice of this issue is brought convincingly before meetings of women's clubs . . . dinners of Kiwanians and Rotarians, and under kerosene and electric lights all over the state and nation.[80]

The NCL also solicited support for the Truth in Fabric bill by interviewing presidential candidates on the issue, and by writing letters to congressional candidates and incumbents, hoping to capitalize on the fact that the election of 1920 was on the horizon.[81]

The NCL was not alone in shifting focus to "truth in fabric." Divisions of the General Federation of Women's Clubs also turned their attention to "honest cloth" and misbranding. Referring to the Barkley Misbranding Bill (a similar act also pending in congressional committee), Mildred Weigley, St. Paul chairman of the home economics committee of the Minnesota Federation of Women's Clubs, declared to an audience at their January 1920 statewide meeting, "We must secure sufficient interest to secure reporting out of committee, discussion and action." "The passage of this bill," Weigley exclaimed, "would mean more opportunity for efficient buying and hence be a step in decreasing the cost of living."[82] The American Home Economics Association, which had strongly supported the campaign of the Women Division, also ultimately focused much of its efforts on honest cloth legislation. Advisory committees of the association secured the endorsement of women's clubs for "truth in fabric" and the association's journal dedicated more attention to discussion in support of honest cloth legislation.[83]

Ultimately, the NCL and its allies had little to show for their efforts. Numerous manufactures and merchants of clothing opposed the bills, calling them "ill-conceived." Many merchants underscored the tension between emphasizing pure or quality fabric and trying to promote thrift. In a letter to the NCL, Richard A. Feiss of the Cleveland Clothcraft Shops explained, "In our efforts to keep down the cost of living and for the conservation of our resources, it is not only essential to the buying public that reworked wool be used as extensively as possible, but that no bad name be attached to its use."[84] Feiss, of course, neglected to mention that reworking fabric was supposed to be the consumer's job and that their main complaint was not the sale of reworked fabric, but dishonest or unclear labeling of it. In a statement to members of Congress and the general public, the National Association of Wool Manufacturers (NAWM) argued that many "shoddy" grades of wool were actually of higher quality than "virgin" wool. Under this reasoning, manufactures would be encouraged to use higher percentages of lower quality "virgin" fabric, a form of deceit that would not be revealed by French-Capper labeling. The NAWM also noted that conspicuous labels on clothing would "put an end to the thrifty practice of 'turning' and remaking dresses." The best solution, the NAWM claimed, was to let free-market competition regulate honesty.[85]

Popular newspapers expressed mixed feelings for the legislation. While some newspapers wholeheartedly backed the French-Capper bill, a *New York Times* opinion piece went as far as stating that the general public opposed the bill. Many articles pointed to the idea that the bill or its proponents had sent contradictory messages regarding thrift. Facing these obstacles, the NCL and other women's organizations failed to convince Congress to pass the bill, though the issue of "honest cloth" did resurface occasionally in the years to come.[86]

Ultimately, the Women's Division faced a difficult task. In addition to battling the tension between thrift and the maintenance of middle-class fashion standards, cooperating women's organizations focused on additional legislative action rather than simply doing the work of the Women's Division. Perhaps most onerous, amid inflated public expectations that the federal government could reduce the cost of clothing, the task was too large of a burden to place on a subdivision of a U.S. government department. As Mrs. J. R. Leighty, chairman of the Missouri Women's Division, noted while publicly criticizing Strauss and the DOJ, "$150 for an executive secretary and a small sum for a stenographer are inadequate" to bring down the cost of clothing.[87]

Yet the Women's Division claimed success, at least in the reduction in prices for women's apparel. As the Women's Division disbanded in mid-late 1920, Figg wrote to the *New York Times*, "The work of the women's organizations cannot be too highly praised," while telling fair price commissioners "the Women's Division . . . has succeeded in turning the trend of prices of women's wearing apparel in the direction of reasonable levels." However, a survey of advertised retail prices for a variety of women's apparel sold at three different department stores suggests that prices for women's apparel actually increased by 48 percent from mid-1919 to mid-1920. Wholesale prices published by the Bureau of Labor Statistics indicate a similar trend.[88]

## Conclusion

Whereas the Women's Division claimed ambiguous success, by mid-1920 many viewed DOJ prosecutions as a universal failure. Attempting to put a positive spin on at least half of the DOJ strategy to bring down clothing prices, a DOJ official wrote to a volunteer reacting to the termination of the Women's Division: "The educational campaign as conducted by the women was of far more value than the prosecutions under the Lever Act." Retail prices for clothing increased by 24 percent from October 1919 to August 1920. The constant battle over the constitutionality of the Lever Act put the Attorney General's Office on the defensive. Every case became a "test case," since defendants only somewhat based their cases on their innocence of the crime. Rather, they focused on the constitutional merits of the Lever Act itself. As an official report of the Attorney General's office recounted, "the Bureau was seriously hampered in its efforts. . . . judges held those sections under which its principal activity was carried on to be unconstitutional." The constraint that judicial readings of the Constitution placed on the fight against profiteering exacerbated the already limited strategy of fighting the high cost of clothing by attacking individual profiteers.[89]

The DOJ strategy also did not adequately assuage the middle class's antipathy toward the supposed growing power of organized labor and its role in causing the high cost of living. As just one discontented voice, the Jacksonville *Fraternal Record*, a bulletin of fraternal organizations, in which at least some members represented themselves as "clean, substantial people of the great middle classes," circulated the question "What is the real business of the Department of Justice besides ignoring profiteers?" Complaining of rising working-class wages, the *Record* also printed the remark that "the one ambition of the salaried man is to live up to the standard established by the unskilled laborer." Many middle-class Americans viewed striking workers as lazy people who lacked thrift and enjoyed the fruits of a consumer society while the middle class struggled. They lacked "true" producer values of industriousness and thrift that middle-class Americans had incorporated into their consumer identity. In a speech to citizens in West Virginia, a High Cost of Living Division official pointedly summarized the sentiments of many in the general public: "they are constantly complaining that nothing is being done, or at least if anything is being done, it is not being done right."[90]

It was continued frustration with the inability of elected officials to solve the high cost of clothing that would encourage many in the white-collar middle class to undertake grassroots organization. The top-down federal government strategy that drew partially on middle-class voluntarism had not gone far enough. The disgruntled "consuming public" responded to these failures of the federal government not just by sustaining their assertions of middle-class victimhood in the postwar economy but also by building on their growing political consciousness as consumers to form new organizations. As Edith Strauss reported while the work of the Women's Division was nearing an end, "Overall and gingham dress clubs have been organized in many states." The middle class would soon don denim to fight the high cost of living and, as consumers wearing the costume of diligent production, call for a return to traditional producer values among the working class.[91]

# 4 • A Nation in Overalls

## Middle-Class Clothing Boycotts

On April 29, 1920, the Reverend New Harris of St. Paul's Methodist Church in Muskogee, Oklahoma, performed not one, but two, weddings. On the surface, the "double header" of ceremonies seemed far from unusual. It was the culmination of two classic war romances. The first couple, Parker Watson and May Gibson, intended to marry in 1917, but Watson was called to arms when the United States entered World War I. At the conclusion of hostilities, Watson returned home and intended to marry "his bride" only to be again summoned for duty. For the next few months he served in France while Gibson longed for his return. When the couple finally stepped to the altar, they were joined by Watson's business partner, Harry Rex Whaley, and his bride, Golda Miley. Like Watson, Whaley had served in the Armed Services during his engagement, delaying his wedding for two years. It seemed only natural that the two men would share the same wedding date. But what united these two marriages was not simply their common war romances or the fact that Watson and Whaley were business colleagues. Rather, the couples also chose to combine ceremonies because both men had decided to abandon formal wear in favor of bib overalls.[1]

The popularity of wearing overalls had recently spread throughout Oklahoma. Across town from the wedding, W. G. Robertson, a trial lawyer, pleaded a case in overalls in the district courthouse. Nine days earlier, numerous citizens paraded in overalls down the streets of Oklahoma City to celebrate the opening of the Western League baseball season. On the same day, a group of students at the local high school forced a classmate to put on overalls after he had remarked that the wearing of such attire was "all foolishness." The students "held him by force, removed his stylish clothes and dressed him in overalls." Reports of the event mentioned no disciplinary action.[2]

By May 1920, similar stories could be found virtually anywhere in the

United States. The "overall movement"[3] had spread to the point that ministers preached in overalls, politicians wore them to appeal to their constituencies, and students attended dances in overalls. Perhaps most noticeable, citizens in localities ranging from Milledgeville, Georgia, to New York City paraded in the streets displaying signs with slogans, such as "To Hell With the High Cost of Living" and "Down With the Profiteers in All Lines," while donning nothing but denim. As economist Henry W. Macrosty recalled, "by the middle of April, the storm broke."[4]

When the overall movement emerged, middle-class citizens were already protesting high food prices by pressing for municipal markets and planting home gardens, and had grown frustrated with the federal government's seemingly failed attempts to address the high cost of clothing. According to many white-collar Americans, the Wilson administration and the DOJ had not been aggressive enough in reducing clothing prices, which, they argued, placed a special burden on white-collar workers, whose salaries had remained stagnant since the onset of the war. With the overall movement, middle-class Americans embraced a new strategy. "Striking" against the high cost of clothing, participants in the movement signed pledges agreeing to wear only overalls until clothing prices returned to more reasonable levels. Newly formed "overall clubs" organized formal protests and in part blamed merchants and middlemen for price advances.

Appropriating of the clothing of productive labor also served as a means for the middle class to protest the working class's supposed role in causing high prices. White-collar citizens, who took part in home garden and municipal market campaigns or eagerly awaited the results of Department of Justice prosecutions, had also frequently lambasted laborers for inflating prices. Overall movement participants expanded on this antipathy toward labor. Responding to an increase in labor unrest during the postwar period, club members and their supporters identified working-class greed and laziness as reasons for the high cost of living. As newspaper reporter Laura A. Smith proclaimed, the movement sought to oppose laborers undertaking a "whirlpool of strikes." In the context of the first red scare, popular fear of bolshevism's influence on organized labor further inflamed passions directed against the working class. Borrowing "the symbol of real work," middle-class Americans responded with direct and abrasive action against actual producers. They defined economic justice using producer values as they expressed the power and importance of their growing consumer identity. Even if asking for more government intervention into the economy, they promulgated a culturally and economically conservative discourse, which nostalgically called for a return to "traditional" producer values of hard work, honesty, and thrift.[5]

## The Early Overall Movement: Origins in Jacksonville

The movement began during the last week of March 1920 in Jacksonville, Florida. Noticing a rise in the price of clothing at local stores, an eclectic group of citizens met to discuss an organized response. Seeking to "dethrone" "the king of high prices," they decided to use their power as consumers to combat profiteering and encourage lower prices. The $2.50 overall in "all [its] glory" would serve as the symbol and strategy of protest. Each participant signed pledges to don nothing but denim until clothing became more affordable. Within days, the Jacksonville overall club had enrolled 1,000 members.[6]

In hopes of universalizing the movement's appeal, many early Jacksonville overall club members aimed for interclass cooperation. For example, the club passed a resolution stating that its membership came "from all walks of life" and that one of its goals was the creation of "a sentiment to put a stop to the great extravagance and waste now prevalent among all classes." The resolution also absolved most local merchants from blame for high prices, so as to gain their support. Sympathetic newspaper reporting emphasized the varied backgrounds of club members, which included machinists and firemen, as well as white-collar professionals, and noted that rising clothing prices affected all consumers.[7]

The nascent organization expressed grand ambitions and sought to rapidly increase its membership. Beyond using the workplace as a site for organization, the overall club set up a registration headquarters on Hogan Street, which enrolled as many as 200 members in one day during the first week of April. The new members "represented more than fifty different businesses, trades and professions." The leadership further announced that they would create a number of regional registration sites located in different parts of the city and that the club would provide overalls for any participant lacking their own pair. Based on this initial success, club leaders optimistically declared that they would secure the names of approximately 5,000 residents on pledge sheets by April 4. As the *Florida Metropolis* reported, "the overall movement has spread with rapidity that seems very remarkable."[8]

Rather than merely seeking to address local price increases, organizers wanted the movement to gain mass appeal. Toward this end, leaders successfully solicited the support of the mayor and members of the city council. Participants suggested that these endorsements represented only the beginning. One organizer hoped the movement would "spread until it becomes a nation wide movement as originated here." On March 30, less than a week into the movement, James A. Davis, secretary of the club, predicted that this would happen "in a short time." While his prediction would hold true, neither Davis nor any other club member had publicly voiced a desire for it to spread as a specifically white-collar, "middle class" movement.[9]

After adding as many members to the association as possible, club leadership called for a parade of overall-clad citizens down the streets of Jacksonville. In actuality, it would be the second overall parade to occur in the city. In late March, fifty employees of the Drew Press Company had marched in the streets in overalls while wearing "little placards" labeled "The Overall Club." Now the overall club leadership envisioned something larger—participation of all members, two brass bands, speakers, the mayor, and a motion picture company to film the event. Leaders initially decided to hold the parade on Easter Sunday. Hoping for maximum publicity and participation, the club twice postponed the event until finally setting April 8 as the date.[10]

The Jacksonville parade lived up to its billing as "one of the most unique demonstrations held in the South." On April 8, scores of Jacksonville residents converged on Hemming Park to march in overalls. Led by the grand marshal, Police Captain W. D. Vinzant Jr., they chanted against profiteers and the high cost of living while "a large number of people lined the streets or hung from windows in stores and business houses to see what was going on." Two brass bands blared patriotic marches. Members of the club carted a stretcher around the park carrying a dummy with "High Prices" written on its body, and E. E. Cohen of the Cohen Bros. Department Store filmed a short movie of the event and forwarded it to a current events film company. Mayor John W. Martin then issued a proclamation stating, "I feel it incumbent upon me to call special attention to these resolutions [of the overall club], and to the parade, and to ask for both the most earnest consideration of our people."[11]

The signs and banners raised by marchers demonstrated the multifaceted nature of the movement, but also hinted at its potential to be co-opted as a middle-class movement, disdainful of the working class. Most signs focused on profiteers, such as one stating "demand value for your money." Others called for thrift by using slogans like "save your money" or "get the saving habit," or appealed to patriotism and the antiradicalism of the red scare by asserting "let's get rid of the red menace and be 100 per cent American by deporting the profiteer." Yet one banner foreshadowed a major characteristic of the movement as it spread from north Florida and entered the national scene. Taking a stab at the working class for the supposed role of underproduction in causing high clothing prices, one marcher's sign declared "dignify the overall." For some at the parade, it was those donning the costume of productive labor, rather than those wearing overalls by trade, who brought dignity to the garb. In the overall movement, the cross-class unifying potential of a shared consumer identity would soon be wrought with tension.[12]

## A Middle-Class Movement: The Overall Campaign in Tampa

Before the movement spread to the rest of the United States, the city of Tampa spurred its growth. In fact, Tampa embraced the movement early enough to confuse newspapers throughout the country into calling it "The Tampa Idea." Tampa served as a logical site for a grassroots and increasingly middle-class movement. The formation of overall clubs continued a tradition of grassroots activism in the city that adapted itself to constantly changing local circumstances. Over the previous decades, Tampa residents had created organizations to address controversies over immigration, labor, urbanization, religion, and patriotism. These groups had featured both combinations and divisions according to class, race, and gender. How each organization formed, networked, and fissured depended greatly on immediate historical context. In 1920, the immediate problem facing middle-class Tampa residents was the high cost of living.[13]

The increasingly antilabor tone of the overall movement resembled the ideology behind previous powerful organizations in Tampa. From the late nineteenth century into the 1920s, elite and white-collar Tampa residents formed "citizens committees" to promote antilabor vigilantism designed to maintain the social and economic order of Tampa. Seeking to prevent tobacco companies, which constituted the backbone of the local economy, from moving elsewhere because of labor unrest, these committees intimidated and lynched labor activists. While the overall clubs were initiated in Jacksonville, it was in Tampa, with a tradition of grassroots activism and antilabor vigilance, where the overall movement grew and received national press.[14]

The Tampa movement began on March 29, 1920, at a meeting place called The Horseshoe. A few men began discussing high prices, and before long a crowd congregated to weigh in on the issue. One of the men mentioned the unique strategy Jacksonville residents had chosen to address the problem.

Within "a few minutes a score of men were enrolled in the club and they started out to get more." Hafford Jones, a fire insurance agent, left the encounter as the president of the new Tampa overall club, telling residents, "Down with the new Easter suits; on with the overalls."[15]

Wasting no time, the club began planning for an Easter overall demonstration. They requested that churchgoers "bloom out" by wearing overalls and solicited the participation of "doctors, lawyers, preachers and business men," but invited all to join. The club held meetings and informed the local press that new members could sign up by leaving their names at The Horseshoe. The leadership and the local media projected a masculine construction of the meaning of work clothing by stopping short of asking women to wear overalls and instead encouraged them to "adopt some method of combating the issue." In the coming days, some local women formed their own Calico Club.[16]

On the morning of April 4, scores of Tampa residents got ready for church. Some pulled the price tags off recently purchased outfits, while others reached into the back of their closets for their oldest work clothes. Before church services, numerous overall-clad Tampa residents converged on Franklin Street and gathered around the bandstand in the courthouse yard. The group included soldiers, high school girls, "bungalow apron girls," as well as many others. As part of the events, participants and observers listened to speeches on the high cost of living, including one by Charles Metcalf, who spoke of the inability of the "salaried man" to "make ends meet." At the conclusion of festivities, attorney Lee J. Gibson presented a petition to Mayor Donald McKay that protested clothing profiteering and the high cost of living.[17]

Even if participants organized in part because of the inability of the government to address rising prices, much of their focus remained on the need for government solutions. The petition presented by the Tampa overall club to the mayor, Governor Sidney Catts, and Florida's two senators called for each "to use your good office" to end profiteering. The petition asserted that signers would cease to purchase clothing "until the different branches of government show an honest effort to curtail profiteering." Through grassroots organization, these Tampa residents took matters into their own hands, but ultimately looked to the further expansion of the state into economic affairs to effect real change.[18]

Tampa's demonstration attracted the attention of the national press. Many newspapers throughout the United States described the Tampa movement as led by "business and professional men," "marching" with "spirit" and determination to "fight," "battle," or "crusade" against rising prices. Within days, newspapers began referring to the formation of overall clubs as "The Tampa Idea," as "the whole country now knows of it and has characterized it." Through the press, Hafford Jones became the face that inspired what soon became a nationwide movement. Despite originating the movement, the Jacksonville club was no more significant in the public eye than overall campaigns that would materialize in Detroit, Kansas City, San Francisco, or anywhere else in North America.[19]

The Tampa overall campaign focused primarily on the plight of the middle class. Accordingly, the leadership and first members consisted of two managers, an attorney, an insurance agent, the president of the Electric Motor Company, a clerk, a real estate agent, and an employee of the Masons Lodge. On March 31, Hafford Jones reported that the club had gained the support of shipyard and railroad workers, but indicated that such support was ancillary to "businessmen and salaried men, who are really the greatest sufferers." Thus, it comes as no surprise that newspapers such as the *Tampa Times* described the movement as made up of "business and professional men." One letter to the *Times* elaborated on the reasons behind such class divisions. The writer declared, "it is not our class who is making the trouble but the ones getting the fat [pay] envelopes."[20] Regardless of their motivations, Tampa club members made little effort to coordinate with working-class consumers.

Even unsympathetic local merchants defined the overall campaign as a middle-class movement. One clothing merchant called middle-class efforts to manipulate the consumer economy "a fool joke." Salaried workers could abstain from new clothing purchases, the merchant argued, but a well-compensated working class would undercut middle-class consumer organizing. "Just as long as folks who work for wages demand $15 silk shirts, $3 silk neckties and $2.50 silk socks," the merchant declared "they will get them." He further added, "and while they're buying that sort of stuff you may lay your heaviest bet on their also buying the best suits of clothing the market affords." The working class, therefore, could not only engender the high cost of clothing through strikes, but also through irresponsible, spendthrift consumption.[21]

To participants in the early movement, the overall garb served not just as a weapon for economic equality but also as a symbol of moral fairness—a promotion of hard work, thrift, and honesty. Looking nostalgically to the nineteenth century, the *Tampa Tribune* noted that participants, in their modern-day effort to create a more just economy, had chosen to wear clothing worn by "all citizens subsequent to the Civil War, then in protest of the high costs." It was no accident that the first parades were set to occur on Easter, a day in which the pulpit could aid in publicizing and expanding the movement. The Jacksonville overall club sent letters to every minister within city limits to urge them to preach on how conservation could reduce the high cost of living. Such a strategy held great potential. First, popular writing on the high cost of living frequently highlighted the plight of ministers alongside of clerks, lawyers, doctors, and people in other salaried professions. More important, the symbolic meaning of the overall garb appealed to many Christian preachers, whose Sunday morning sermons recounted New Testament tales celebrating thrift and discouraging greed, gluttony, and sloth. The use of overalls as a means to discuss thrift represented one way to relate these lessons to everyday life. As Josiah Morse, professor of philosophy and religion at the University of South Carolina, would later state, "I look upon it as a religious movement."[22]

Some early participants in the overall movement drew inspiration from the story of John the Baptist, a biblical figurehead of thrift. One banner in the Jacksonville parade, for example, declared "John the Baptist went to Church in sack cloth and ashes and so will we." John the Baptist was attractive to club members, because he wore clothing made of camel's hair, told tax collectors to "exact no more than which is appointed to you," advised soldiers to "be content with your wages," and told the rich not to hoard, specifically mentioning clothing. Nearly two thousand years later, these were the concerns of white-collar citizens as they protested the high cost of living. In associating the movement with religiously driven moral teachings, overall club members could further claim the universal righteousness of their values.[23]

Before long, speakers from both the pulpit and the soapbox were gaining fame as they appealed to Americans to wear overalls in order to fight two central foes of the immediate postwar middle class: elite profiteers and organized labor. Perhaps no other figure embodied the enthusiastic, yet self-serving, leadership of this increasingly popular movement more than Noel Mitchell, the president of the St. Petersburg overall club.

## "The Sand Man" in Overalls

The home of Noel Mitchell was in many ways an unusual New South city. Although only 30 miles across the bay from Tampa, St. Petersburg seemed a world apart. Lacking a major productive industry like Tampa's cigar trade, St. Petersburg resembled a backcountry town until tourists began to choose its sunny location as a popular destination in the early twentieth century. By 1920, the approximate beginning of the great Florida Land Boom, St. Petersburg had witnessed the arrival of scores of northern tourists.[24]

Aggressive city promotion by the *St. Petersburg Times*, the *St. Petersburg Independent*, the Chamber of Commerce, and its leading citizens recruited a new, diverse, and itinerant citizenry. The arrival of tourists and winter residents added regionalism to race, gender, and class as markers of distinction in the city. Local politicians and prominent citizens often had to appeal to divergent groups to achieve their goals, and the surest way to achieve this task was to foster more sensational city promotion. Newcomers migrated at least in part because of this grand advertising, and long-standing residents depended on it economically. Each St. Petersburg subcommunity ultimately had an interest in selling the city. Nobody sold St. Petersburg better than Noel Mitchell.[25]

A shrewd businessman, Mitchell drew on his eccentricity at a young age to build his entrepreneurial enterprises. Mitchell was born on Block Island, Rhode Island, and moved to Providence as a teenager to take business courses and work for a sewing machine company. By the age of 18, Mitchell had created the Original Atlantic City Salt Water Taffy company, first selling his product while on the road exploring northeastern resort towns. Mitchell's company soon took off nationally and he began to develop other enterprises. Among them were a circus "freak show," amusement parks, and numerous real estate ventures.[26]

One day, Mitchell's wife overheard a fellow shopper in a Block Island store praise St. Petersburg. Noel Mitchell had a long-standing affinity for Florida, dating back to his visits to market taffy, but he preferred Daytona Beach as an eventual destination for his family. The couple decided to settle the disagreement on a coin flip. Fate would have it that the Mitchells would move to St. Petersburg.[27]

The individual described as "colorful, zany, a genius, an eccentric a man with a slogan or a gimmick for promotion of everything," turned heads almost immediately. After he became the first man in St. Petersburg to pay $1,000 for a lot of land, residents began referring to him as "The Crazy Yankee." Within a few years, Mitchell bought numerous properties, including the beachfront land known as "treasure island." He established a real estate office on Fourth Street and Central Avenue, advertising himself as "the Sand Man, the Man Who Never Sleeps." The "Sand Man" gained even more notoriety when he started a trend of building park benches in the city. The first bright orange bench (later repainted green) stood in front of his real estate office, encouraging tired city strollers to rest and peruse his advertisements for available properties. A seat on his bench was in such high demand, that crowds would converge, each person waiting for one to become vacant. In the meantime, they would "talk, bask in the sunshine, flirt a little," a scene that became known as "Mitchell's prayer meeting." Before long, the benches graced the entire city.[28]

Mitchell also spent many of his waking hours promoting St. Petersburg to residents elsewhere in the United States. His boosterism expanded beyond the soapbox to a wide variety of methods. Mitchell placed postcards that depicted St. Petersburg as a desirable destination in each of his taffy containers, dug into his own pockets to place an ad in *Saturday Evening Post* for the "sunshine city," filmed a 1912 city celebration of George Washington's birthday and sent copies of the movie around the county, and constructed billboards for St. Petersburg tourism throughout the East Coast. Years later, Newton O'Berry, an associate of Mitchell, recalled one of his billboards on a main corner in West Haven, Connecticut, that displayed a map of Florida with St. Petersburg "as the only spot on the map." According to O'Berry, "Miami howled about it."[29]

Of course, Mitchell's boosterism of St. Petersburg also served as a means for self-promotion. Mitchell embraced nicknames like "the crazy Yankee" and created a number of his own slogans to gain greater notoriety. On each of his green benches, Mitchell printed "Mitchell, the Sand Man. The Honest Real Estate Dealer. The Man With a Conscience. He Never Sleeps." On other occasions, Mitchell referred to himself as "The Singing Auctioneer," or implied that under his leadership "a star will guide you." Mitchell also used anecdotal fame to heighten his local celebrity. He and his wife became the first to travel in an automobile from Tampa to St. Petersburg, a three-and-a-half-day trip that included flat tires and a forest fire, among other obstacles. In 1914, Mitchell reportedly became the world's second commercial airline passenger. In an attempt to become the first, he agreed to pay $175, only to be outbid by A. C. Pheil, a former mayor, who offered $400.[30]

It seemed only natural that Mitchell would enter politics, using his flair for creative advertising to enhance his many campaigns. Mitchell began his political career in 1916 by becoming a candidate for governor in a losing effort. Shortly after, he entered the race for sheriff, running on a curious slogan, "See No Evil, Speak No Evil, Hear No Evil." He sold thousands of toy Siamese monkeys to accompany the slogan, much to the chagrin of political opponents who felt that the catchphrase was inappropriate for law enforcement. Mitchell lost the race, but continued to attempt to appeal to the masses by casting himself as an eccentric man of the people.[31]

The strategy worked to his advantage in the mayoral election of 1920. Mitchell was able to get away with holding a number of controversial positions, because many St. Petersburg residents viewed him as a lovable maverick. It was widely believed that Mitchell had ultimately done more to promote St. Petersburg than perhaps any other citizen. Accordingly, his uncharacteristic views in some ways added to his appeal as a "colorful, zany"

Mitchell promoted his personal real estate business and St. Petersburg tarpon fishing through spectacles such as the one pictured here (taken in 1908 and sold as a postcard). Postcard in author's possession.

and, for many, likeable man. And he did indeed express controversial positions. In the context of the first red scare, the Jim Crow South, and, at best, mixed local opinion of organized labor, one of Mitchell's newspaper campaign advertisements pushed for "Free speech," "Justice to all, white or black," and "a living wage." But, above all he was the "people's candidate," who had shown "loyalty" and a dedication to "boosting for this city for the last 17 years." On April 6, Mitchell was pleased to learn that he had been elected mayor by a margin of nearly 17 percent of the vote.[32]

After the election, Mitchell realized that gaining the approval of residents who were less willing to accept his controversial views would be a formidable task. The *Independent*, a paper that was partially financially backed by Mitchell, noted how those unsupportive of Mitchell made "it appear that he was a regular devil with horns and a tail and would devour the city." Others called the election "a calamity." But, the *Independent* reiterated why Mitchell had been elected: "He has been for many years a persistent and active booster for St. Petersburg" and "has the good of the city at heart." Mitchell did not have to win the support of organized labor, African Americans, or women, whose newly granted right to vote helped propel him to victory. To become more popular and powerful, Mitchell needed to appeal to a segment of the middle class that was disdainful of organized labor, but wiling to adopt unusual political strategies if the cause was worthy. Embracing overalls provided him with an opportunity to apply his talents as an eccentric leader to a popular and increasingly middle-class movement. As a leader of the movement, Mitchell promoted what had become a symbol of middle-class promulgation of "traditional" conservative values of thrift and hard work even as he developed a celebrity image through his support of the consumerism of St. Petersburg tourism. Mitchell and middle-class Americans did not cease to participate in consumer culture. In performing and extolling a selectively defined culture of production, they made these producer values a part of their consumer identity.[33]

As the president of the St. Petersburg overall club, Mitchell took an active role in building the movement, even as he used it for self-promotion. Having been the first person in the city to drive a car from Tampa to St. Petersburg and the second to fly as a commercial airline passenger, Mitchell was never one to pass up a chance to become the face of a new social fashion. In this case, he would literally embrace a new fashion to gain favor as the local leader of what the *St. Petersburg Times* called "organized protest" and a "rebellion against the cost of living" that took "the nation by storm."[34]

By the time Mitchell took charge of the St. Petersburg movement, it had already gained a clear middle-class orientation. Mitchell's own *Independent*, for example, pointedly declared, "The men who now propose to wear overalls are the salaried men and those with fixed incomes who have been caught between capital and labor and are being ground to jelly." They "are professional and business men, clerks and newspaper men." The *Independent* further stated its distain for the irresponsibility of organized labor by attacking blue-collar spending habits. "Union workmen," the paper asserted, "are drawing big pay" and "not saving anything." Similar statements arose from commentary on the movement from many different places in the United States. According to such statements, participants in the overall movement spoke in favor of thrift and resented working-class consumer indulgence. Simultaneously, they were organizing to protect their own ability to consume up to the standards of a middle class identity and to maintain the visual markers of their class positioning. The *Lowell Sun* defined the movement as a an uprising of "professional men" borrowing "the badge" of "hard soiling manual labor" to "demand of the powers of government that the necessities of life be placed within the financial reach" of them. More pointedly, the *Chicago Daily Tribune* described overall clubs as made up of "white collar boys" who want "to see if [they] cannot feel like a carpenter or a bricklayer or a plumber."[35]

Mitchell's efforts as a leader of the St. Petersburg movement surpassed those of many overall club organizers. As the mayor-elect, he took it upon himself to give every St. Petersburg resident a chance to don denim. On April 15, Mitchell announced that he would take orders for army surplus overalls for 50 cents a pair. He used city hall to as the venue in which to secure orders and distribute the overalls, obtained from the South Carolina Army Warehouse Co. Two hundred people took him up on the offer, with more willing buyers to follow. Mitchell also set up the first major St. Petersburg overall club meeting at city hall, which drew approximately 400 citizens. Shortly after, residents flocked to sign pledges to buy no new clothes. Included in the standard pledge was a declaration that blamed high prices in large part on "lack of production."[36]

Following the meeting, Mitchell's *Independent* identified the culprits for high prices and explained the cultural significance of overalls. "Overalls spells work," the *Independent* declared. If true to the garb, "One doesn't loaf when one dons overalls. One produces." The paper continued by declaring that "never was there a time when this country needed more work, greater production." William J. Carpenter, a local minister, was one white-collar resident who seconded this opinion. In support of the overall movement, Carpenter wrote that "we have too many [people] who never do enough real hard work." To individuals like Carpenter and the editors of the *Independent*, overalls provided the means for a clothing boycott, but also carried the cultural significance of promoting diligent production.[37]

While overall club members mainly focused on clothing prices, Mitchell and other participants also organized in the name of lower prices for all commodities. Shortly after ordering army surplus overalls, Mitchell ordered 4,608 pounds of army bacon and 1,800 pounds of canned beef to sell to St. Petersburg citizens for approximately one-third of the normal cost. His actions, described as giving "the cost of living in the Sunshine City another hard blow," received publicity in the both St. Petersburg and Tampa newspapers. In addition, at overall club meetings, members took pledges to fight high sugar prices by refraining from sugar or candy purchases for a period of 60 days, and discussed the idea of bringing ocean shipping lines directly to St. Petersburg.[38]

Despite his support of the overall movement, Mitchell suffered from increasingly hostile coverage of the movement from the rival newspaper, the *St. Petersburg Times*. Ultimately, his position as the face of the St. Petersburg overall movement did not help him in his efforts to gain greater appeal; at least for the time being, clothing prices remained high.[39]

Yet, from the first day of his short run as mayor, Mitchell had larger problems. At the first city council meeting he got into a fistfight with a city employee over a denied appointment for sanitation officer. During the scuffle,

Dr. W. J. Tanner, who had been passed over for the position, broke Mitchell's wrist. In spite of his injury, Mitchell did not hold a grudge. According to Tanner, "Next Day, Mitchell saw me across the street and hollered 'Hi Doc, I didn't know you had it in you." Facing a hostile city council, Mitchell managed to create more trouble by authorizing the use of city property for a "tent city" for migrants who traveled to St. Petersburg to enjoy its warm winters. The visitors, described as "tin can tourists," enjoyed free city water, lighting, garbage collection, and bathrooms and were known by their tendency to cook beans over a fire as a means of daily subsistence. Mitchell's actions led the angry city council to pass a resolution "in favor of no tent city within corporate limits." A "liquor party in the mayor's office" just months after prohibition took effect across the country finally paved the way for Mitchell's political demise. Mitchell's opponents jumped at the opportunity to amass the necessary signatures to submit a petition for a recall election. In the December 20, 1920, election, Mitchell lost in a landslide, receiving 39 percent of the vote to Frank Pulver's 60 percent.[40]

The remainder of Mitchell's life was symbolic of both his glory as perhaps the city's most recognizable man, and the humiliation of his political downfall. Still a memorable figure, Mitchell generated headlines by running for city council in 1935. Soundly defeated, Mitchell again found himself at odds with the authorities, this time for becoming so rowdy at a beer party that "a sanity petition" had to be taken out. Mitchell, whose sanity had been confirmed, made one final push for glory by announcing his candidacy for governor in 1936. Just a month later, a police officer found him passed out on one of his very own green benches. The irony was not lost on the public. In court, the arresting officer stated, "I straightened him out three times but each time he fell over again." Mitchell then stood before the judge and exclaimed, "I suffer from auto-intoxication and after I eat a big meal I usually relapse into slumber." "What's more," Mitchell continued, "the St. Petersburg Police Department has been persecuting me for years." Mitchell did not get another chance to rebuild his political career. Within months, his health declined and he died of pneumonia. Despite Mitchell's recent brush with the headlines, journalist Paul Davis recalled that "many old friends did not even know of his passing."[41]

Mitchell's efforts embodied those of many of the prominent leaders of the overall movement. While middle-class participants rallied passionately against high prices, those who rose to the forefront of the movement often basked in publicity. The movement provided yet another means for the Noel Mitchells of the country to generate headlines that would associate them with a cause of the masses.

## The Overall Movement as National Popular Culture

By the third week of April the overall movement had become a major feature of national popular culture. Virtually every newspaper in the United States chronicled the growth of the movement, often on almost a daily basis. Magazines, including the *Nation*, *Life*, *Literary Digest*, *Leslie's Illustrated Weekly*, *Outlook*, the *Independent*, and *Current Opinion*, published articles discussing the new use of overalls. Analysis of the movement appeared in academic journals and was the subject of poems. Organizations such as the Oakland Housewives League and Norfolk Federal Employees Union passed resolutions urging members and local business and professional men to wear denim, and for government authorities to help reduce clothing prices. In fact, the overall movement expanded beyond American popular culture. Clubs, demonstrations, and press coverage surfaced in Canada, Great Britain, Argentina, and France.[42]

Wearing overalls had become such a popular action that college students and even elementary and secondary school students formed clubs and donned denim to school. Overall clubs were organized at colleges ranging from Wesleyan College to the University of Texas. At Wesleyan, students punished club members who were seen to be wearing normal clothes by throwing them into a local pond. At Chicago's Lakeview High School, Harry Rumsfeld and Frank Pollen, both members of the Junior Chamber of Commerce, formed an overall club and graced school hallways in the clothing of labor. The junior class of Passaic High School in New Jersey was one of many groups of students across the nation to designate overalls and calico as the official clothing for prom or other events. Senator Nathaniel Dial (D-South Carolina) took special notice of students' efforts and how high prices impacted their parents. Dial declared to the Senate, "It is an encouraging thought to see the school and college boys falling so readily into line. Sometimes the young are too inexperienced and too self-centered to consider the pocketbooks of their elders; but not so now."[43]

The overall campaign in New York City showcased the popularity and spectacle of the movement. The Cheese Club, a group of actors, writers, and producers, stood at the forefront of the New York City overall club. Altogether, the club enjoyed the participation of numerous theater men, the Rotary Club, students from Columbia University and Jamaica High School, and a host of other individuals. As a "strike" against the high cost of clothing, they agreed to "wear the garb of labor" on the streets of New York to publicize their grievances. And publicity they achieved. So much so that newspapers from Atlanta to Los Angeles covered the planning and results of the spectacular parade down Broadway on April 24. If New York did not originate the movement, club leaders would attempt to surpass the showmanship of other clubs.[44]

On April 24, thousands of onlookers watched a few hundred people march down Broadway in overalls. Also present were newspaper reporters, circus elephants, camels, motion picture men, and numerous signs condemning the high cost of living. A supporter contemplated "adorning the whole neck of the camel with a white collar . . . to stiffen the backbone of the revolting 'white collar boys.'" Nils T. Granlund, "a press agent," led the parade, "having nothing to do with the cause." According to Harry Hershfield, a member of the Cheese Club, "Time and place had no special meaning for Granlund, so long as he could get publicity." Ben Atwell, another leader in the parade, guided participants in such a way so as to make sure that those filming it would get a clear shot of marchers in front of a sign for "the Capitol Theater," with which many Cheese Club members were affiliated. As a result, some New Yorkers believed that the Cheese Club merely sought to use the movement to bring more business to Broadway. A few people even subscribed to the rumor that "a New York newspaper man . . . got the idea into his head and he went to some makers of overalls and got $10,000 for an idea out of which they made millions and are still making millions." Whether defined as success or failure, the parade turned heads. If the parade had not already seemed unusual, it ended with an "elephant being stranded on Broadway." As one account stated, "Worldwide Interest Aroused Through Publicity."[45]

Not only did spectators on Broadway experience the overall movement, so too did those who attended Broadway plays, operas, and films. The Capitol Theatre began advertising "opera at overalls prices," and actively sought to connect their productions and films to the popular movement. In an attempt to advertise the silent film adaptation of Rex Beach's *The Silver Horde*, a group of women dressed in denim and posed for a photo while holding a sign stating, "If you see Rex Beach's The Silver Horde at the Capitol Theater You'll Know How to Fight the Profiteers." Directors, actors, and actresses also promoted their own careers by donning denim. In Hollywood, noted filmmaker Marshall Neilan drew the attention of the press by showing up at his studio dressed in overalls to "cut the high cost of clothing," and by urging his employees to do the same. "Heartily in favor of the movement," Helene Chadwick "enjoyed" wearing overalls on the Will Rogers film *Alec Lloyd, Cowpuncher*. Just down the road, members of the Burbank Theater Chorus abandoned their expensive bathing suits in favor of "overall bathing costumes." They boasted of making car repairs en route to the beach, while proclaiming, "We think that we are doing our bit to help reduce the high cost of

New York City Overall Parade. Assorted Materials, scrapbook "Cheese Club," "1920, re overall parade" MWEZ X n.c., Billy Rose Theatre Collection, New York Public Library.

The Capitol Theater using the overall movement to promote the Silver Horde. Assorted Materials, scrapbook "Cheese Club," "1920, re overall parade" MWEZ X n.c., Billy Rose Theatre Collection, New York Public Library.

living." Ironically, the theater and film industries used overalls, symbolic of hard work, thrift, and moral fairness, to make an extra buck—a process of commodification present in many consumer movements.[46]

Plays, films, and music inspired by the movement expressed the producerist themes articulated by middle-class consumer activists themselves. In these productions and pieces, overalls represented a longing for an American tradition that celebrated the producerist values and simplicity of the past. In the Mack Sennett comedy *Gingham Girl*, a film playing at the height of the overall movement, the protagonist, a "country girl" who inherits millions of dollars, decides to embrace the values of her simple past by thwarting the advances of high-society suitors in favor of a butler. Dedicated to the Cheese Club, the song "Overalls and Calico" by Gus Kahn and Jean Schwartz, ideal-

*Overalls and Calico* by Gus Kahn, an example of the overall movement in national popular culture.

ized the simplicity and thrift of childhood dress. To a moderate melody, an alto voice sings, "Styles in clothes are always changing, I suppose they always will, but the clothes we wore in childhood, somehow dear I love them still" leading to a chorus, "overalls and calico, each recalls the long ago . . . we miss the tattered clothes." The picture on the cover of the sheet music for "Overalls and Calico" depicts a refined man standing in front of his automobile wearing overalls with a collared shirt, vest, and tie underneath. The image shows middle-class attachment to both the producerism conveyed by the overalls and to consumerism, represented by the automobile and the formal clothing under the man's overalls.[47]

Magazine and newspaper commentary similarly celebrated the overall movement as a means of incorporating the producerist values of yesteryear into a modern consumer society. Edwin E. Slosson of the *Independent* magazine (New York) wrote, "the first fight for American freedom was won when the colonists boycotted British cloth and pledged themselves to wear nothing but homespun." Continuing the tradition of thrift, "in our Civil War again economy became fashionable . . . and now look at our streets. . . . one would think that the white collar men, finding that the overall men had gotten ahead of them in salary, had suddenly shifted to the better paid profession." "But no," Slosson asserted approvingly, "it is merely a consumers strike on a large scale." The *Newark Evening News* more pointedly concluded, "overalls are . . . the symbol of honest work, service and sacrifice. . . . putting on overalls is putting on democracy."[48]

Part of this romanticized traditional American past was a celebration of American manhood expressed through hard work and a belief in economic fairness. Promoting the movement to the press, Judge William E. Fort, of the Birmingham, Alabama, overall club, proclaimed, "This movement is a protest of American manhood against conditions which have become a shame. It is a return to the old days when principle meant more than the almighty dollar." Fort was by no means the only one who made a connection between the overall garb and masculinity. When scores of male residents joined the Birmingham overall club, women were turned away, prompting one women's activist periodical to declare, "Sex discrimination is now raging in Birmingham, Alabama."[49] Since women often held the socially ascribed role of being the primary consumer for the household, price increases placed a particular burden on their labor as household managers.

Rather than standing pat, women in Birmingham and elsewhere organized gingham and calico clubs, and appealed to largely the same producerist themes as overall clubs, portraying these values as equally applicable to women.[50] Drawing on the notion of an American tradition of thrift and the

This depiction of the overall movement showcased the sentiment that representing hard work by wearing overalls to protest the high cost of living was a demonstration of American values. *Chicago Daily Journal*, April 21, 1920.

particular emphasis on a gender-segregated role of women in wartime, one Columbia, South Carolina, resident suggested, "the women of the [18]60s should get the women of the 20s together." They should "tell them some things about the Confederate war times and how they lived and prospered." The movement was hampered, but not crippled, by the masculinization of this consumer protest; women found ways to participate, in spite of male leaders' mixed opinions about their inclusion.[51]

Similar to middle-class anti-high-food-price activists, overall movement participants and proponents claimed that they were acting in the name of the "people" by associating their consumer identity with the apparent established American values of hard work, masculinity, honesty, and thrift. Theodore Lamar, a Birmingham overall club member, bluntly summarized the movement by stating, "the people have gone on strike." Others, like a Richmond resident writing to the *Richmond Times*, used similar language and connected the movement directly to the values of the previous generation. "The people are rebellious," the resident declared. By "go[ing] back to overalls and ginghams," they are appearing "in the garments which our parents wore and made honorable." With widespread participation nationally and claims that they represented the public, many club members looked to multiple levels of government to effect change.[52]

## The Government in Overalls

Noel Mitchell represented just one of many examples of local government officials who seized the opportunity to gain mass appeal by joining the overall movement.[53] Such individuals hoped that embracing the movement would represent an adequate response to persistent calls for them to use their offices to address the high cost of clothing. The scope of and manner in which public officials took control of the movement varied. Some mayors, councilmen, judges, and city officials merely wore the garb and condemned the high cost of living. Others set up commissions to investigate local influences on rising clothing costs, or amended dress codes to allow city employees to wear overalls. Ultimately, however, local, state, and federal politicians passed few new laws, and little evidence exists to suggest that they made notable improvements in their attempts to enforce any pertinent existing statutes. In sum, government participation was largely symbolic. Nevertheless, they further legitimized the overall campaign as a movement of the people. Significantly, even though not all overall club members or the officeholders who supported them were politically conservative, they advanced a popular antilabor and culturally conservative discourse that ultimately favored a conservative politics.

In many locales, the courts, city officials, state legislatures, and governors joined the movement. Los Angeles Superior Court judge Fred Taft, a supporter of the campaign for state-run municipal markets in California (see chapter 2), led the overall movement at the Los Angeles County courthouse, telling people to "wear them until prices break." "The cry used to be 'Back to the farm,'" Taft proclaimed. "Today it is back to overalls."[54] San Diego allowed its employees to wear working clothes, and, in South Carolina the Supreme Court changed courtroom rules so as to allow attorneys and court employees to wear overalls in litigation, helping to lessen the burden placed on them by high suit prices. This prompted one resident to declare that "it shows that our supreme court is not out of touch with the new thought of the age."[55] Beginning on April 20, Idaho governor David William Davis and his entire cabinet showed up to work at the statehouse dressed in overalls. With the press looking on, they signed overall pledges and encouraged others to do the same. The Davis administration was not alone. *Literary Digest* reported that "the State Capitols of Texas and Michigan have welcomed overalls," listing merely two of the numerous examples of state governments with politicians endorsing the garb.[56]

Hoping to appeal to their constituents, many members of both parties in the U.S. Senate and House of Representatives embraced the movement. Overalls first graced the House Chamber on April 17 when Rep. William Upshaw (D-Georgia) interrupted a debate on tobacco manufacturing to read a telegram from a resident of Atlanta that had asked him to endorse the local overall club. Casting himself as a man of the people, Upshaw declared, "Naturally I could not indorse it without practicing what I preach. So I went downtown and spent $4 for this good suit of overalls, which I am now wearing." Upshaw continued, "Let us set a good example and help still the tempest of unrest and bring a speedy return of peace to the land we love so well." The House applauded and many of Upshaw's colleagues crowded around him to admire "the time honored garb of the working man." Roughly a dozen congressmen immediately agreed to wear overalls and according to the *Charlotte News*, the ordeal "created such a sensation that it was almost impossible to continue the business of the house."[57]

In the U.S. Senate, Sen. Nathaniel Dial (D-South Carolina) took charge of the movement. A few days in advance, Dial created anticipation among the media by announcing that he would deliver an extensive message in support of overalls. As promised, on April 19 Dial stood up and addressed the Senate. He began by identifying the roots of the high cost of living: first, the indolence of striking labor; second, extravagance; and lastly, profiteering. Playing on widespread antiradical and antilabor fears of the first red scare, Dial gave special attention the influence of the "I.W.W. and the bolshevistic crowds" in encouraging strikes and an idle workforce. Against these threats, the people, Dial asserted, were beginning to respond with "the right spirit." To striking laborers, Dial admonished, "Let them know that the public can also organize."[58]

In spite of the fact that many participants in the overall movement still ultimately placed their hopes in the government to lower the cost of clothing, Dial deemphasized government action. Of "overall clubs," Dial declared, "I am delighted to know that the people are beginning to realize that it is not in the province of Government to set styles and prescribe what one should wear or eat." Dial elaborated by stating, "There has been too much looking to Washington and the people have been too prone to complain to and of their representatives. . . . prosperity, like their salvation, is in their own hands." While the overall movement was a response to government failure to meet the public's heightened expectation that the state could solve the high cost of living, Dial understated the role overall club members expected the govern-

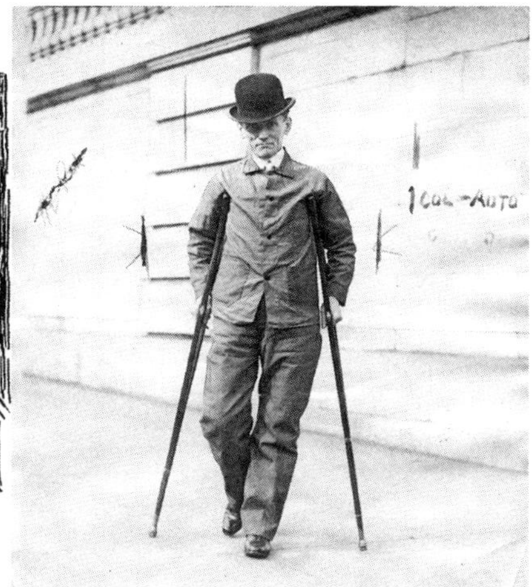

The cartoon (*on the left*) from *Life* magazine captures the use of the overall movement by politicians as a means to gain popularity (in this case, commenting on the 1920 presidential race). Rep. William Upshaw (*pictured on the right*) is shown posing in overalls. At least one presidential candidate (Massachusetts governor Calvin Coolidge) wore overalls in public. Editorial cartoon, *Life*, June 10, 1920; *Boston Daily Globe*, May 8, 1920; *Oelwein Daily Register*, May 15, 1920; Upshaw press photo in author's possession.

ment to play in reducing prices. Nevertheless, participants did believe that their "buyers strike" could have a direct effect on prices. Dial sought to praise the middle class and lend his symbolic support without taking further legislative action or inflating expectations that the federal government would lower prices.[59]

The other congressmen and senators who supported or joined the movement generally shared Dial's methods, but stopped short of stating precisely what the public should or should not expect from the government. This approach allowed politicians to become visible leaders of the movement and latch on to its producerist messages, but also implied that consumers were the only force in society that could decrease prices. In essence, most governmental figures understood their role to be symbolic. By wearing overalls, encouraging production, and condemning extravagance, politicians would become role models for American citizens and cause the press to take notice. Such a strategy did not address the issue of whether Congress needed to pass new legislation. It was ideal for politicians who identified with the cultural messages of self-reliance, thrift, hard work, and returning to a traditional

America. It further played to the economic conservatism of using the government to oppose the labor movement, but otherwise expressing faith in the people themselves to be arbiters of economic justice. Sen. Charles Thomas (D-Colorado), for example, called the "overalls brigade . . . a beginning," reiterating that normalcy would return with a decline in spendthrift habits and labor unrest.[60] On May 19, Senator William Kenyon (R-Iowa) similarly stated that "the need for more production is at the base of our trouble," but any reduction in clothing prices could be attributed to that fact that "people were stopping buying." "The nation," Kenyon declared, "must look to the great middle class to save it in its hour of stress."[61]

## A "Fad"?

While the sight of senators, governors, mayors, and actors wearing overalls promised to expand the visibility of the movement, to many it signified its faddish nature. Citizens demanded that the high cost of clothing receive serious attention and a number of people insisted that political rhetoric, publicity stunts, and circus elephants did not qualify. For example, Austin Potter, a business manager and the president of the Lima, Ohio, Kiwanis Club, exclaimed, "It's just one more fad." A number of press accounts and editorials began to share Potter's sentiment. Editorials in newspapers throughout the United States carried headlines such as "Faddism Will Fail," "The Overalls Folly," "Unnecessary Overalls," and "The Truth about the 'Overall Fad.'" Arguments about the overall movement's effectiveness and longevity served to divide prospective participants. Overall clubs had real meaning to many people as an important part of a trend of middle-class consumer protest. Yet in many ways the spectacle of the movement stymied its potential.[62]

Some called the movement a fad or spectacle, because many middle-class Americans were genuinely hesitant to completely abandon formal dress. White-collar workers were accused of wearing expensive clothing underneath the overalls "costume." An Appleton, Wisconsin newspaper, as just one of many examples, reported, "Don't be startled if you observe one of the city's prominent business or professional men hiking to the office covering up a silk shirt with a new suit of overalls."[63] Some participants did merely seek to latch on to a fad, but others, like Fred Haight, a music teacher in Medford, Oregon, truly struggled with such a drastic change in fashion. Haight wrote in his diary of "quarrelling between Myself and me"—in other words, a disconnect between his thoughts and his desires. According to

Mrs. Joseph T. Bowen Jr. and W. J. Howland Jr. of Lake Forest (metropolitan Chicago area) wearing formal clothing underneath denim, demonstrating the performative nature of their actions. *Chicago Herald and Examiner*, May 3, 1920.

Haight, "If I clothe him comfortably enough he objects and cry for a new $75 suit when overalls are more comfy. I become conscious of his existence and the power of his errors at such times, and am weak before it for a time." Eventually, "weakness" prevailed. On June 7, Haight called himself a "fool" for paying a profiteer $50 for a new suit, blaming his actions on his tastes, but also his profession. Haight wrote, "A music teacher is being watched constantly and judged according to his outward makeup as much as his inward." Ultimately, by wearing overalls in his white-collar profession, Haight could both help and hurt himself. Some patrons and colleagues would applaud his demonstration of thrift, whereas others would look upon him as a faddist and question his professional credibility. The tension between thrift and the desire to wear normal middle-class fashions in the overall movement resembled a similar tension in the DOJ-High Cost of Living Division Women's Division. Also representing the conflict between thrift and consumer expectations, municipal market supporters struggled to keep the markets up to the cultural standards of a middle-class shopping experience even as their purpose was in large part to promote thrift. Middle-class participants found that making thrift a part of their culture placed a difficult strain on their consumer behavior.[64]

This tension was also on display in popular discourse on the relationship between consumerism and American identity amid the first red scare. Popular writings commonly portrayed Bolshevik Russia as repressive of individual liberty, including the ability to freely consume. If free consumption served as a differentiating point in American identity from Bolshevism, then the overall movement's emphasis on thrift stood on tenuous ground. As *Life* magazine reported in an article titled "The Overall Movement in Russia," two women in Russia "were recently arrested and convicted on a charge of needless extravagance and ostentation, publicly stripped of their finery, and sentenced to ten years' *hard labor*." The magazine concluded sarcastically that this "gives us one more cause to lament that we do not have a Soviet form of government in the unenlightened United States." Even if such writings could suggest that repressing consumption mirrored Bolshevik practices, others played on red scare language to support the movement in its efforts to combat the supposed disorder and discontent promoted by labor unions and profiteers. For instance, while wearing overalls at a local meeting, Massachusetts Rep. Thomas A. Niland (D-Boston), proclaimed, "the profiteers have caused more discontent and unrest in this country than Bolshevism could do in a hundred years," and suggested deporting them all.[65]

Further narrowing the scope and potential effectiveness of the overall movement, overall clubs made little or no effort to involve racially or ethnically diverse consumers. Critiquing the economic impact of the movement, *El Heraldo de Mexico*, a Spanish-language newspaper in Los Angeles, noted how it led to a rise in the price of overalls. Published African American sources not only indicate that African Americans typically did not form their own overall clubs, they also include cynical analysis of the movement. Calling the movement a "fad," the *Chicago Defender* reported that "we have not heard of any man in Harlem donning overalls." The *Tulsa Star*, an African American newspaper, stated in an editorial titled "Southern White 'Ge'mmen' to Wear Overalls" that high prices "have caused the prominent white citizens of [Birmingham] to put aside thoughts of Negro domination . . . and discard their woolen business suits and wear overalls. Now this course is especially odd because for generations, the Colored laborers in the fields, factories and other commercial activities have always worn overalls." "But now," the editorial sarcastically proclaimed, "'Col.' Bill and 'Massa' John are to make the overall suit eminently respectable, thus discarding it as the insignia distinguishing a white gentlemen from a Negro." Elevated clothing prices did affect African American consumers, but overall clubs primarily concerned themselves with the impact of economic change on the *white* middle class, and used a disparaging symbol to express their protest. Much like in discussions of food profiteering in Los Angeles, profiteers took on many white and racialized forms, but, in the eyes of white middle-class Americans, the victims looked like themselves. The "public" was decidedly white collar and white.[66]

While the white middle-class, antilabor identity of the overall movement energized many white-collar consumers, it eliminated the potential participation of a range of people who could have otherwise fallen under the category "consumer." Not only were working class and African American consumers overtly or tacitly excluded from the movement, the embedded tension between a consumer identity and the values of thrift and sacrifice in the overall movement created further barriers to full middle-class participation. Men like Fred Haight wanted to wear overalls for either political purposes or for comfort, but also the suits that seemed to represent the very middle-class lifestyle they hoped to protect. They were attached to the moral value of sacrifice at least in part for the purpose of protecting their right to *spend* in a "fair" marketplace.

## Backlash from Labor and the "Old Clothes" Movement

As a predominantly middle-class endeavor, the overall movement suffered from a lack of working-class participation. Many labor unions were experienced in using consumption as a strategy to influence both wages and prices, having organized boycotts and consumer cooperatives. But, since many overall club leaders placed blame on organized labor for the high cost of clothing, the potential for interclass coordination was limited. Many laborers did not respond kindly to frequent middle-class accusations that they had extracted excessive wages in the postwar upsurge of strikes. As Samuel Gompers, president of the American Federation of Labor, declared, "The appeals of wage earners for relief from profiteering, relief from the high cost of living . . . have been made under conditions most aggravating. . . . Abuse has been heaped upon them and they have been charged with every manner of social crime."[67]

Perhaps most damaging to the possibility of interclass cooperation, the overall movement mocked and criticized the working class culturally. Members of labor unions resented the very idea of the middle-class appropriating the symbol of "hard work" from the working class. For many, it carried the assumption that white-collar workers deserved to wear the garb more than plumbers, builders, coal miners, railroad workers, and other members of the working class. A statement by the International Brotherhood of the Steam Shovel and Dredge Men exclaimed, "After getting into a pair of overalls . . . a good test of the sincerity of the motive behind the movement would be to hand to the newly dressed a pick or shovel and see how ready the action might be to utilize these implements of everyday usefulness." Similarly, a wage earner discussing contemporary issues with William M. Leiserson, chairman of the Rochester Labor Adjustment Board, declared facetiously, "This overall movement is great. Let the . . . middle classes wear overalls now. We'll wear the good clothes." To many, the middle class merely wore a "costume" and "performed" hard work symbolically.[68]

Making matters worse, the overall movement brought hardship to the working class economically by driving up the price of overalls. Within a month of the inception of the movement, the price of overalls skyrocketed in response to increased demand from the middle class. Laborers who needed to wear overalls for their work were left to spend up to triple the normal amount. Price increases were reported heavily in the press, and government officials received complaints about "the advance in prices in overalls."[69]

Organized labor fumed over the rising price of overalls engendered by middle-class demand. The Marysville, California, Carpenters Union represented just one of many union locals that passed resolutions condemning overall clubs. It promised to boycott any business that endorsed the movement. Explaining their opposition, the *Labor World*, the voice of the Duluth, Minnesota, Central Labor Body, stated, "Think of beating down the cost of living by wearing the blue jeans of the proletariat. . . . The working people must wear overalls and they will have to pay more. . . . it will result in a lot of injury to the workers and their families." The Boot and Shoe Workers' Union protested that "the artisan must pay twice as much for the overalls necessary to him because of the recent overalls hysteria." The union further claimed, "All makers of overalls must have reaped a golden harvest through the increased demand for their goods." Radical organized labor reacted just as fervently. The socialist *New York Call* concluded, "The net result of the overalls craze is to increase the cost of living for the workers which will certainly be followed by strikes for more wages and a middle class yowl because of the 'Red specter.'"[70]

Many farmers shared the complaints of the urban working class. One New England farmer called the movement a "mania" and worried that it would expand to a boycott of foods that would "result in bankrupting farmers." An Indiana farmers' periodical exclaimed, "Overalls constitute [the] uniform" of "farmers, mechanics and others," and elaborated, "it means a real hardship to them . . . and gives the manufacturers of overalls an excuse for boosting the price of their product." Making specific reference to the overall movement, E. G. S. Gagnler, a farmer from Plattsburgh, New York, wrote to his local newspaper, "People are attempting to lower the HCL in every way but the proper way." While many donned overalls, Gagnler reasoned that only the "the 16-hour a day farmer" was "producing." The *Iowa Homestead* issued even greater criticism, asserting that the middle class in overalls had "paraded like clowns." The *Homestead* declared, "Leave the overalls for the farmer and the laboring man."[71]

In addition to the backlash from farmers and the working class, numerous white-collar workers themselves abandoned overall clubs in favor of "old clothes clubs." Members of old clothes clubs complained that overall clubs had increased the price of overalls, further enabling profiteering. For example, Gilbert P. Shafer, a student at the University of Michigan, reasoned that wearing overalls only tended to cause a "rise in price . . . [and] defeat the original purpose." Within days, Michigan students joined many other Americans in signing "old clothes pledges" in place of promises to wear overalls. Concurrently, old clothes clubs surfaced in localities ranging from New Orleans to Cambridge, Massachusetts. The days of the "blue denim revolution" were numbered.[72]

As more and more citizens opted for old clothes clubs, many politicians followed suit. Ogden, Utah, mayor Frank Francis, previously a strong supporter of the overall movement, quickly shifted his allegiances to old clothes. Senator James Reed (D-Missouri) took a more vehement stance. "If men and women of the United States could be persuaded . . . not to go through this silly performance of wearing overalls, but to wear old clothes," Reed declared, "there would be a surplus of dress goods and of suitings in the United States at the end of six months and the prices would go down." Choosing not to address the growing concerns over the movement's strategy, Rep. Upshaw conveniently ceased wearing the garb by claiming that the "cool weather and a cold he had contracted" forced him to find more suitable clothing.[73]

Despite lacking longevity as a practical social movement strategy, the overall campaign empowered the conservative politicians and rhetoric that came to characterize much of the political history of the 1920s. Officeholders and candidates embraced and enlarged the movement's traditionalist discourse, which called for a return to the values of self-reliance, honesty, individualism, hard work, and thrift. Activists and politicians joined hands in condemning labor unions for indolence and greed during a period of significant labor unrest. Seeing themselves as protecting traditional masculine values, the movement often eschewed women's participation unless they took part through gender-segregated "calico" or "gingham clubs." Many politicians latched on to the movement's conservative messages, while ignoring a number of activists' calls for more government action to reduce prices. Rather than advocating the power of government to effect change, they promulgated business conservatism by emphasizing their faith in the people and their consumer power to fix the unjust economy.

Politicians who latched on to the overall movement not only used conservative rhetoric, they also frequently supported conservative policies before and during the 1920s. Throughout his political career, Rep. William Upshaw was one of the most passionate supporters of prohibition, making speeches for the antisaloon league, and he befriended the Ku Klux Klan, going as far as writing for the Georgia KKK periodical, the *Searchlight*. Upshaw's cultural conservatism gained him the title the "Billy Sunday of Congress" and he sat on the board of trustees for the conservative Bob Jones University.[74] Sen. Nathaniel Dial, another chief supporter of the overalls/old clothes movements, also championed culturally and economically conservative messages and policies throughout the 1920s. As one biographer notes, "Dial sought to retain fiscal conservatism" and "enforce the public values of thrift, honesty and responsibility." He supported prohibition and opposed the minimum wage, a constitutional amendment banning child labor, unions' right to strike for higher wages, and woman's suffrage (under the logic that it interfered with states' rights).[75] Fitting his conservative beliefs, he sidestepped the overall movement's general, though largely unspecific, call for more government intervention in the economy to address high prices, instead reiterating his faith in the public to bring about economic justice.[76] Meanwhile, Sen. Charles Thomas, a supporter of overalls in the Senate, saw labor unions as making "exorbitant" demands, and, in his retirement, became a strong opponent of the New Deal.[77]

Conservative presidential candidates of the 1920s also promoted themselves through the overall or old clothes movements. Calvin Coolidge, as one newspaper put it, "joined the movement" by wearing denim in front of Boston newspaper reporters and movie operators. Warren G. Harding endorsed the old clothes movement and called for a more traditional way of living. He asserted, "The only way to bring down the high cost of living is to return to simple ways of living."[78] In his famous "return to normalcy" speech, Harding celebrated "simple living and thrifty people." He proclaimed, "It is utter folly to talk about reducing the cost of living without restored and increased efficiency or production on the one hand and more prudent consumption on the other," adding that "[w]e might try repairs on the old clothes and simplicity for the new." Celebrating the old clothes movement but also recognizing its purpose of defending people's ability to affordably consume, Harding concluded, "I rejoice in our normal capacity to consume our rational, healthful consumption."[79] Fitting these words, at least one delegate to the 1920 Republican National Convention showed up wearing the placard "I am wearing out my old clothes."[80] Noted conservative presidential hopeful and Attorney General A. Mitchell Palmer also supported the old clothes movement. Although a Democrat in the Wilson administration, Palmer built his conservative credentials by fanning the flames of the first red scare, during which he ordered the arrest of alleged radicals and labor activists in a series of DOJ raids.[81]

Despite their political and cultural prominence in the immediate postwar period, the overalls and old clothes campaigns failed to last. Even if offering a more practical solution to the high price of clothing, old clothes clubs hindered the coordinating ability of a general middle-class anti-clothing-profiteering movement, and lacked the same degree of headline-generating symbolism and shock value of white-collar workers parading in the clothing of productive labor. While the importance of exercising thrift in clothing consumption continued to hold a prominent place in popular culture, by July 1920 few overall or old clothes clubs remained. Nevertheless, the movement empowered a conservative, antilabor, and culturally traditional rhetoric, which helped to abet the conservative politics of the 1920s, and further entrenched the idea of the white-collar "middle class" as guardians of the public interest.

## Conclusion

Disgruntled over the state's inability to lower the cost of clothing, scores of middle-class Americans formed grassroots organizations to influence prices, assert their values, and encourage more aggressive government action. To the organizing middle class, the high price of clothing was an issue of moral fairness. As part of overall or gingham clubs, they continued to attempt to self-righteously impose on the consumer economy the producerist values of industriousness and thrift, which they connected nostalgically to an older American identity, masculinity, Christianity, and whiteness (at least indirectly). They claimed to be acting in the name of "the people" based on their consumer identity and their association with these values, and suggested that they would bring fairness to an economy that was seemingly favoring profiteering laborers, middlemen, and merchants. As newspaper reporter Laura A. Smith proclaimed, overall club members adopted "the insignia of manual labor" to call for a "return to the pioneer days." The "descendants" of these pioneers "are saying, 'Strike without reason and we will show you that we can keep the wheels moving ourselves.'" Bridging the home garden and overall movements, Smith declared, "Force up the prices of vegetables and fruits and we will have our own gardens and fruit trees. Put clothing beyond our reach and we will go back to overalls." Many overall movement proponents resented not just the impact of strikes on prices but also the idea that higher wages enabled workers to indulge in consumerism. Overall movement participants were part of a broader opposition to working-class "extravagance," and an "orgy of spending," as one newspaper editorial phrased it. Protesting both the greed of capital and the underproduction and overconsumption of the working class, the overall movement claimed to stand for diligence in production and consumption. It suggested that middle-class Americans were the proper, moral consumers and held the right to demand adherence to producer values, as they defined them, by the working class and elites. Like the consumer activists that came before them, they believed that they as consumers could and should exercise both economic power and moral righteousness.[82]

The "blue denim revolution" ultimately fell apart for a few reasons. While numerous public figures and politicians, such as Mayor Noel Mitchell, Governor D. W. Davis, or Rep. William Upshaw, helped to energize the movement, they had seemingly latched on to the movement as a means of self-promotion. Many politicians chose to publicly identify themselves with the conservative strands of the movement's rhetoric, and fittingly did not use government power to undertake any new grand strategies to combat high clothing prices, despite calls for them to do so. Even though large numbers of women took part in the movement, middle-class men placed constraints on their participation by defining overalls as a masculine symbol of protest and expressing ambivalence over their involvement. Club members also made no efforts to involve nonwhite consumers and appeared to see only white Americans as victims. Equally significant, middle-class demand for overalls placed an economic hardship on manual laborers, who were also mocked and criticized for indolence. This alienated and angered a large group of consumers and dissolved any potential for cross-class cooperation, thereby limiting club members' ability to affect prices. The movement had also exhibited a tension within many consumer boycott movements throughout American history. This was the tension of a group exercising and promoting thrift in order to protect their ability to more easily consume. Participants in the movement attached themselves to the values of sacrifice and thrift at least partially in pursuit of the goal of creating a "fair" marketplace in which they could maintain a consumer lifestyle befitting their class. Finally, when many individuals began to question the practicality of purchasing and wearing overalls to reduce prices, white-collar activists fissured into proponents of overalls, old clothes advocates, and general antifaddists.[83]

The desire among the middle class to organize as consumers remained, but overall clubs would no longer provide the basis for organization. Some hoped that the growing middle-class "tenants' protective unions" would achieve greater success. Sometime in the summer of 1920, John R. Patterson, one of many tenant activists, walked into his apartment on the North End of Chicago and removed his overalls. Stepping outside for a stroll down the streets of his middle-class Rogers Park neighborhood, he would have seen numerous signs hanging in apartment windows foretelling a continuing series of "rent strikes." They read: "Unfair. The landlord demands an unreasonable advance in rent. This apartment will not be vacant."[84]

# 5 • Rent War!

## Middle-Class Tenant Organizing

Post–World War I Chicago took on many different meanings for its increasingly diverse citizenry. It was a center of progressive reform, home to a tradition of political corruption, a site of labor unrest, a destination for immigrants from eastern Europe and African American workers, and a city undergoing a housing crisis. In the midst of rapid industrialization, Chicago's population grew from 1.7 million in 1900 to 2.7 million in 1920. Over the course of the late nineteenth and early twentieth centuries, scores of middle-class Chicagoans settled down in "family homes" in "safe" and "sanitary" communities away from many in the city's growing working class. In the wake of World War I, as rents increased along with the price of other commodities, Chicago's white-collar tenants grew increasingly worried about their ability to afford a middle-class lifestyle in a middle-class neighborhood.[1]

Reflecting this deepening frustration, on March 18, 1920, A. E. Jessurun, treasurer of the self-proclaimed "middle class" Chicago Tenants Protective Association (CTPA), addressed a pig before an audience of 500 disgruntled tenants at the Graeme Stewart School. In an "apologetic" tone, Jessurun asked the "real, live, kicking, poker" for forgiveness. "I did you an injury whenever I called a landlord a 'rent hog,'" Jessurun declared. "I take it all back. You certainly did nothing to deserve having your name transferred to the landlord." Following a lengthy applause from the crowd, the pig "grunted forgiveness."[2]

With each meeting, membership in the Chicago Tenants Protective Association had grown. White-collar tenants, who had seen their rents raised along with the cost of other necessities, had become increasingly frustrated with all groups that they believed played a role in causing exorbitant rents. According to the CTPA, striking laborers and grafters in the construction industry had increased rents by inflating building costs, while landlords had capitalized on the large demand for housing by extracting additional profits. Chicago's organizing middle-class tenants demanded that the local and state governments bring these groups to justice and pressed for rent reform to give renters protection from profiteering landlords.

In their neighborhoods and in their writings and public statements, these tenants created a middle-class consumerist space and portrayed themselves not just as defenders of the public, but as *the public*. Chicago tenants used the terms "middle class" and "the people" or "the public" interchangeably. Casting themselves as "the people," they used producer values—industriousness, honesty, and thrift—to define what was fair in the local housing market. They demanded justice against profiteering landlords, as well as against greedy and corrupt labor unions whose alleged opportunism opposed "the people's" interests and epitomized the opposite of these values. Drawing on producerist rhetoric, symbols, and organizing strategies, the middle-class tenant movement, along with the municipal market, home garden, and overall movements, represented an aggressive attempt by middle-class activists to define a consumerist politics as a neutral and righteous defense of the public against supposedly selfish groups.

## The Building Shortage and Graft in Early Twentieth-Century Chicago Politics

Among the primary grievances of Chicago's postwar middle class was the role that a building shortage played in raising rents. At the onset of the World War I, companies and laborers associated with the building industry directed their efforts toward war industries, a trend that coincided with a 20 percent growth in Chicago's population between 1910 and 1920. As a result, demand for housing outweighed supply, leading to what one commentator called a "virtual famine in housing accommodations." Indeed, whereas in 1916 there were 12,437 total building permits in the city, by 1918 the number had dropped to 1,853, climbing only modestly to 6,316 in 1919. Many residents believed that indolence, greed, and general corruption in the building industry exacerbated the situation. One local organization, of which Jessurun, the tenant leader who had apologized to a pig, was a member, spoke of the need to "expose crime in the building industry, and to assist in abolishing all restrictive agreements or practices which tend to increase the cost of building." Summarizing these common sentiments, a national law journal observed that the "mania" for rent-fixing is "no doubt due to the desperation of the people, who found themselves threatened with extinction as to the extortionate demands of those who controlled the necessaries of life," not the least of which included "higher wage demands."[3]

Middle-class residents implored members of the government to take action against striking or underproductive laborers and corrupt unions and contractors in the building industry. National, state, and local politicians read complaints in the press and received many letters discussing how striking construction workers and profiteering in "building material" caused the high rents and housing prices. For example, in a letter to Illinois politician Charles Merriam, Paul Perry, a fellow progressive, declared "Real Estate [in Chicago] is dead" and cited "[t]yrannous exactions, grafting labor officials, exorbitant wages [and] idleness" as reasons. An Illinois General Assembly commission on building in Chicago reported that "the public demands relief against the manipulations and extractions of price-fixing combinations." After defining the middle class as "the public," a *Chicago Daily Tribune* editorial pointedly declared, "The white collar job holder, the salariat, the small tradesman and professional worker . . . living in No Man's Land between organized labor and capital, have for five years been suffering under the fire of opposing forces." According to the *Tribune*, middle-class citizens "have seen wealth amassed on one side and wages going up on the other, while the only advance which touched on them was the advance in the cost of living." Economist Royal E. Montgomery later reflected that "the public was coming to feel that the building trades needed a policeman."[4]

The housing crisis occurred in the midst of a long tradition of graft and graft accusation in Chicago politics. Union corruption accusations were frequent and sensational enough during the 1910s for the labor-friendly *Chicago Day Book* to refer to "the crusade against labor grafters" undertaken by the press and government officials.[5] Throughout the 1910s and 1920s, many Chicago politicians made their careers by accusing labor unions, as well as contractors, and other politicians of taking bribes or making excess profits. Union corruption continued to be a primary feature of public discourse and a means to attack labor unions beyond the 1920s, when exposés of New Deal era labor union corruption by reporters such as Westbrook Pegler both promoted their own fame and helped to set the stage for the long-term decline of the labor movement.[6] During the immediate postwar period and beyond, this discourse about graft offered real estate developers, investors, and large employers in the building industry the opportunity to speak in terms that resonated with sympathetic politicians, newspapers, and middle-class tenants.[7]

Aiming to reduce labor costs, real estate developers pressed the issue of graft by portraying labor union corruption as a matter of public interest. Large real estate developers, such as Julius Rosenwald of Sears and Roebuck and members of the Chicago Real Estate Board, publicly linked labor graft to the building shortage and high rents. One of many statements by the Chicago Real Estate Board explained that rental increases were caused by a lack of building, transpiring from "[u]nregulated associations and combinations [that] have been formed enabling enemies of society to injure the public and themselves through profiteering and restriction of production." According to this and similar appeals, the high cost of labor represented the most prohibitive factor in new building. Since middle-class Chicagoans had also called for the government to lower the cost of housing by addressing striking and grafting labor, local real estate interests framed the issue in terms of protecting "the public" or "the people." Such statements encouraged middle-class Chicagoans to join with real estate interests in an effort to suppress strikers and labor graft. However, in large part this would take shape after a series of direct battles between tenants and their alleged "profiteering" landlords, who had taken advantage of the situation.[8]

## "Coin Hungry" Landlords

To many middle-class Chicagoans, opportunistic landlords had unfairly capitalized on the building shortage to squeeze additional profits out of renters.[9] Scores of tenants objected to excessive rents before the city council, so much so that the council's Judiciary Committee referenced frequent complaints from "many citizens" and from the "public press" concerning the "vital importance" of addressing "extortionate rentals." White-collar renters in Chicago and elsewhere in the United States frequently called on local, state, and federal officials to address the problem. Summarizing the situation, U.S. Rep. George Huddleston (D-Alabama) proclaimed, "No wonder we find a loud outcry going up because of the extortion that is being practiced."[10]

Escalating rents were a national reality. Along with a rise in the price of coal, building materials, and other housing-related commodities, average rents in the United States increased by 11 percent from 1914 to 1919. The cost of housing in Chicago (rents included), in which 73 percent of residents were renters, climbed by 14 percent. But the greatest increases occurred during 1920 and 1921, when, as a result, tenant activism blossomed. From December 1919 to December 1921, housing costs in Chicago jumped by 62 percent (see figure below). In this same period the general cost of living in Chicago, while nearly double that of 1914, marginally decreased. This trend encouraged Chicagoans to pay special attention to housing in these months.[11]

Chicago's middle-class tenants cited their ability to maintain a single-family rented home in a middle-class neighborhood as a primary concern. The paragon of middle-class single-family occupancy grew in the late nineteenth and early twentieth centuries with the rise of consumer culture and mass advertising in America. During this time, Americans witnessed a boom in mass culture led by popular magazines with middle-class readership in mind. Widely distributed periodicals told middle-class readers to buy myriad items to put in their homes. These items, the home itself, and where it was located to a large extent defined middle-class status. Magazines and advice manual writers such as Ellen Richards suggested to middle-class readers that an independent single-family home would protect against "communal pleasures" that could expose middle-class families to the dangers of socialism, immigrants, the working class, and "primitive" communities. While many white-collar Chicagoans chased the dream of home ownership, the ideal of single-family occupancy also applied to renters. In the post–World War I period, it was an ideal that many middle-class tenants steadfastly defended.[12]

At least some middle-class renters resented the idea that common laborers could now afford housing in middle-class neighborhoods. Julian Yurman, a doctor living in a South Side apartment, wrote to a Chicago judge not only to protest escalating rents but also to complain about the nature of his new neighbors. Coinciding with an increase in rent, a streetcar driver, his wife, and five kids moved into a "small five room flat" directly above Yurman's apartment. Yurman called the environment "unsanitary and a danger to the neighborhood," and declared that because of all of the commotion he and his

Table 1. Relative Housing Costs and Cost of Living in Chicago, December 1914 to March 1922

| Month/Year | Housing Costs | Cost of Living (All Commodities) |
|---|---|---|
| December 1914 | — | 1 |
| December 1916 | 1 | 1.095 |
| December 1917 | 1.007 | 1.42 |
| December 1918 | 1.019 | 1.72 |
| June 1919 | 1.073 | 1.74 |
| December 1919 | 1.126 | 2 |
| June 1920 | 1.342 | 2.14 |
| December 1920 | 1.527 | 1.933 |
| May 1921 | 1.77 | 1.784 |
| September 1921 | 1.786 | 1.75 |
| December 1921 | 1.827 | 1.72 |
| March 1922 | 1.828 | 1.65 |

*Note:* For Housing costs, December 1916 = 1, while for cost of living, December 1914 = 1.

Cartoons in the Chicago press featured families dressed respectably (rather than in penury), but looking visibly distressed over how profiteering might threaten their future, whether it involved seeking to remain in their home, renting an apartment, or buying a new home. *CT*, April 2, 1921 (Rent Hog); *Southtown Economist*, February 21, 1921 (Home Hunters).

wife got "no rest." Yurman lamented having "to work nights at the University of Chicago to pay rent."[13]

In addition to their housing concerns, many middle-class tenants also lamented that wage earners were increasingly experiencing other parts of consumer culture that had hitherto signified middle-class status. In particular, a supposed decline in middle-class marriage rates troubled white-collar workers and sympathetic reporters. Representing this anxiety, a 1920 study conducted by S. C Legner, the chief Cook County (Chicago) marriage license clerk, concluded that "the number of licenses issued to members of the 'salaried' class is steadily decreasing, the number issued to members of the laboring class is steadily growing." A similar *Providence Journal* study of marriage rates more directly probed into the reasons why. Finding their quest for an affordable flat "in vain," and suffering from the high costs associated with a respectable wedding, white-collar men were less likely to enter matrimony than their working-class counterpart, whose pay had increased with the cost of living. The *Journal* concluded that unmarried "white collar daughters will pay the greater part of the toll," as the primary victim of the "tragedy" of the high cost of living.[14]

In defending their ability to consume up to the standards of their class, middle-class tenants claimed to be righteously defending "the public" from

**1910 Census Occupations of a Sample of Residents in a Location with Tenant Activism (Based on Heads of Households Listed on Two Census Sheets Corresponding with the Addresses Below)**

| Street/ House # | Profession | Street/ House # | Profession |
|---|---|---|---|
| **Lunt** | | **Morse** | |
| 1404 | Landscaper | 1406 | Shoemaker |
| 1404 | Tire nursey | 1408 | Cleaner |
| 1404 | Dry goods examiner | 1408 | Plasterer |
| 1415 | Restaurant | 1415 | None |
| 1425 | Publisher | 1419 | Civil Engineer |
| 1425 | Clerk | 1419 | Broker |
| 1427 | Printing foreman | 1424 | Minister |
| 1431 | Own income | 1430 | Manufacturer |
| 1441 | Actor | 1434 | Clerk |
| 1505 | Physician | 1440 | Bookkeeper |
| | | 1444 | Teacher |
| **Unclear** | | | |
| 1960 | Manager | | |

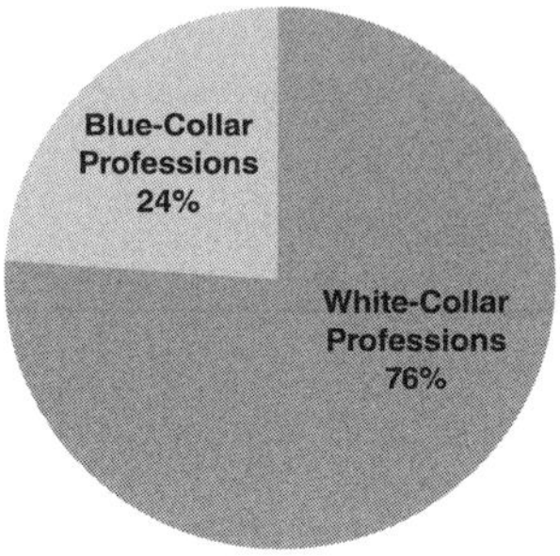


**1920 Census Occupations of a Sample of Residents in a Location with Tenant Activism (Based on Heads of Households Listed on Two Census Sheets Corresponding with the Addresses Below)**

| Street/ House # | Profession | Street/ House # | Profession |
|---|---|---|---|
| **Morse** | | **Lunt** | |
| 1415 | Carpenter | 1411 | None |
| 1417 | Cobbler | 1415 | Janitor |
| 1417 | Milkman | 1425 | Superintendent Library Binding |
| 1419 | Teacher | | |
| 1419 | Osteopath | 1427 | Auditor |
| 1420 | Washer | | |
| 1421 | Physician | **Greenview** | |
| 1424 | Wire/Agricultural Commission | 6927 | Treasurer |
| | | 6957 | Instructor |
| 1425 | Florist | | |
| 1429 | Fireman | | |
| 1431 | Florist | | |
| 1434 | Housekeeper | | |
| 1435 | None | | |
| 1440 | Cashier | | |
| 1441 | Bookman | | |
| 1441 | None | | |
| 1443 | None | | |
| 1443 | Practitioner | | |
| 1445 | Storekeeper | | |

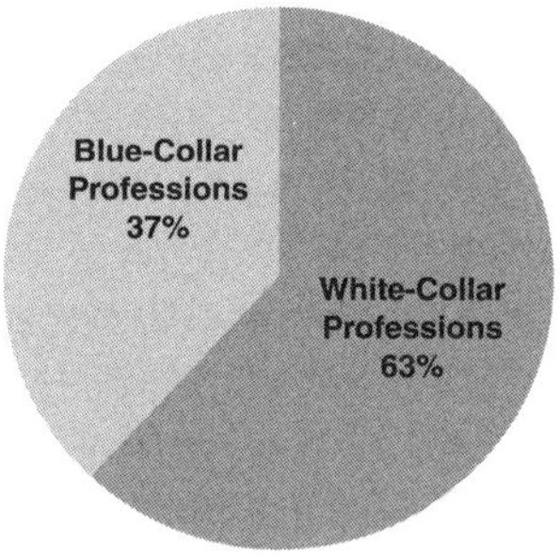


The tables and charts show a proportionate increase in working-class settlement in this Rogers Park block, though it remained largely white collar. The data is a sample, which includes only "heads of households" on two census sheets for each census, but it is worth noting that most heads of households shared apartments with their families, and, in some cases, boarders. See endnote 23 in chapter 5 for additional methodological discussion.

"Cupid Studies the Dollar Market," *Providence Journal*, April 4, 1920.

self-interested groups, and promoting universal American values. While describing the agenda of a self-proclaimed "middle class" group of Rogers Park tenants, John R. Patterson stated that "the public has a right to protect itself." Patterson argued that curbing rent increases was not only desirable but critical to the standard American principles of "life, liberty and the pursuit of happiness." Further universalizing the principles and priorities of organizing middle-class tenants, Patterson claimed to be working on behalf of the common interest, stating, "The unreasonably high rents prevailing in so many quarters are demoralizing the people, demoralizing the profiteer, unfair to the fair minded landlord, [and] robbing the tenant of money that ought to be expended on his family."[15]

Along with middle-class citizens themselves, local and national newspapers frequently defined middle-class concerns as those of "the people." The *Englewood Times* (South Side Chicago) used the term "middle class" interchangeably with "the public" and "the majority" in a diatribe against strikes, high wages, and profiteering. The *Times* asserted that both organized labor and real estate investors "punished" the "middle class," and lamented that members of the "the public generally pay for the sins of both labor and capital." Similarly, the *New York Times* stated that when faced with "increased prices" and "profiteering in rents," white-collar workers make up "a formidable total" and "their influence is bound to be felt."[16]

At the municipal level, the Chicago City Council reacted to citizens' complaints by passing resolutions that condemned the popular culprits for high rents—striking labor, grafters, and profiteering landlords—and established a committee to investigate excessive rents. A July 1919 city council resolution declared that the cost of labor had "so greatly advanced" that the city was in the midst of a "long-continued building shortage," adding that "landlords and agents throughout the city are taking unfair and intolerable advantage" of these conditions. The resolution further called for the Judiciary Committee to investigate high rental charges and to figure out a "practical legal measure" to prevent landlords from raising rents by more than 10 percent. Five days later, the city council authorized the superintendent of public service to collect data on rent profiteering, receive tenants' complaints, and forward them to a special city council committee. The council instructed the committee to send these complaints to the Board of Review of Cook County with a request that "the property taxes of said landlords be increased proportionately with the increase in rentals demanded by them." This strategy involved multiple levels of local bureaucracy and would only penalize profiteering landlords by making them pay a percentage of their newly found profits. Otherwise, the Judiciary Committee "found that there was nothing it could do." To many Chicagoans, this was not enough.[17]

On August 14, 1919, middle-class Chicagoans transformed their grievances into organized action, forming the Chicago Tenants Protective Association. At the 1021 Garrick Building, approximately 400 tenants came together to protest rent increases of as high as 600 percent.[18] The CTPA had a strong white-collar orientation. The original chairman and treasurer of the CTPA were a manager and a broker, respectively; and the president of the CTPA for most of time frame of the organization's existence was the manager of the book binding division of the Chicago Public Library. Describing the organization's "middle class" membership, CTPA president John Patterson stated that the CTPA was made up of "the clerk class, the salesman class, the professional men's class, the small-business men."[19]

Very quickly, the CTPA expanded. Just three days after its founding, William S. Forman, a CTPA organizer, announced to the city council, "We have hundreds of complaints every day and some of them come from the best known and most respected persons in town." The CTPA promised an "aggressive campaign" against landlords who had "robbed" "the people" "of $50,000 every day through unfair transactions."[20]

## "Rent Strike"

As landlords across Chicago continued to increase rents, organized middle-class tenants announced plans for "rent war." In February 1920, borrowing the strategy of working-class tenants before them, middle-class Chicagoans declared a "rent strike" beginning May 1. When landlords raised rents, they would neither pay the increase nor move out. Over the course of the next two months, tenants, landlords, politicians, and local newspapers anticipated potential chaos.[21]

Prior to the postwar period "rent strikes" and tenant organizing had taken place exclusively in working-class neighborhoods. Working-class renters across the United States had used the "rent strike" since 1904, beginning with socialists on New York City's Lower East Side. During these strikes, working-class renters, living side by side, relied on each other in tenant organizing, a practice that was mostly possible because of the spatial segmentation of many cities by economic and social class. They exerted power through spatially grounded collective organization.[22]

When middle-class tenants faced rent increases in the postwar period, they too organized in accordance with the class-based demarcation of the city. Just as their working-class counterparts generally lived side by side, many middle-class tenants resided in predominantly white-collar neighborhoods. For instance, one North Side block that was located in a neighborhood that was active in tenant organizing consisted of a strong majority of heads of households with white-collar professions, ranging from auditor to lawyer (a statistical breakdown is shown in the nearby graph). Other areas often followed the same pattern (for an additional example, see earlier data and graphs on the Lunt and Morse Street area; for methodology, see endnote 23).[23]

Leading up to the strike, the most vocal landlords and tenants spoke confidently and prepared for a showdown. "We should get as much as we can," shouted George W. Torpe, president of the Lake View Property Owners and Improvement Association before fellow landlords at a February 27, 1920, public meeting. According to a press account, landlords at the meeting encouraged each other to "shove it to the tenants," and when tenant-friendly Alderman Robert Mulcahy failed to show up for an invitation to speak, landlords reportedly called him "a coward." Gaining wind of the landlords' sentiments only emboldened tenants planning the May 1 rent strike. "We have organized a strike," CTPA officer H. S. Standish declared, "and we intend to see who is running this city—the public or the landlords." By "the public" Standish had the white-collar class in mind. At the next meeting, the CTPA discussed for the first time the idea of establishing a "white collar league" of "professional men and office workers."[24]

On May 1, Chicagoans witnessed what participants and the media called "rent war." Many striking tenants publicly condemned their landlords as they steadfastly refused to move from their homes. Among the scenes in Chicago flats was a fight between tenant Rose Mistretta and a new tenant who sought to move in "before she was ready to vacate." During the altercation, the new

**1920 Census Occupations of a Sample of Residents in a Location with Tenant Activism (Based on Heads of Households Listed on Two Census Sheets Corresponding with the Addresses Below)**

| Street/ House # | Profession | Street/ House # | Profession |
|---|---|---|---|
| **Windsor** | | **Wilson** | |
| 920 | None | 902 | Assistant Agent |
| 922 | Manufacturer | 926 | Salesman |
| 922 | Contractor | 927 | Brush Maker |
| 922 | Cook | 928 | Lawyer |
| 922 | Plumber | 936 | Salesman |
| 926 | Salesman | 938 | Stenographer |
| 928 | Manager | 942 | Manager |
| 930 | Retired | | |
| 930 | Agent | | |
| 934 | Auditor | | |
| 936 | Buyer | | |
| 940 | Salesmen | | |
| 942 | None | | |
| 946 | Salesman | | |
| 948 | Salesman | | |

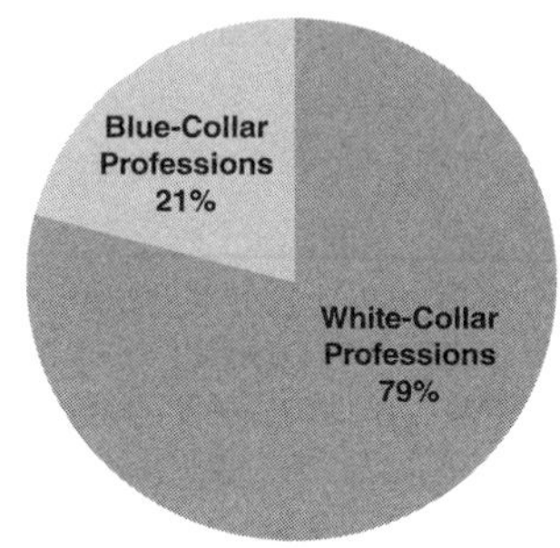


Residents' occupations in a location with tenant activism (heads of households, 1920)

tenant managed to give Mistretta "many bruises, pull out sections of her hair and break her glasses." While most tenants did not experience that kind of violence, they did prepare for a different kind of battle—in municipal court. Acting collectively, individual tenants hoped to force landlords to sue for forcible detainers. The CTPA envisioned that by jointly stretching the capacity of the municipal court, tenants would force the local and state governments to enact landlord-tenant reform.[25]

Even from the early planning stages of the May 1 rent strike, striking tenants aimed to convince local and state governments to develop more aggressive strategies to prevent rent increases. Politicians, did, indeed, give the CTPA reason for optimism. Led by Democratic alderman Robert Mulcahy, many members of the city council investigated high rents and publicly advocated penalties for rent profiteers. Aldermen and former judges attended CTPA meetings, and board of education officials had offered schools as meeting places for tenant organizing. With renters having rhetorical and logistical support from key politicians, a letter to the editor of the *Chicago Daily Tribune* summed up their goals. "Take [cases] to court," the writer advocated. "Should the decision be against the tenant, file an appeal, give bond, and let the [rent] hog wait for his year's rent until the decision is handed down. . . . The Illinois legislature convenes in 1921 and it is hoped that a bill may be passed. . . . If the poor white collar slaves will only stand together it can be done in Illinois."[26]

Chicago's real estate interests were alarmed by the growing tenant organization, and publicity that portrayed landlords as profiteers. As a result, the Chicago Real Estate Board attempted to minimize further collective tenant organizing by individualizing landlord-tenant conflict. They set up landlord-tenant arbitration committees, at first using their own arbitrators, who presumably would be friendlier to landlords' interests, but eventually agreeing to have joint boards with the CTPA. In any case, this strategy not only worked against collective action by tenants but also sought to prevent tenants from flooding the courts. Without these weapons, tenants seemingly would be unable to convince the state legislature to pass rent reform.[27]

Members of the Chicago Real Estate Board also shifted blame for high rents almost entirely on supposedly greedy, corrupt, and striking workers in the building industry, as well as on grafting contractors. The board noted that after the signing of the armistice, "construction costs were constantly increasing and maintenance and repairs were correspondingly excessive." The problem, according to the official organ of the Chicago Real Estate Board, was "the attitude of contractors and employers [and] . . . laboring men." Playing to the popular fears of the first red scare, the board warned of "radical elements in the labor movement" and complained of a lazy working class, stating, "until labor realizes that anything less than a man's maximum production in exchange for an agreed wage is not just to the employers and is decidedly unjust to the entire public . . . he need expect no great sympathy for his wage demands." As these strikes "paralyz[ed] the building and construction work of this community," "unregulated associations and combinations" exacerbated the situation, which served to "injure the public." This "restriction on production" caused an undersupply of places to live, leading to rent increases commensurate with ongoing demand for housing.[28]

In candid moments, Chicago Real Estate Board members did occasionally complain of the "unreasonable" demands of tenants, but generally had to avoid lashing out against them publicly. Vilifying tenants would problematize the idea that they could be unbiased arbitrators in middle-class tenant-landlord disputes. In fact, the board made great efforts to cast themselves as protectors of the public interest. For example, Adolph Kramer, the president of the Renting Division of the board, told a reporter for the *Chicago Daily Tribune*, "The courts are being cluttered up with rent cases. There are many cases where both tenant and landlord are wrong. There is no reason why these difficulties cannot be settled out of court." Yet, in a speech to members of the board, Gerhardt F. Meyne claimed that a 1920 comparison of property values and rents in "a middle class neighborhood" yielded no evidence of profiteering; in fact, Meyne maintained, landlords were charging too little. Publicly, the board seemingly sought to depict themselves as evenhanded before middle-class tenants. Privately, the board gave little legitimacy to middle-class concerns and blamed the press for a "campaign" to sensationalize the scope and nature of rent profiteering. Above all, Chicago's real estate interests sought to prevent the government from involving itself in the real estate market in any manner that would limit their profits.[29]

The limited evidence of the outcomes of the arbitrations suggests that many of them did result in minimizing rent increases for individual tenants. Edith Rockwood, of the Chicago Women's City Club, noted, "In certain [cases] the tenants were convinced that the increase was reasonable, and in others the landlords were persuaded to reduce their demands." But even in cases that were decided in favor of a tenant, Real Estate Board arbitrators sought to serve a greater purpose: to forestall legislation that would either fix rents or give tenants more rights. While publicly stating "[l]et the board take a public stand against profiteering," Real Estate Board president L. M. Smith mentioned the board's true motive for arbitration by asserting that "[t]his will take the wind out of the sails of the thousands of tenants who plan to go to Springfield and get rent legislation."[30]

As rents continued to climb, an aggressive approach from the government was precisely what many organizing tenants demanded.[31] In fact, many members of the CTPA only joined the organization in anticipation of future rent increases, as well as in sympathy for defiant neighbors. Lacking significant change in the local housing economy or immediate reform to curb rent profiteering, middle-class tenant activism only stood to increase.

## The Rogers Park Tenants Protective Association and Rent War in Court

The Rogers Park affiliate of the CTPA stood at the forefront of this continued activism. Situated on Chicago's far North Side, Rogers Park consisted of a number of smaller neighborhoods. Most of the reported postwar tenant activity occurred in the Morse/Lunt Avenue area. While these blocks had long been residential, the early twentieth century brought many new two-story apartment buildings and stores to Pratt Boulevard, Touhy, Sheridan, and a number of side streets. The 1910 census lists residents with predominantly white-collar professions,[32] and local sources emphasize Morse/

Lunt (and Rogers Park in general) as a family-oriented neighborhood.[33] One resident, who lived "at 6928 N. Lakewood, near Morse Avenue" next to "an apartment house at Morse and Lakewood," described Rogers Park as "a very simple, family-oriented neighborhood" and remembered "Morse Avenue as being a tree-lined, quiet street." Drawing on a national middle-class antiprofiteering discourse and responding to local rent increases, residents of Rogers Park in the postwar period transformed their image of Rogers Park as a family-oriented neighborhood into a public middle-class neighborhood identity. This identity would soon play out not only in their apartments and meeting places, in courtrooms and legislative halls, but also in the national media, wherein dozens of newspapers drew on their example to help shape the very national discursive space of middle-class consumer activism that reinforced local organization.[34]

John R. Patterson, the president of the Rogers Park Tenants Protective Association (RPTPA), served as an ideal representative of middle-class consumer discontent. A lover of books since reading rags-to-riches Horatio Alger novels as a child, Patterson worked at the Chicago Public Library as the manager of the binding division, a white-collar position. Rather than simply being known as a binder, he preferred to be thought of as "doctor to 1,750,000 books." Although Patterson made a comfortable living, his salary, and those of many of his colleagues, had increased very little in the previous 5-7 years. In keeping with the identity of the area, Patterson was a family man, living with his wife and two daughters at his 2437 Lunt Avenue apartment. Patterson spent his free time studying history, and reading and lecturing to children.[35]

A veteran of the overall movement, Patterson's grievances were not limited to housing.[36] Just as the overall movement had often reflected consumer discontent beyond high clothing prices, Patterson's tenant activism served as a platform for organizing middle-class citizens against all types of profiteering. Unlike the overall movement, which depended on organization across a wider range of space, tenant activism relied on neighborhood and often block-level organization. While some tenants such as Patterson had already identified individually as members of the middle class through previous or concurrent antiprofiteering movements, they had not necessarily always done so alongside of their neighbors. Led by Patterson, Rogers Park, and particularly the Morse/Lunt blocks, transformed itself from a neighborhood with middle-class residents to a politically conscious *middle-class neighborhood.*

Patterson and the RPTPA often issued the most virulent antilandlord statements among Chicago tenant organizations, and made the most pointed appeals to the state for rent reform. In September 1920, for example, the RPTPA told the *Chicago Daily Tribune* that candidates for Illinois House and Senate seats would be required to "declare themselves on the rent situation." Perhaps seeking to gain favor among Chicago's middle class or for fear of specific opposition from the RPTPA, three state representatives, one senator, and a candidate for senate spoke at RPTPA meetings. Even more daunting to some politicians was Patterson's threat that "we'll throw 100,000 votes against those who have not a clear record on the rent question."[37]

Claiming to simultaneously represent "the public" and "the middle class," members of the RPTPA paid special attention to the impact of high rents on middle-class family life. To many in the RPTPA, rent profiteering was not simply an attack on their pocketbooks; it represented an attack on the family. At a March 1920, meeting, for example, William Forkell declared, "If it [rent profiteering] keeps on, the children as well as the wives and husbands, will be deprived of many necessities in order to pay the rent." Summarizing the beliefs of his fellow tenants in the "middle class" RPTPA, John R. Patterson declared, "They feel that they are fighting for the preservation of the home, for a wholesome community, in which to bring up their children."[38]

Whether involving Rogers Park tenants or those residing elsewhere in Chicago, the flood of landlord-tenant cases heard before the Chicago Municipal Court featured many of these same themes. For example, one tenant complained to Judge Arnold Heap that his landlord had not only evicted him but also his wife and his two-week-old baby. Heap instructed the family to move after a ten-day stay of the eviction. In another case, Judge Heap granted a tenant permission to temporarily remain in her flat after she came home one day to find her children sitting on the doorstep. Her landlord had kicked them out and locked the door. Heap, while respecting her landlord's right to raise rent, found this behavior to be extreme.[39]

Because the municipal court lacked the authority to control rent increases, tenants only achieved, at best, mixed results in court.[40] In a best-case scenario, tenants were given an extra 60 days to move, or, in cases of poor building maintenance by flat owners, they received financial restitution. For the most part, tenants had to confine their legal defense to arguing that they had not been given sufficient notice that a lease would not be renewed after stating that they refused to pay higher rent. Faced with limited options, tenants sometimes attempted to create legal technicalities that would allow them to remain under the old terms of a lease. In one case, a tenant fought a forcible detainer on the logic that the landlord had sent her a notice that her lease "expires April 30, 1920 and will not be renewed," when the written lease had specified May 1, 1920, as the end of the rental agreement. According to the tenant, because the landlord's specific language differed by one day, the notice of termination was null and void, thus requiring her to renew the old lease.

Neither the municipal court nor the appellate court agreed. If anything was clear from the rent court cases of 1920, legislation that would empower tenants and provide them with more options in the courtroom would be necessary. Chicago's tenants "storming the corridors of the city hall courtrooms," as the *Chicago Herald-Examiner* concluded, "were fighting a losing battle."[41]

Of course, organized tenants knew that their legal options were limited before participating in rent strikes. While some tenants marginally improved their individual situations in court, they all succeeded in flooding the courts and generating publicity in the Chicago area press. Chief Bailiff Dennis J. Egan noted, "More suits have been filed than ever before." But would politicians respond?[42]

## Action from the State: The Kessinger Rent Bill

While continuing to plan for further landlord-tenant confrontation, the RPTPA and CTPA focused on maintaining pressure on government officials throughout mid-late 1920 and early 1921. On May 3, 1920, alarmed by the magnitude of ongoing tenant activism, the city council pressed the state government to address the situation. Determining that "the City of Chicago has not the power" to control rents, it passed a resolution imploring the State government to "compel landlords . . . to desist from charging exorbitant and unfair rental." The council added that the states of Maryland and New York had enacted legislation that enabled Baltimore and New York City, respectively, to regulate rents.[43]

Tenants also shifted their attention to the Illinois House and Senate, which were set to convene in the early months of 1921. After gaining the support of the city council for new state landlord-tenant legislation, the CTPA invited state legislators to attend their meetings and sought their public endorsement. Many senators and representatives responded favorably, even as CTPA rhetoric intensified. By November 1920, RPTPA president John R. Patterson had classified landlords as not just "hogs" but also "cockroaches."[44]

At the beginning of the 1921 session, Senator Harold Kessinger, a Republican, sponsored legislation designed to address tenants' call for reforming Illinois landlord-tenant law. The "Kessinger bill" contained two main provisions, which were technically part of different bills, but often referred to singularly. First, it provided tenants with the right to trial by jury, even if they had waived that right in a lease. Second, it empowered municipal court judges to grant a stay of up to six months before executing a forcible detainer. During the stay, tenants would be liable for rent at the same rate charged one month before the expiration of the lease, thus denying landlords the ability to force tenants to pay higher rents for as long as six months. With the support of the governor, the Kessinger bill stood a significant chance at becoming law. The *Chicago Evening Post* concluded that the bill's prospects left tenants "sitting pretty."[45]

Attempting to create a sense of urgency for the bill's passage, CTPA leaders coordinated another rent strike. The May 1, 1921, rent strike promised to be every bit as dramatic and contentious as that of the past year. Hoping to forestall or at least minimize the chaos and conflict of another rent strike, legislators promised to vote before May 1. However, when a number of representatives failed to show up for a planned vote on April 27, the provision calling for six month stays had to be postponed until after "moving day." The legislature did pass the jury waiver measures and Governor Len Small added his signature, leading the *Chicago Daily Journal* to proclaim, "the powerful lobby formed by the landlords of Chicago surrendered to the tenants in the fight over these measures." The landlords, however, "have not given up hope," the *Daily Journal* warned, and "intend to carry on this fight." Tenants were reportedly equally ready for a conflict. Charles S. MacCubbin, a manager in the advertising industry and member of the CTPA, told reporters, "We are determined to oppose in every possible way the increases demanded." In anticipation of May Day tenant activism, the city positioned extra police outside of many apartment buildings, and municipal court judges held an emergency meeting "for the handling of the great number of eviction suits expected to follow the 'strike' threatened for May 1 by 20,000 tenants."[46]

Those anticipating a dramatic May Day were not disappointed. Signs with the words "rent hog," "rent war," or "unfair" graced the windows of apartments all across Chicago. The local news media reported "numerous fights" between landlords and tenants. C. D. Behan, scoffing at a 110 percent rent increase, purportedly waited in front of his apartment with a "Babe Ruth ball bat" "for those who wished to evict him." On 4518 Sheridan Rd., Dr. L. C. Zeigler barricaded his door with numerous chains and a piano, and "armed himself with a revolver and a supply of roman candles." This followed a "continuous fight with [window] placards," in which Zeigler and his landlord had denounced one another over a two-month period. Zeigler wanted the entire community to know that he would not accept a 60 percent increase in his rent for the upcoming year. His neighbors gathered on the street and cheered.[47]

With the courtroom dockets once again filled with forcible detainer cases and the legislature set to vote, no less than the fate of the CTPA strategy stood in the balance. "We are pinning our hopes on the passage of the Kessinger Bill," John R. Patterson declared. The CTPA held rallies for the "anti rent hog bill" at the Le Moyne and Swift Schools and sent its officers to Springfield to lobby the legislature. Alderman Robert Mulcahy and John R. Patterson were part of the delegation. Upon arrival, they were met by the local "Anti-Gougers" league and a band. They processed to the capitol with a style of pomp and circumstance that reiterated the whiteness of their middle-class victimhood, and the power of symbolically racializing their profiteering villains. As the *Chicago Daily Tribune* described it, "Bringing up the rear [of the parade] on the way to the state house was a colored man with a canvas smock inscribed 'Rent Hog.' He was cuffed and dragged—mock stuff—all the way up to the steps and earned his $10 all right." It was a symbolic dehumanization of their white landlord enemies (and a literal dehumanization of the "colored man"), and a metaphorical demonstration of their desire to shift who held power in the Chicago rental market. The racial symbolism of this procession played to the discursive space of middle-class white consumer victimhood, represented in settings ranging from the racialized visual images of profiteers in popular magazines to the anti-Japanese character of Los Angeles municipal market campaigns. The racial component of this discursive space was capable of crossing class boundaries, as the interclass boycotts against George Shima, the "potato king," suggest (discussed in chapter 2). However, it was also a crucial part of more exclusively white-collar middle-class expressions of consumer activism.[48]

CTPA officers and allies were not alone in Springfield. After declaring its opposition to the bill, the Chicago Real Estate Board sent a contingent of its members to lobby the legislature. Both sides invoked the versatile language of the red scare, which, as scholars have noted, came to represent anxieties over anything from changes in family life to race relations.[49] "Now they try to call us bolshevists," Patterson proclaimed at a hearing at the state capitol. "We are not bolshevists; we're real red blooded Americans. I say the rent gougers are bolshevists." Despite these attacks on tenant activists' patriotism, Patterson remained confident, stating, "We have the assurances of all the leaders in the legislature that the bills will go through Tuesday . . . the tenants who strike now will be the ones to profit." Patterson declared that any Chicago politician who opposed them would be committing "political suicide."[50]

After moving through the Senate, the legislation passed the House by a "close vote." The 104-29 vote, while seeming like a wide margin, was only two votes above the 102 vote minimum due to emergency clauses in the legislation. Shortly after the vote, Patterson and two other CTPA officials presented Governor Small with a gold pen that they had jointly purchased. The collectively owned pen represented the group effort required to achieve their

Delegation of CTPA members to Springfield. Press photo in author's possession.

goals. It embodied the realization of tenants that their fates were tied together. With cameras flashing, Small accepted the pen and signed the six-month stay bill. The "tenants rejoice[d]." Shortly after, CTPA officers announced that they would stage a "tenants' festival" on May 12 in celebration of their victory. At the "Jubilee" tenants would enjoy music, dancing and a carnival. "We intend to make the carnival the biggest event ever known in the history of Chicago tenants," declared one CTPA official. With a sigh of relief, Patterson stated "[the] new laws will protect us from profiteers."[51]

Within days of the enactment of rent reform, striking tenants began to see relief. Isaac Sharashaw was just one of the tenants to reap the "first fruits of the tenants' victory at Springfield." Told to leave his flat on May 1, Sharashaw testified that his wife was sick and he did not want her to undertake "the strain of moving." Judge John J. Rooney granted a stay of 60 days without any increase in rent. Others achieved similar results. But perhaps more telling of the tenant victory was the "sudden drop" in the number of eviction suits filed by landlords, who did not want to fight a losing battle. Those that did file forcible detainer cases faced delays from the new system of jury trials. After a tumultuous few months, Dr. L. C. Zeigler moved the piano that he had placed in front of his door and put down his revolver. Not only had he threatened his allegedly profiteering landlord, but on moving day he had fired a shot at the new tenant. With the option of a jury trial and the prospect of a six-month stay, Zeigler decided to claim his rights.[52]

Six-month stays and the right to trial by jury represented important victories for Chicago tenants, but these measures stood to provide them only temporary relief from rent increases. After six months, many of Chicago's tenants would have to pay higher rent elsewhere—at least until the housing market offered lower rents. All seemed to agree that more building was necessary to bring the supply of housing up to the demand. Doing so would require addressing the "greed" of striking workers in the building industry and delving into the "corrupt" and "grafting" world of Chicago's construction contractors and labor organizers.

## Building Graft and Reform

Nearly one year after publicly apologizing to a pig for associating the animal with profiteering landlords, A. E. Jessurun testified as representative of the CTPA before the Illinois Assembly Building Investigation Commission (Dailey Commission), which had been formed with the goal of encouraging new construction by rooting out graft in the Chicago building industry. In addition to hearing testimony from a CTPA officer, the Commission called prominent Chicago landlords on the Chicago Real Estate Board to answer to rumors that they had conspired to oppose new building operations in the city with the objective of maintaining high rents. However, the Commission mainly focused on testimony from a variety of people in the building industry who detailed how labor unions' and contractors' corrupt practices poisoned the housing market.[53]

Meeting from March until June of 1921, the Dailey Commission exposed shocking forms of apparent graft in the building trades and construction materials manufacturing involving both unions and contractors. It called witnesses to testify on illegitimate strikes and graft in janitorial service, terra cotta work, carpentry, brick manufacturing, and numerous other parts of the building trades and related areas. Witnesses recalled forms of graft ranging from labor unions calling strikes if contractors obtained parts from outside of Chicago to simple cases of bribery. As just one example, Chicago millwork manufactures allegedly conspired with the Carpenters union to have them refuse to use millwork produced outside of the city. After reaching this agreement, the manufacturers supposedly raised prices by 300 percent and split the profits with the union.[54]

Although the character and extent of union corruption was likely exaggerated by the Dailey Commission, a number of Chicago unions had pressured or colluded with contractors to use only local unionized labor for the production of building materials and the construction of homes. This practice limited the range of product choices available to builders and consumers, and increased prices. In the most extreme cases, laborers policed job entry by throwing bottles and bricks at businesses that hired nonunion or non-Chicago workers, and even set off bombs.[55] As Andrew Wender Cohen notes, Chicago craft unions protected their interests and fought corporatization by enacting "self-styled laws that favored small, local, and labor-intensive businesses at the expense of large national firms," enforcing these laws "through fines, strikes, boycotts, pickets, assaults, bombings, and shootings."[56]

By exposing and sensationalizing the impact of existing corruption on high rents, the press and the Dailey Commission helped to solidify the notion that grafters and, more broadly, labor unions, were enemies of middle-class tenants.[57] The *Chicago Daily Tribune* reported that contractor and union graft "are costing tenants from $2,000,000 to $5,000,000 annually in increased rents."[58] For its part, in addition to having one of its officers testify before the Commission, the CTPA had passed resolutions (shortly before the Commission met) that congratulated U.S. District Attorney Charles F. Clyne for indicting corrupt union officials and contractors, and called on the state's attorney to do the same.[59] Much to their liking, the Commission worked with the state's attorney and the U.S. Department of Justice to prosecute 124 defendants for graft, among whom were union leaders, contractors, and business agents. The specific offenses ranged from bribery to restraining trade. Ultimately, however, only 18 were found guilty.[60]

Amidst the Dailey Commission hearings, the Building Construction Employers' Association (BCEA) and the Associated Builders, as Chicago's most powerful contractor organizations, aimed to reduce wages for workers in the Chicago building industry, claiming that it would lead to an increase in construction. After having agreed to a horizontal wage scale of $1.25 an hour for skilled workers and $1.00 for unskilled workers in the building industry in 1920, contractors affiliated with the Associated Builders and the BCEA sought a 20 percent wage cut for skilled workers and a 30 percent cut for unskilled workers during the spring of 1921. According to Edward M. Craig, secretary of the BCEA, "Persons contemplating building will not undertake it until the cost of labor is reduced."[61] The CTPA partially agreed, blaming *both* unions and contractors "for stopping the construction of apartment buildings."[62] On January 21, 1921, representatives from 32 unions in the Building Trades Council voted to oppose the proposed reductions, a position reaffirmed by referendum votes among the rank and file.[63] The two sides were unable to find a compromise, leading the employers to begin a general lockout on May 1—nearly a month before the expiration of the previous agreement. Building in Chicago had been at a standstill for six weeks when on June 11, 1921, the Joint Arbitration Boards of the BCEA and the Building Trades Council agreed on an arbitrator to settle the dispute.

The two major parties agreed to have Judge Kenesaw Mountain Landis determine wage scales in what came to be called the "Landis Award." Facing negative publicity, fueled by newspaper accounts of the Dailey Commission testimony, building trades unions decided that it would be in their interest to agree to have the seemingly fair-minded Landis make the ultimate decision. Landis, who had recently taken the post of commissioner of Major League Baseball, had previously made headlines for fining Standard Oil $27 million in a 1907 antitrust case. For their part, business interests and many politicians claimed that setting wage scales for each type of worker in every trade would limit the opportunity for graft.

Landis, however, did not confine his decision to wage scales. Influenced by the publicity of the Dailey Commission,[64] Landis, in his ruling on September 7, 1921, not only lowered wages for virtually all trades, he also rewrote work rules, effectively opening the door for the Chicago building industry to henceforth operate on an open shop basis. Such a ruling struck at the vitals of the building trades' unions' efforts to control access to jobs and on-site conditions.[65] Organized labor was furious with the result. A public memorandum issued by the Chicago Federation of Labor declared, "Judge Landis, with no building trade experience, after considering the situation for the short period of three months during which time he was occupied on the bench, giving some attention to his job as chief base ball umpire, some at playing golf," mandated "impractical and unjust working rules."[66] While Landis granted a rehearing and lessened some of the wage cuts, labor certainly did not come out on top.[67]

The Landis Award provided a prime opportunity for Chicago businessmen to appeal to middle-class residents who themselves condemned the alleged exorbitant demands of organized labor. Realizing that unions would fight the implementation of the Award, on November 15, 1921, a group of Chicago businessmen associated with the Chicago Association of Commerce formed an organization called the Citizens' Committee to Enforce the Landis Award (CCELA). The Committee sought to "protect against strikes, graft, sabotage and boycotting of materials," and claimed that "the Dailey legislative investigation exposed the true state of affairs in the construction industry in Chicago."[68] They asserted that it represented the citizens of Chicago, but, in reality, the organization was comprised of 176 wealthy bankers, manufacturers, merchants, and other members of the business elite.[69] More than 80 percent of the 176 CCELA members were owners, principal officers, directors, and trustees of companies, and many of them had been listed in the *Directory of Directors in the City of Chicago*. A number of CCELA members were well-known philanthropists, leaders of social clubs, or served on city boards or commissions.[70]

In the press and in its literature, the Committee portrayed itself as the "people's" committee, guarding the interests of the consuming public. One booklet written under the auspices of the Committee, "The Giant, We the People and the Landis Decision," serves as one of the most glaring examples of the Committee's use of language that played to middle-class readership. Using phrases such as "We the People" and "the Public," the booklet outlined how "the Snake of Selfishness and Greed," organized labor, sought to poison the public. It stated that "[t]he free-lunchers and grafters tear apart Giant We-The-People and throw him into the ditch." Of the impact of labor on "the public" the booklet elaborated, "The union rules got so snake-ridden in Chicago that one-fifth to one-fourth of all the millions paid for building was wasted by these overcharges! . . . So it was that Giant We-The-People rose in his wrath. . . . But Judge Landis said . . . get the Snake!" The booklet also reiterated how building strikes and graft led to increased rents, noting "the high cost is added on to rent." Using phrases such as "the public" and "the people" and referring to these groups as victims in antilabor graft, antiunion, and antiprofiteering tirades, the booklet's words closely resembled the manner in which middle-class Chicago residents referred to themselves. Further, it contrasted the selfishness of labor unions with "architects, engineers, doctors, lawyers [and] teachers," who "see how much they can give and how they can improve and set higher standards for themselves." Other CCELA publications portrayed the organization "as drawn from every profession" with "no axes to grind." Characterizing the CCELA as disingenuous, the Chicago Federation of Labor's newsletter accused the Committee of seeking to "crush labor unions," and proclaimed that "to cover its real purpose, it blathers about graft in the building industry; it palavers to rent payers."[71]

A number of white-collar citizens supported the CCELA. When, in July 1922, the Committee set up a free training school to bring more nonunionized employees into the building trades, white-collar workers reportedly flocked to school. The CCELA reported receiving hundreds of letters that resembled the words of a "white collar" man who stated that he was a "full fledged American," who completed "six months of business college" and "would be pleased to have a personal interview" for an opening in the trade school. Attending the school served as a way for these middle-class Chicagoans to both support the Committee's antiunion agenda and supposedly enjoy the higher pay of blue-collar construction work. As one newspaper stated of the white-collar middle-class man enrolled in the Committee's school, he "no doubt hates to trade his linen collar for a cotton jumper, but the economic pressure is forcing the change." The paper specifically identified them as "stenographers, office clerks, minor salesmen, and bookkeepers." After training at the CCELA school, one former clerk reportedly increased his weekly pay by 35 percent as a sheet metal worker. To maintain white-collar support, the Citizens' Committee continued to remind CTPA members and other tenants of how CCELA actions would reduce rents. A CCELA "Talking Points" summary instructed members to state that "[l]iving expenses cannot reach the normal [levels] while the cost of building remains high. . . . A lower building cost is the first step toward lower rents." Making a similar argument, a February 1923 Chicago Association of Commerce publication printed the headline "Building Trade School Growing Rapidly: Rapidity With Which Construction Is Going Forward Indicates, It Is Held, That Drop in Rents Is Likely."[72]

With a significant measure of white-collar support, the CCELA did more than just use pamphlets, public statements, or even training schools to "enforce" the Landis Award. The Committee arranged for building contractors to make bids on jobs in Chicago when competition seemed lacking, monitored and exposed individuals and groups that did not abide by the award, and wrote companies with impending construction projects to encourage them to only engage in business with firms and unions that worked under Landis Award terms. It also brought new workers to Chicago to replace strikers and employed approximately 700 guards to "protect" work sites.[73]

Chicago Building Trades workers expressed outrage over the CCELA's tactics and the strain that it placed on their earning power amid the high cost of living. The Amalgamated Sheet Metal Workers lamented how the Landis Award lowered wages when "the price of food, clothing and other living costs maintained the same average as before the reduction," and criticized the CCELA for "forcing" the new wage on the workers.[74] Condemning the CCELA's efforts to "smash" unions, members of the Chicago Federation of Labor attempted to turn the tables on the CCELA's appeals to middle-class consumers by marshaling their own working-class consumer power against CCELA businesses. They boycotted businesses that were owned by CCELA members and located in working-class neighborhoods, ultimately forcing at least one banker to resign from the committee after neighborhood residents withdrew their deposits. The Chicago Federation of Labor bulletin proudly declared that it "didn't pay [for] him to line up with the labor fighters."[75]

Nevertheless, the Committee claimed success, as more than 85 percent of building in Cook County occurred under Landis Award guidelines.[76] In a

July 1922 letter to a supporter, one member of the Committee wrote, "Since the Committee began functioning, there have been no strikes, no delays in construction, no restrictions as to where material should be bought, and no graft." One newspaper noted approvingly that "there is now for the first time in five years a real healthy surplus of flats in this city, which means a lowering of rentals and increased purchasing power for this great middle class."[77] This success came at the expense of Chicago building trades unions, which encountered open shop conditions, intimidation, and little public sympathy.[78]

Although Chicago building trades union membership remained strong by the end of the 1920s, these unions operated in an increasingly hostile climate. The Landis Award and the CCELA enhanced employers' ability to use nonunion labor instead of local union workers, and instructed them to pay workers according to the relatively low Landis Award wage scales. In addition, rhetoric that accused organized labor of corrupting the building industry contributed to a broader antiunion discourse that affected unions in all industries throughout the 1920s.[79]

Similar to William Wood's treatment of workers at the American Woolen Company (see chapter 3), Chicago builders exploited and enlarged "public" sentiment against unions to help usher organized labor into a decade of "lean years" for activism and employee rights. White-collar Chicagoans' political organizing and consciousness of themselves as the consuming public not only served to protect their interests against profiteering landlords, they also provided a backdrop for the business conservatism that came to characterize the decade.

## Conclusion

Facing stagnant salaries and a building shortage that precipitated high rents, white-collar Chicagoans drew on an accepted and growing national discourse of middle-class consumer protest, and organized to pressure the state to enact landlord-tenant reform. During the immediate postwar period, CTPA members undertook "rent strikes" and aired grievances to politicians and the press, both of which reinforced and heightened already extreme antilandlord, antigraft, and antilabor rhetoric. They also transformed some Chicago neighborhoods into politically conscious middle-class spaces where residents organized to defend their consumer identity. Significantly, like participants in the home garden, municipal market, and overall movements, middle-class renters claimed to be neutral defenders of the public. They cast consumers as the "people" and equated their needs with those of the middle class. Appropriating the "rent strike" strategy from the working class had served the CTPA well. By employing this tactic CTPA leaders achieved landlord-tenant reform on the state level. As the housing crisis waned and the prices of most commodities stabilized, middle-class consumer organizing faded. However, throughout the 1920s, aided by the publicity of the Dailey Commission and acting through the Citizens' Committee to Enforce the Landis Award, organized employers continued to appeal to the antilabor sentiment that was prevalent among white-collar tenants in the immediate postwar period.

# Epilogue

## Toward a "Middle Class Union"

Even before the Dailey Commission returned its findings, Chicago tenants attempted to broaden their organization. The CTPA was a tenants' organization, but a number of its members had also protested the high prices of other commodities, whether by donning overalls and scorning profiteering of clothing, or by condemning food profiteers and striking workers in a variety of industries for failing to produce. In the midst of the Illinois building graft investigation and their tenant activism, some Chicago tenants sought to build on their recent success by forming a more permanent organization that would continue to protect them in the face of future exploitation by capitalist profiteers and organized labor: the Middle Class Union (MCU). The idea was not specific to Chicago. Throughout the United States, consumers who had formed overall clubs, tenants' unions, or simply protested the high cost of living, attempted to organize "middle class unions." To many middle-class consumers, it represented the culmination of their activism.

These consumers looked for inspiration not only in their own past and current organizing but also from the growing British Middle Class Union. The idea of a "middle class union" originated in Great Britain in March 1919 to enable the "middle classes to act collectively . . . to protect themselves . . . against the inflated prices of the necessaries of life." MCU organizers asserted that membership would protect "the consumer whose necessities are exploited both by Labour and Capital." The British movement sought to use its own power, as well as the state, to "protect" against the supposed excesses of profiteers and the working class.[1] Their goals mirrored those of many American overall club members, municipal market proponents, home gardeners, tenant activists, and DOJ-High Cost of Living Division volunteers. In fact, middle class union leaders sponsored the overall movement in England. In addition, the British Middle Class Union consciously employed the organizing tactics of labor by forming a "union." Far from sympathetic to the gains of labor unions, the MCU not only marshaled its consumer power, it also used its members as volunteer strikebreakers. Developing a collective consciousness as middle-class consumers, the Middle Class Union aimed to attack organized labor—the very group that had given them the strategic basis for organizing.[2]

Unsurprisingly, the CTPA stood at the forefront of white-collar Chicago's attempt to form a U.S. middle class union. After the passage of the Kessinger landlord-tenant reform bill, John R. Patterson and a number of other CTPA members hoped to translate the "jubilation" over their success into a conversion of the CTPA into a middle class union. CTPA leader J. B. Strauss summarized the aims: "To organize the great unorganized middle class so as to protect it from many small but well organized divisions that will take advantage." Among its stated goals was "to undertake the extermination of all profiteering" and "to break down the unlawful building combinations now restricting the construction of homes and apartments."[3] MCU organizers claimed to be acting valiantly in the public interest against selfish parties.

Similar to public discussion over the specific issues of high rents, clothing costs, and food prices, politicians and the press reinforced middle class union rhetoric. In a June 1921 speech, for example, former Illinois governor and presidential candidate Frank Lowden discussed profiteering by capital and labor. "For a time it was feared that the public was helpless against this condition," Lowden declared. "And then occurred what was popularly called the "Buyers' Strike." Lowden concluded, "It was thus shown that what is vaguely called the public after all is more powerful than either an organization of employees or employers in any industry or a combination of both." In speaking of the power of the "buyers' strike," a term typically used to describe a middle-class boycott of any commodity (including the clothing boycotts of the overall movement and rent strikes), Lowden reminded his audience of the potential power of an organized middle class.[4]

To white-collar Americans, a "middle class union" represented far more than a solution to the immediate problem of the high cost of living. It gave them the potential of having a permanent organization to selectively inculcate the consumer economy with the older middle-class producerist values of industriousness and thrift. Middle-class Americans would thus be able to build on the power they expressed in overall clubs, tenants' unions, home garden committees, and through the DOJ-High Cost of Living Division and municipal market campaigns. As consumers they could police the fairness of the economy to ensure that the working and elite classes abided by their own self-righteous understandings of hard work and thrift. With this power, middle-class unionists believed that their ability to afford a middle-class lifestyle would seldom be compromised. Deciding where to live, what to buy, and where to shop served as important entry points into the middle class, but so too did political assertions as to what was fair or unfair in the marketplace. Even as consumer behavior in large part determined their class belonging, it was the seemingly impartial language of producerism that defined much of their political ideology.

MCU organizers cast their own values as the universal values of the broader citizenry. The New York State Middle Class Union proclaimed to secure "fair play for all classes" "against aggression of whatever nature," even as their specific goals were antilabor and anticapital. Both the press and the middle class union members referred to members and MCU aims by using broad terms such as "the people" or "the public." Receiving extensive press coverage for traveling the country in an attempt to support the formation of branches of a national MCU, former senator Chauncey Depew (R-New York) reportedly called for "a square deal for the general public." New York City featured both "Public's Union" and the "People's League." Defined as "middle class unions," these organizations, according to the *Christian Science Monitor*, were "composed of members of the intermediate classes which bear the brunt of the struggles between Capital and Labor." Joseph Wolf, a leader of the Middle Class Union of New York State, referred to the organization as "a body of people," and exclaimed that "its immense power is latent." Gerald E. Forse, another MCU organizer, declared that "it will prove that the people as a whole are greater than even the most powerful and thoroughly organized minority."[5]

The MCU and the other forms of middle-class consumer activism discussed in this book represent a number of attributes of what Lawrence Glickman has termed "modern consumer activism." They took advantage of the wide-ranging category "consumer" to unify spatially separated people, and represent the consumers' interest as the interest of society at large. They understood consumption to be a political act, in which the purchasing decisions made by consumers impacted a larger "web" of producers who made goods, merchants who sold them, and other consumers who might buy them. The decision of whether or not to help or punish people in this web through the purchasing of goods was political and understood to be moral. Also, by exercising moral authority as the "public" through their consumer organizing, they reconciled consumption, an act often understood as passive and self-centered, with active citizenship.[6]

In their expressions of this active citizenship, middle class unionists attempted to coordinate the local and discursive spaces of post–World War I middle-class consumer activism. Individuals ranging from Chauncey Depew to the editors of the *Chicago Daily Tribune* referenced the success of local and commodity-specific activism and fueled a national discursive space of middle-class consumer activism. One New York MCU leader reiterated that "the public has too long been made the plaything of powerful class interests" and stated, "We hope to co-ordinate all useful existing groups, leagues and associations of citizens which have already been formed to assist the public cause, and we invite such bodies to join hands with us in fighting greed and oppression." Even though middle-class consumers often already took part in multiple forms of activism, MCU proponents beamed at the idea of a nationally coordinated union with local organized participation. As Depew exclaimed, a national organization would ensure that the public would be treated "fairly, squarely, rightly, justly and righteously."[7]

Unfortunately for organizers, what constituted a middle class union was unclear. For example, the *Chicago Daily Tribune* applauded the New Jersey Tenants' Association for being "the first middle class union" and bringing "landlords to their knees." There is no evidence that the CTPA and these New Jersey tenants ever communicated, though some communication did occur between the CTPA and a New York middle class union. The *Survey* even suggested that groups of college students offering to serve as strikebreakers in a railroad strike were part of a middle class union trend. It also indicated that organizing teachers were a component of this burgeoning social movement. Yet, the AFT and NEA organized at the workplace (rather than through consumption), and the AFT was affiliated with American Federation of Labor, an enemy of many middle-class consumers. Middle-class Americans wrote Chauncey Depew, requesting to become secretaries of a middle class union, but no existing evidence suggests that this correspondence continued over time.[8]

Perhaps more so than communication problems and the ambiguity of the MCU, broader economic trends and social changes quashed the hopes of middle class union organizers. Many Chicago tenants were at least partially satisfied by rent reform, lessening their outrage over the postwar political economy. More importantly, by 1923 the economic recession had largely ended. Middle-class cost of living concerns persisted into the mid-late 1920s, but more typically in scattered, disorganized forms. Throughout the 1920s the prices for necessities and other commodities remained relatively constant.[9] Perhaps most of all, organized labor, a major culprit for their economic woes, had left the immediate postwar period badly damaged by failed strikes and open shop drives, such as the one conducted by the Citizen's Committee to Enforce the Landis Award. There was often little remaining power in the labor movement to fight. Overt middle-class consumer activism faded along with price decreases and the declining power of the labor movement, but it left important legacies and reflected significant changes in the meaning of middle-class identity over time.[10]

Before these developments derailed their organizing efforts, middle class unionists had aimed to continue the strategy of state-centered voluntarism employed in the other post–World War I middle-class organizing campaigns. As middle class union proponents pressed for stronger legislation to protect consumers and to limit the excesses of labor organizations, they also were willing to help facilitate these goals not just through buyers' strikes, but also by participating in federal wage arbitration conferences and by serving as temporary scabs in labor strikes.[11] Even though their goals differed from most progressives, the postwar middle-class activists discussed in this work continued Progressive Era organizing tactics by calling for reform and simultaneously providing the state with much of the necessary organizational muscle to accomplish it. Whether through the DOJ-High Cost of Living Division, city council home garden committees, or other groups and agencies, middle-class Americans were committed to state-centered voluntarism.

Expanding on this tradition, through the MCU and other organizations, an increasing number of middle-class Americans looked to the state to be immersed in the economy more forcefully than before. They pressed for laws that would limit the power of landlords, and rallied for federal, state, and local government stimulation of building and the creation of "a service bureau for the renting public." They also advocated the expansion of state and local market departments, government supported gardens, and a substantial growth in the power of the Department of Justice to police labor organizations, large corporations, and the corner grocer. These endeavors necessitated an enlargement of government bureaucracy, only partially dependent on middle-class voluntarism. Middle-class Americans continued to believe in privatism and individualism, which made voluntarism so appealing, but became more and more comfortable with a transparently activist state.[12]

Yet, conservative politicians and business leaders, who largely eschewed further government involvement in the economy, benefited significantly from middle-class activists' blending of a producerist rhetoric and consumerist politics in the name of defending the public. In the face of urbanization, growing immigration, and social change, cultural traditionalists found common ground with middle-class activists by appealing to the traditional values of hard work, self-reliance, and thrift. Some politicians, such as Los Angeles city councilman Neal Olsen, further contrasted these traditional values with supposedly dishonest "profiteering" immigrants, inflaming the nation's culture war over immigration that pinnacled with the enactment of the National Origins Act of 1924.

Meanwhile, business conservatives seized upon middle-class activists' mutual distain for the labor movement. Parroting the activists themselves, they referred to the middle class as the public or the people, and worked to undermine the labor movement by appealing to middle-class victimhood. Employer assaults on unions, cast as a defense of the middle-class consuming public against greed and corruption, persisted beyond the period of rapid price increases that took place until 1922. Embodying this continued effort was the Minute Men of the Constitution, which mobilized both elites and white-collar workers in order to further weaken the labor movement.

## The Minute Men of the Constitution

Controversy over the immediate postwar high cost of living helped to set in motion additional antiunion employer appeals to the non-working-class "public" throughout the 1920s. Adding to the repression of labor activism undertaken by the Citizens' Committee to Enforce the Landis Award, Charles G. Dawes, claiming to be acting in the public interest, organized the Minute Men of the Constitution (MMC) in April 1923. Focusing mainly on the Chicago area, the organization aimed to support Illinois politicians willing to limit the power of unions, particularly through the use of injunctions to stop strikes. A major public figure, Dawes was a big-business owner, and Warren G. Harding's director of the Bureau of the Budget. He was a supporter of the national open shop campaign known popularly in the 1920s as the American Plan, and praised the Citizens' Committee to Enforce the Landis Award, of which his younger brother and business associate, Rufus, was a member.[13]

Dawes, however, had other motives for taking a strong position against labor organization. In addition to having connections to and business interests in common with large employers as a bank president, Dawes was a rising star in the Republican Party. His public statements against the power of unions stood to help him and the Republicans receive the backing of antilabor constituents. The newsletter of the United Garment Workers (citing a newspaper correspondent) accused him of as much, asserting of Dawes that "a clear-cut declaration of the anti-union shop will gain [him] the support of businessmen (and make party contribution easy)." In addition to currying the favor of businessmen, Dawes used an antilabor politics to cast himself as a man of the people during a decade that had become generally unfavorable to the labor movement.[14]

Dawes's Minute Men of the Constitution served as an active political constituency for antiunion politicians under the guise of neutral values. Members were instructed to back candidates for the Democratic and Republican state and national conventions that would embrace the MMC's platform. Circulated widely, the platform included "[a]dvocating . . . respect for the law and the Constitution," and asserting "the right of a citizen to work without unlawful interference." Under Dawes's leadership, the MMC formed local companies throughout Illinois, which were responsible for promoting the MMC's platform locally and marshaling support for politicians who agreed with it. Within six weeks, the organization reportedly had 6,000 members. By December 1, 1923, that number had grown to an estimated 30,000.[15] The Minute Men consisted of mostly salaried white-collar workers, who worked in professions in which relatively fewer employees associated with organized labor. For example, 92 percent of "Lieutenants" in the Evanston MMC held white-collar professions, 85 percent of whom were salesmen, managers, attorneys, bankers, brokers, and clerks.[16]

Business leaders and white-collar workers in the MMC found common ground by claiming to represent the public and its supposedly neutral values against the selfishness of labor leaders. They drew on the long-standing narrative in Chicago that labor leaders were selfish and corrupt people, who exploited the public and the rank and file, and were "pretending to speak for organized labor."[17] Mirroring CCELA rhetoric, Dawes contended, "I have opposed the kind of union tactics that have made building operations in Chicago dangerous to human life, where corrupt men have used their influence to extort vast sums from the contractors."[18] The Minute Men contrasted themselves with these allegedly greedy union officials by claiming to stand for "all good citizens," "the law," and "the Constitution."[19]

Much like the middle-class activists of the immediate postwar period, the Minute Men represented their efforts as an embodiment of patriotism and "American" values. Dawes, who had received the commission of brigadier general for his World War I service, other Minute Men, and their supporters, portrayed the organization's actions as a continuation of war themes. Local MMC chapters used militaristic language in defining their chain of command. A chapter was known as a "company," the director of which carried the title "captain" with lieutenants under his leadership. The MMC's "patriotic" language also reinforced the words of the broader national open shop campaign, which had been characterized as the American Plan, as well as the earlier discourses of the home garden and overall movements.[20]

Armed with the rhetoric of selflessness and patriotism, the MMC waged their "first fight" against the Chicago Federation of Labor's campaign in the fall of 1923 to oust two local judges who had impeded the labor movement through injunctions. Repeatedly during the early twentieth century, Judges Denis E. Sullivan and Jesse Holdom of the Cook County Superior Court issued injunctions to stop strikes conducted by unions ranging from teamsters to cooks. Sullivan had additionally sided with the CCELA in a January 1922 case, in which the Carpenters' union requested an injunction of its own to prevent the Committee from pressuring contractors to remove union members from jobs.[21] After holding a conference on the topic of injunctions against labor on August 16, 1923, the CFL mobilized its members to oppose Sullivan and Holdom, as two of the most aggressive "injunction judges," in the November 26, 1923, election. The MMC rushed to the defense of the judges and campaigned on their behalf.[22]

Organized labor in Chicago and elsewhere expressed outrage over the Minute Men's attempts to promote injunctions against unions and establish the open shop behind the veil of "neutral" values, such as "the right to work" or patriotism. The official organ of the International Association of Bridge, Structural, and Ornamental Iron Workers referred to the MMC as Dawes's "pet union-hating organization," while the Chicago Federation of Labor's newsletter called him "Mussolini Dawes" and noted its false neutrality and appeals to wealthier white-collar workers by stating, "while the chief organizer explains that membership is open to 'the white-collar man and the man in overalls,' it is noticeable that the organization's meetings are still being held exclusively in the best residential districts."[23] Perhaps most pointedly, John L. Walker, president of the Illinois Federation of Labor, connected the Minute Men's efforts to organizations similar to the CCELA: "The enemies of labor under the guise during all the years have been fighting to prevent the establishment of the labor movement . . . as citizens' alliances, then as open shop movements . . . and now the Minute Men of the Constitution (so called)."[24]

Despite Walker's and other labor leaders' appeals, the Minute Men were successful. Both Sullivan and Holdom won reelection. The judges called Dawes's office to thank him, and privately stated, according to a Minute Men leader, "that they owed their election to the support and work of the minute men."[25] Portrayed by newspapers across the country as a hero fighting against the selfishness of the labor movement, Dawes, in June 1924, received the Republican nomination for vice president, an office he occupied from 1925 to

1929.[26] Whereas many newspapers applauded the Republicans' choice, labor leaders expressed their displeasure. Matthew Woll, vice president of the American Federation of Labor, stated that with its nomination of Dawes, the Republican Party had endorsed an antilabor platform. According to Woll, the party "accepts and endorses his peculiar views—his championship of the divine right of Judges to do as they please with union men."[27]

The MMC's effect on the labor movement extended beyond raising Dawes's political profile. As one Dawes biographer put it, the Minute Men helped to elect a slate of "law and order" candidates to statewide offices, and brought about "a public awakening on the part of the citizens to the necessity of . . . counteracting unfair propaganda."[28] Whether or not the MMC can be credited with turning the public against labor organization, it represented an example of the all too common antilabor alliance between the interests of employers and white-collar workers that was set in motion by the immediate postwar high cost of living, and continued through the narrative that greed, corruption, and indolence in unions threatened the common people. By the end of the 1920s, the power of the labor movement had deteriorated.[29]

## Legacies of Post–World War I Middle-Class Consumer Activism in the 1930s

Despite furthering the discourse and aims of 1920s conservative politicians and business leaders, postwar white-collar consumer activists' call to use the government to defend the interests of consumers also represented an important step toward the often more liberal middle-class activism of the New Deal era. During the 1930s, in the midst of economic depression, a number of middle-class-led organizations became leaders of what was termed "the consumer movement." Existing and newly formed groups, ranging from the League of Women Shoppers to the Consumers' National Federation, advocated several government policies to promote economic justice and address a struggling economy. Putting the "high cost of living on trial," the Consumers' National Federation in 1937 pressured the government for rent control, greater action against monopolies, and federal housing programs. The organization also lobbied President Franklin Delano Roosevelt and Congress for "a central consumer agency," or "bureau," to promote the needs of consumers. These calls came even after the federal government created an unprecedented number of agencies, programs, and laws to intervene in the economy. The National Recovery Administration, one of a multitude of such New Deal agencies, featured a Consumer Advisory Board. Composed of consumer activists, the board sought to ensure that maximum prices were not set too high and that consumers enjoyed quality standards and proper product labeling to help them achieve the best value for their purchases.[30]

Middle-class activists' characterization of the consumers' interest as the public interest had become a trend by this time. During the Great Depression, many middle-class consumer activists expressed interests that came closer to actually reflecting those of the masses, compared to their post–World War I counterparts. Middle-class consumers often spent their money selectively in politically conscious ways, choosing to support companies that offered fair prices, but also paid reasonable wages to blue-collar workers. In contrast to the immediate post–World War I period, these middle-class Americans frequently worked toward the same goals as the working class in their consumer activism. Both classes faced significant levels of unemployment, and many in the middle class believed that giving all consumers purchasing power would provide the best chance to bring the entire country out of the Depression. Despite this apparent "purchasing power" alliance, the consumer movement suffered from internal divisions over whether to privilege support for mistreated workers as a primary objective, or to focus chiefly on the needs of consumers themselves. As Lawrence Glickman has noted, this division came into focus during a strike at Consumers Research, a "consumer education organization," in which workers walked off the job over poor wages, oppressive working conditions, and the dismissal of three co-workers. A strike taking place at a celebrated epicenter of the consumer movement called into question whether consumer activism should prioritize the main objective of Consumers Research, expert-driven product testing designed to educate consumers, or whether consumption should centrally be used as a collective tool to achieve better conditions for workers.[31]

Amid these schisms, new calls emerged for an assertive "middle class" collective consciousness to defend itself from elites, and, to some extent, the working class. Equating the middle class with the people, writers like Gilbert Seldes condemned corporate robbery of middle-class pocketbooks and advocated for greater justice for the middle class in significant measure through its careful use of its "spending power." Noting in *Your Money and Your Life: A Manual for the "Middle Classes"* (1938) that "the basic law in America has enormously favored the producing interest and has been extremely casual about the consumer," Seldes pushed for middle-class Americans, as the foundation of the nation's economy, to become more politically aware and active. This would counteract attacks on their "pocketbook" and "their peace of mind."[32]

Renowned author Walter Pitkin stood at the forefront of this strand of middle-class activism. Best known for his book *Life Begins at Forty*, Pitkin was a prolific writer and professor at Columbia University who saw himself as a tireless advocate for the interests of the middle class, a mission that he took on as both a writer, and soon as an organizer. In his 1935 polemic *Capitalism Carries On*, Pitkin lamented, "The middle-class man is being ground exceeding fine between the upper millstone of Croesus and the nether millstone of Cyclops. He is caught between the powerful rich and the powerful poor," evidenced by the unequal "records of spending since 1930," wherein excessive government relief was given to corporations and the poor. Celebrating the middle class's desire to defend a regulated form of capitalism that would safeguard middle-class interests, Pitkin exclaimed that it "stands overwhelmingly with the old American system," rejects "anticapitalist leaders, Socialist and Communist," and believes "that careful reorganization will whip capitalism into shape." Pitkin optimistically suggested that the middle class would demand change and that government and society would respond accordingly.[33]

On June 29, 1939, Pitkin put these words into action, forming the American Majority in Elyria, Ohio, a location he described as "a typical American community." Nearly two decades after Elyria residents had protested the high cost of living by donning overalls, and the *Elyria Chronicle-Telegram* had declared that the "middle class" was being "ground into a pulp," Pitkin announced the formation of the organization as "A League of the Middle Class in Revolt Against the Predatory Rich and the Predatory Poor." Trumpeting the type of nationalistic and producerist rhetoric that had pervaded the post–World War I discursive space of middle-class activism, Pitkin declared before a crowd of approximately 600 at Elyria High School that "ward heelers," "cheapskate politicians," and "rackets in the labor movement" had attempted to destroy "hard-working Americans." According to Pitkin, "the next American Revolution" was to begin among Elyria's middle class, and would soon spread to other communities to become a nationwide movement. Following Pitkin's remarks, Mayor Joseph Petro appointed a committee "to make the plan effective." On that day, the American Majority was born.[34]

Throughout the following months, the founding chapter of the American Majority sent "twenty young people" to distribute anonymous surveys to Elyria residents, which asked them to identify their pressing concerns. A committee of local professionals, under the guidance of Pitkin, reported the results. The respondents focused on a number of common desires, from more transparency in government to the consumer-driven concern of wanting more housing with cheaper rents, a priority that mirrored the objectives of the Chicago Tenants Protective Association two decades before. At another public meeting Pitkin suggested that these grievances embodied the seemingly overlapping "middle class" and "American" identities of this "middle class" city. "You aren't a 100 percent American city," Pitkin exclaimed, "you are about a 325 per cent American city." Pitkin included in his praise the responsible spending of local middle-class residents by lauding their "expenditures of money for good purposes." A celebration of producerism also accompanied this rhetoric, with the American Majority pointing out Pitkin's producerist credentials as a farmer, in conjunction with his occupations as an educator and writer.[35]

Armed with the information in the surveys and Pitkin's praise, the Elyria American Majority became an active organization of middle-class residents over the course of at least the next seven years. Although the organization formed on the broad basis of opposing the "predatory rich and the predatory poor," a mission that could have immersed it in a host of political, economic, and cultural issues, the Elyria American Majority came to focus on efficiency and transparency in government. Members lobbied the local government on issues connected to these themes and criticized its conduct through it regular publication, *Everybody's Business*. In this publication, they decried the cost of meals for prisoners in the county jail, expenditures on local election supplies, the debt burden of a local school, and a number of other matters of governance. Despite their primary emphasis on good government, they still brought consumerist language to their analysis, with *Everybody's Business* lauding itself for keeping its readers "informed about affairs which concern them and their pocketbooks" and condemning "purse draining practices."[36]

The American Majority movement received significant national publicity and spread to at least one other community. Out-of-state newspapers carried such headlines as "Pitkin Summons the Middle Class for a 'Revolution'" and "United Movement Growing to Save Middle Class from Destruction," and, in September 1939, Pitkin announced "organization work" in New Jersey, Pennsylvania, and Michigan. In 1942, the American Majority worked with a "public-spirited group of leading citizens" to establish a chapter in Richland County, Ohio. Similar to the Elyria chapter, it often focused on efficiency and transparency in local government, and, in the context of World War II, the chapter connected many of its issues to the war, or, in the words of *Everybody's Business*, "the country's No. 1 problem—defeating Hitler and the Japs."[37]

The American Majority, much like many of the activists in the immediate post–World War I period, in significant ways advanced the priorities of the Republican Party. On the one hand, in criticizing the actions of both the rich and the poor, their political rhetoric does not neatly fall into the categories of "Right" and "Left." Yet, as the *New Republic* noted in an article titled "Rabble-Rouser of the Right,"

> Elyria was chosen as a national headquarters and guinea pig of the movement because this city of 26,000 "so thoroughly typifies the solidity, energy, and patriotism of American civil life." The fact that Elyria has no CIO, no liberal group . . . may also have been considered. Lorian County, of which Elyria is the seat, has frequently been described as the most solidly Republican county in the United States.

Moreover, the magazine noted Pitkin's "record of antagonism" against "labor unions in general." Speaking to its procapitalist orientation, one of the "fundamental aims" of the Richland County Unit was "maintaining our system of free enterprise," and *Everybody's Business* referenced disparagingly the Congress of Industrial Organization's "plans to take over the Democratic Party." Altogether, the American Majority's populist and yet largely conservative rhetoric and agenda eschewed neat political categories, but ultimately fell more in line with Republican discourses on cultural traditionalism, limited government, and skepticism of the working class.[38]

## Middle-Class Consumer Politics in Modern America

After World War II, middle-class Americans continued to represent their consumer interests as those of the nation, in spite of the ongoing tensions in popular conceptions of who was considered a legitimate consumer. In the post–World War II period, citizens lived in what Lizabeth Cohen calls the "Consumers' Republic," marked by a belief that "satisfying material wants actually served the national interest." Above all, many middle-class Americans in the Consumers' Republic sought to pursue *their* own ability to partake in mass consumerism even if their actions were couched in the framework of benefiting the nation. They sought suburban homes in middle-class neighborhoods, furnished with the latest consumer goods and featuring quality local school systems. Even as their goals differed from those of Depression era "citizen consumers," who made selective politically conscious purchases, middle-class Americans proclaimed that they consumed as representatives of the people at large.[39]

Far from politically neutral, middle-class Americans continued to impose variations of their own set of "universal" producerist values on the consumer economy. As a result, the middle class maintained a tenuous relationship with the working class. The nature of their "universal" values shifted in accordance with their perceived position compared to the working class. During the Great Depression, while a number of white-collar consumers continued to demonize the working class, many other consumers saw them as fellow sufferers and their lack of spending power as an impediment to economic recovery. Accordingly, they worked concurrently with many blue-collar laborers to advance a "purchasing power" solution to jump-start the economy. In this context, creating jobs with adequate wages would best promote industriousness among the working class, and, by extension, create economic opportunity for the middle class. Yet, the tension between high wages and high prices—so prevalent during the immediate postwar period—was latent. During the post–World War I period, many middle-class Americans had defended their pocketbooks by arguing that high wages represented working-class excess, indolence, and luxury. In the post–World War II period, high wages again seemingly threatened middle-class Americans' ability to freely consume. While protecting their own self-interests, a number of middle-class Americans once more sought to impose on the working class the value of industriousness. As one professor declared, to prevent price increases, laborers would have to learn to "work harder."[40] Similar to the post–World War I period, these calls for greater working-class industriousness were enlarged by companies seeking to minimize labor costs. Many middle-class Americans privileged their desire for cheaper goods over working-class wage concerns, and alliances between working-class Americans and middle-class consumers often fell apart.[41]

While the middle-class producerist value of industriousness remained an important part of middle-class consumer identity, thrift fell into the distant background. It was less compatible with the blatant and celebrated excesses of the Consumers' Republic. As William H. White, editor of *Fortune* magazine, noted in 1956, "thrift is now un-American."[42] While their values shifted in conjunction with their changing priorities and alliances over the course of the twentieth century, middle-class consumers continued to define themselves as "the people" and characterize their values as universally fair and just.

## Echoes of Post–World War I Middle-Class Consumer Activism in the Recent Past

On October 8, 2011, more than nine decades after the nation's first overall club held a mass demonstration in Jacksonville's Hemming Park, scores of local residents converged on the same park to begin the Occupy Jacksonville movement. Their protest was part of a national revolt of the "99 percent" against economic injustices stemming from corporate power, federal financial policy, and other factors. With John Lennon's "Working Class Hero" blaring on loudspeakers, one organizer carried an upside-down American flag, while other protesters held signs condemning the government for "Driving up Prices" or proclaiming "We are the 99%," "WTF? Public Need vs. Corporate Greed," or "Eat the Rich." One of a number of speakers that day called on Americans to "[b]e the people behind 'we the people.'"[43] Across the street, a member of the Tea Party, another movement contending to represent the public, held a sign in protest of Occupy activists. The crowd at Hemming Park stood among the distant shadows of overall-clad protesters demanding economic justice in their own time.[44]

The connections between the cultural categories of consumer, producer, citizen, and middle class have continued to carry significant discursive power in multiple strands of middle-class politics even in the not too distant past. Participants in movements as politically disparate as Occupy Wall Street and the Tea Party claimed to represent the public, partly on the basis of celebrating various expressions of producerism in the interest of justice for consumers against the undue influences of centralized forces, whether corporations, the U.S. government, or labor unions.

Advocating in the name of the 99 percent amid government bailouts for large banks and growing corporate power, protesters in the Occupy Wall Street movement took to the streets and public squares of cities from New York to Los Angeles during the fall of 2011. Occupy supporters protested for a myriad of reasons, but many drew on the mutually reinforcing identities of consumer and middle class in positioning themselves as representatives of the public. As one supporter proclaimed, "The rich have become enormously so and the middle class is now declining . . . unable to maintain a standard of living. . . . The population understands quite well that something must be done."[45] Accompanying such pronouncements were representations of producerism through protest language that contrasted corporate greed with the struggles of hardworking people, and through public displays of thrift, self-reliance, and rugged living conditions in tent communities throughout the nation's public parks. By categorizing the victims of corporate greed as the 99 percent and intermittently extolling time-honored producerist values, the movement could purport to speak for the people, despite, according to one survey, being disproportionately comprised of Caucasian white-collar professionals (with only 8 percent of participants identifying as blue collar), even if often friendly to the aims of the labor movement.[46]

Despite aiming to protect consumers from corporate greed, the Occupy movement, much like the post–World War I activists, held an uneasy relationship with consumerism. The post–World War I activists celebrated thrift and condemned greed, but did so with the goal of gaining greater relative purchasing power. Participants in the Occupy movement similarly emphasized how the greed of the 1 percent had squeezed the living standards of the masses, a grievance predicated ultimately on the desire of the common people to be able to more comfortably consume. Yet a number of Occupy activists defined consumerism as a symptom of corporate control and injustice.[47]

Standing on the opposite side of the street at Hemming Park, and on the opposite end of the political spectrum, were the Tea Party protesters. Representing a conservative politics, the Tea Party movement also embraced the language of middle-class victimhood, wherein, according to many of its popular assertions, taxpayers and consumers suffered from government regulations, corporate welfare, and working-class laziness and greed. Much like Occupy Wall Street, Tea Party activists drew on diverse motivations, and yet, as Abby Scher and Chip Berlet have noted, "behind much Tea Party rhetoric is the claim that hard-working productive middle-class citizens are being squeezed in an economic vise—from above by high government taxes, onerous regulations, and monetary policies set by greedy bankers, and from below by lazy, sinful, and subversive parasites."[48] In one expression of this rhetoric, Nancy Ripley, a retired counselor/mediator and Tea Party supporter, used the language of producerism in a *New York Times* video feature, to call for the furtherance of a robust capitalist system for "the majority of the nation's citizenry." She proclaimed, "We of the Tea Party are the backbone of this nation. . . . we of the Tea Party are hard-working, and self-sufficient people. . . . we of the Tea Party want to stay a capitalistic democracy, where all do the work for the few who can't work, instead of a few doing the work for the many who won't work."[49]

Despite the antielite overtones in some Tea Party critiques of corporate bailouts, business conservatives operating through such groups as Americans for Prosperity and FreedomWorks helped to facilitate the Tea Party movement and worked to shape a common ground with many of its participants on a number of issues, including weakening labor unions.[50] In Wisconsin, Gov. Scott Walker, who became popular with Tea Party supporters and received campaign contributions from a number of corporate leaders and small donors, successfully reduced the collective bargaining rights of Wisconsin public employees in a 2011 nationally publicized showdown with organized labor, political opponents, and a number of pro-labor protesters.[51] In order to gain support for his policies and his gubernatorial and presidential candidacies, Walker professed to stand for the middle class against big government and labor unions, while projecting producerist values and imagery through references to his teenage job at McDonalds, by boasting of his $1 Kohl's sweater, and through a campaign advertisement in which he drove a 12-year-old Saturn and celebrated his thrift in packing a lunch instead of eating out.[52] In a similar vein to William Wood, Charles Dawes, and the businessmen in the Citizens' Committee to Enforce the Landis Award, each of whom helped to usher organized labor into the 1920s "lean years" by playing to middle-class antilabor activism, corporate and political leaders, like Walker, drew on the antilabor elements of the Tea Party to further their own political visions or financial interests.[53]

Although separated by nearly a century, the Tea Party and Occupy Wall Street movements echoed significant features of the middle-class politics expressed by the post–World War I activists who planted gardens, patronized municipal markets, wore overalls, conducted rent strikes, and attempted to form middle class unions. Even though their post–World War I activism fizzled with an improved economy, a middle-class political citizenship that blends the priorities of a consumer identity with an attachment to the symbolic and rhetorical power of producerism has remained a persistent force in American politics and culture.

# Appendix

Ratio of the White-Collar Worker Earnings to Average Manufacturing Worker (Blue Collar), and Food and Clothing Prices

| | 1912 | 1913 | 1914 | 1915 | 1916 | 1917 | 1918 | 1919 |
|---|---|---|---|---|---|---|---|---|
| **Clerk, male** | | | 1.676 | | | | | 1.202 |
| **Clerk, female** | | | 2.073 | | | | | 1.525 |
| **Assistant professor** | 2.309 | 2.193 | 2.251 | 2.396 | 2.156 | 1.866 | 1.548 | 1.366 |
| **Associate professor** | 2.751 | 2.559 | 2.675 | 2.849 | 2.491 | 2.202 | 1.818 | 1.688 |
| **Full professor** | 3.659 | 3.575 | 3.635 | 3.903 | 3.406 | 3.014 | 2.418 | 2.175 |
| **Average of earnings for sample of white-collar professions versus blue-collar wages** | | | | | | | | |
| | | | 2.462 | | | | | 1.591 |
| **Retail food prices (relative to 1912)** | | | | | | | | |
| | | | 1.04 | 1.03 | 1.16 | 1.49 | 1.71 | 1.9 |
| **Clothing prices (relative to 1912)** | | | | | | | | |
| | | | 0.977 | 0.983 | 1.27 | 1.75 | 2.28 | 2.52 |

*Sources:* Earnings data taken from Claudia Goldin and Lawrence F. Katz, "The Returns to Skill in the United States across the Twentieth Century," Department of Economics, Harvard University, and National Bureau of Economic Research, 36–39. Food prices taken from Department of Commerce, Bureau of Foreign and Domestic Commerce, *Statistical Abstract of the United States 1921* (Washington, DC: Government Printing Office, 1922), 631. Clothing prices taken from U.S. Department of Commerce, *Statistical Abstract of the United States 1928* (Washington, DC: GPO, 1928), 318.

# Notes

## Introduction

1. "Tenants 'Sit Tight,'" *Chicago Daily Journal*, May 2, 1921; "Rent War Signs Halt Traffic," *Chicago Daily Tribune*, March 7, 1921 (hereinafter *CT*); "Tenants Enlist Evanston Corps for Rent Battle," *CT*, March 21, 1921; "Revolt of the Consumer," *San Antonio Evening News*, June 9, 1920.

2. "Rent War Signs Halt Traffic"; "Tenants Enlist Evanston Corps for Rent Battle."

3. See chapter 5. "Tenants Hold Up Rent Cases," *Chicago Daily Journal*, May 9, 1921; "Tenants' Unfair Rent Signs Are Declared Legal," *CT*, March 19, 1921.

4. See appendix for data on the changing ratio between white- and blue-collar earnings during the war; data calculated from U.S. Department of Labor, Bureau of Labor Statistics, "The Cost of Living in the United States," *Bulletin of the Bureau of Labor Statistics* 357 (May 1924): 457; "Relative Retail Prices of Food," in Department of Commerce, Bureau of Foreign and Domestic Commerce, *Statistical Abstract of the United States 1921* (Washington, DC: Government Printing Office, 1922), 631. For dry goods prices, see U.S. Department of Labor, Bureau of Labor Statistics, "Retail Prices 1913 to December 1919," *Bulletin of the Bureau of Labor Statistics* 357 (February 1921): 58. Retail prices of dry goods were not taken by the Bureau of Labor Statistics in 1913 or 1914. Date range: May 15, 1915–October 15, 1919.

5. United States Senate, Select Committee on Reconstruction and Production, *Reconstruction and Production: Hearings before the Select Committee on Reconstruction and Production, United States Senate, Sixty-sixth Congress, Third Session, Pursuant to S. Res. 350 . . . to Stimulate and Foster the Development of Construction Work in All Its Forms* (Washington, DC: Government Printing Office, 1921), 941–44; John Corbin, *The Return of the Middle Class* (New York: C. Scribner's Sons, 1922), 15.

6. Many scholars have used the terms "new" or "old" middle class, or both, as frameworks to distinguish between blue-collar producers and white-collar workers (as a "new" middle class), while often acknowledging and analyzing the subtleties of middle-class identity within and between these categories. C. Wright Mills's *White Collar* is a foundational work in this area. See also, for instance, Oliver Zunz, *Making America Corporate, 1870–1920* (Chicago: University of Chicago Press, 1992); Christopher P. Wilson, *White Collar Fictions: Class and Social Representation in American Literature, 1885–1925* (Ath-

ens: University of Georgia Press, 1992); C. Wright Mills, *White Collar: The American Middle Classes* (New York: Oxford University Press, 1953). The statistical calculation for the growth in the white-collar labor force is based on data listed in a 1924–26 *Handbook of Labor Statistics* occupational distribution table. Total data for professions under the categories "professional service" and "clerical occupations" (both categories include only white-collar professions) for 1880 were calculated and compared to totals (per million in population) from the same categories for 1920. U.S. Department of Labor, Bureau of Labor Statistics, *Handbook of Labor Statistics, 1924–1926* (Washington, DC: GPO), 420.

7. Though not always using the word "respectability," many historians have identified cultural practices that came to denote a middle-class identity during this period. See, for instance, Marina Moskowitz, *Standard of Living: The Measure of the Middle Class in Modern America* (Baltimore: Johns Hopkins University Press, 2004); Amy Blair, *Reading Up: Middle Class Readers and the Culture of Success in the Early Twentieth-Century United States* (Philadelphia: Temple University Press, 2011); Jennifer Scanlon, *Inarticulate Longings: The* Ladies' Home Journal*, Gender and the Promises of Consumer Culture* (New York: Routledge, 1995); Marjorie Murphy, *Blackboard Unions: The AFT and the NEA, 1900–1980* (Ithaca: Cornell University Press, 1990), 4–5.

8. Susan Porter Benson, *Counter Cultures: Saleswomen, Managers, and Customers in American Department Stores 1890–1940* (Urbana: University of Illinois Press, 1986).

9. Similarly, David A. Horowitz notes that the corporate "organizational revolution produced a white-collar culture of salaried professionals whose institutional loyalty was in marked contrast to the individualism of independent entrepreneurs." Michael Zakim, "The Business Clerk as Social Revolutionary; or, a Labor History of the Nonproducing Classes," *Journal of the Early Republic* 26, no. 4 (Winter 2006): 577; David A. Horowitz, *Beyond Left and Right: Insurgency and the Establishment* (Urbana: University of Illinois Press, 1996), 3.

10. Jerome Bjelopera, *City of Clerks: Office and Sales Workers in Philadelphia, 1870–1920* (Urbana: University of Illinois Press, 2005), 18.

11. Ibid., 113; Moskowitz, *Standard of Living*; Carole Srole, *Transcribing Class and Gender: Masculinity and Femininity in Nineteenth-Century Courts and Offices* (Ann Arbor: University of Michigan Press, 2010); see also Scanlon, *Inarticulate Longings*.

12. Corbin, *Return of the Middle Class*, 9, 11; "Incorporate Union of Middle Class," *Washington Post*, February 8, 1920. See also Daniel Horowitz, *The Morality of Spending: Attitudes toward the Consumer Society in America, 1875–1940* (Baltimore: Johns Hopkins University Press, 1985).

13. Records of the City Council of Los Angeles, November 4, 1919, Los Angeles City Clerk's Office, Records Management Division, Los Angeles, CA (hereinafter LACCR); 1920 U.S. Census, Los Angeles, Los Angeles County, California, digital image, s.v. "Newton M. Allen," *Ancestry.com*; "The Short Way Home," *New York Times* (hereinafter *NYT*), May 23, 1920; "The Great Middle Class Is Beginning to Turn," *New York Tribune*, January 11, 1920.

14. Thomas R. Marshall, "The Awakening Middle Class," *NYT Magazine*, October 5, 1919; Corbin, *Return of the Middle Class*, 12.

15. Many historians and commentators have discussed the significance of the "middle class" to American political and cultural discourse during the post–World War II period, and its relationship to literature, political realignment, and other themes. These works range from Andrew Hoberek, *The Twilight of the Middle Class: Post–World War II American Fiction and*

*White-Collar Work* (Princeton: Princeton University Press, 2005), to Matthew Lassiter, *The Silent Majority: Suburban Politics in the Sunbelt South* (Princeton: Princeton University Press, 2006). Bolstering this centrality to postwar discourse is the fact that a strong majority of Americans have identified as middle class since 1940, even if other identities add complexity to this common attachment to the term. See Marina Moskowitz, "'Aren't We All?' Aspiration, Acquisition, and the American Middle Class," in *The Making of the Middle Class: Toward a Transnational History*, ed. A. Ricardo Lopez and Barbara Weinstein (Durham: Duke University Press, 2012), 75; "Middle Class Union Urged," *Oregonian*, April 11, 1920; "What Is the Middle Class and What Does It Want?" *NYT*, December 22, 1935.

16. For instance, in the post–World War II period political and cultural discourse often included blue-collar workers in the middle class, and yet at times included critiques of the impact of high wages on consumers. See Meg Jacobs, *Pocketbook Politics: Economic Citizenship in Twentieth-Century America* (Princeton: Princeton University Press, 2005), 250–61; Lizabeth Cohen, *A Consumers' Republic: The Politics of Mass Consumption in Postwar America* (New York: Vintage, 2003), 152–64; "Sees Return to Old Time Thrift in Overall Move," *CT*, April 19, 1920.

17. Jeffery M. Hornstein also suggests that the "imprecision and amorphousness" of the term middle class "inheres the political and cultural power of the category." For historiographic representations of the deconstructionist critique of the middle class, see Carol E. Harrison, "The Bourgeois after the Bourgeois Revolution: Recent Approaches to the Middle Class in European Cities," *Journal of Urban History* 31, no. 3 (2005): 388; Dror Wahrman, *Imagining the Middle Class: The Political Representation of Class in Britain, c. 1780–1840* (Cambridge: Cambridge University Press, 1995); Maris A. Vinovskis, "Stalking the Elusive Middle Class in Nineteenth-Century America: A Review Article," *Comparative Studies in Society and History* 33, no. 3 (July 1991): 582–87; Burton Bledstein and Robert D. Johnston, eds., *The Middling Sorts: Explorations in the History of the American Middle Class* (New York: Routledge, 2001); Patrick Joyce, *Democratic Subjects: The Self and the Social in Nineteenth-Century England* (Cambridge: Cambridge University Press, 1990), 19, 163.

18. See, for example, Cohen, *Consumers' Republic*; Jacobs, *Pocketbook Politics*; or Regina Lee Blaszczyk, *American Consumer Society, 1865–2005: From Hearth to HDTV* (Wheeling, IL: Harlan Davidson, 2009). For discussion of how consumer identities have interacted with or incorporated the value of thrift, see Lawrence Glickman, *Buying Power: A History of Consumer Activism in America* (Chicago: University of Chicago Press, 2009), 59; Horowitz, *Morality of Spending*. Similar to this book, Daniel Horowitz analyzes the tensions between thrift and consumer society for the early twentieth century middle class, often in the context of inflation. He notes how a number of writers considered thrift to be an important part of a proper middle-class consumer identity, while others shifted from this emphasis.

19. See, Moskowitz, *Standard of Living*; Blaszczyk, *American Consumer Society*.

20. Lawrence Glickman has noted that generally in the 1920s "many Americans, far from losing interest in politics, developed new political engagements based in large measure on their identities as consumers." Lawrence Glickman, "Rethinking Politics: Consumers and the Public Good during the 'Jazz Age,'" *OAH Magazine of History* 21, no. 3 (July 2007): 16–20.

21. Charles Henry Meltzer, "The Intermediate Millions," *North American Review* 209 (February 1919): 233.

22. Otto P. Geier, "The High Cost of Living vs. the High Cost of Dying," *Nation's Health* 1, no. 6 (October 1919): 487.

23. "Overalls Signal for America to Return to Work," *Indianapolis Star*, May 10, 1920; "Topics of the Times," *NYT*, April 17, 1920; "Beating the H.C.L.," *Los Angeles Times* (hereinafter *LAT*), February 8, 1920.

24. Entry for April 29, 1920, Diary of Fred Alton Haight, Medford, Oregon, 1918 and 1920–21, Ms. 338, Southern Oregon Historical Society, Medford, Oregon.

25. The percentage includes discontinuous strikes. David Montgomery, *Workers' Control in America* (New York: Cambridge University Press, 1979), 97.

26. Corbin, *Return of the Middle Class*, 8.

27. In many cases, it appears that middle-class activists and sympathetic writers used the language of antiradicalism as a powerful vocabulary to describe profiteers and striking workers without necessarily expressing a specific fear of a radical revolution in the United States, or of their potential role in such an event. A number of scholars have illustrated how the red scare and its language represented and reflected versatile meanings. See, for example, Kim Nielsen, *Un-American Womanhood: Antiradicalism, Antifeminism, and the First Red Scare* (Columbus: Ohio State University Press, 2001); Erica Ryan, *Red War on the Family: Sex, Gender, and Americanism in the First Red Scare* (Philadelphia: Temple University Press, 2014); Theodore Kornweibel, *"Seeing Red": Federal Campaigns against Black Militancy, 1919–1925* (Bloomington: Indiana University Press, 1999); Mark Robbins, "American Anxiety and the Reaction of Michigan Agricultural College to the First Red Scare," *American Educational History* 31, no. 1 (Spring 2004): 72–79.

28. *Beatrice (NE) Sun* article quoted in "Middle Class Sense," *Omaha World-Herald*, April 6, 1920; "A Get-Together Industrial Committee," *Shiner (TX) Gazette*, September 29, 1921; "A Game That Two Can Play," *Cincinnati Enquirer*, June 18, 1919.

29. Using Portland, Oregon, as a case study, Johnston mainly focuses on the petite bourgeoisie's radicalism, anticapitalism, and relationship to the working class, but also includes white-collar workers in his argument. Johnston mostly discusses the pre–World War I period, but notes that middle-class anticapitalism did not die out in the 1920s, and draws examples of its persistence from the immediate postwar period. The differences between the interpretations of middle-class activism in this book and Johnston's narrative can be attributed to a few reasons. In addition to his primary focus on the Progressive Era, an earlier period in which the middle class is acknowledged by many scholars to often have a pro-labor orientation, Johnston covers a single location that might well have had a stronger presence of a competing strand of middle-class politics. While the political behavior and aspirations of the middle-class activists discussed in this book are a strong counterpoint to Johnston's argument, it is worth emphasizing that I do not claim that their story represents the only strand of middle-class politics. It is, however, a strand that reflects an important window into the political and cultural behavior of many early twentieth century middle-class Americans, and which left significant legacies. Furthermore, Johnston states that he wants to "rehabilitate" the middle class from disparaging treatment by historians, who have purportedly portrayed it as anxious, fixated on its own status, and failing to meaningfully challenge capitalism (largely regardless of the era). While Johnston's critiques can be applied to works that focus on the middle class in many historical moments, his general expectation of middle-class radicalism is less conducive to an analysis of middle-class identity that is historically contingent, wherein the middle class has the potential to express radical anticapitalist beliefs in some eras and regions,

and not in others. This book situates middle-class consumer activism in a specific historical moment, while suggesting its long-term legacies. It further acknowledges that the middle class's identities and political expressions continued to shift across time and place. Robert D. Johnston, *The Radical Middle Class: Populist Democracy and the Question of Capitalism in Progressive Era Portland, Oregon* (Princeton: Princeton University Press, 2006).

30. Johnston's *The Radical Middle Class* is the most notable example of a recent work that emphasizes the connections between the working and middle classes. By analyzing middle-class appropriation of working-class culture alongside of its criticism of the working and elite classes, this book chronicles the ideological and cultural separation of the middle class from labor and capital, while still analyzing the lines of power and culture that flowed between these groups. Johnston, *Radical Middle Class*. Kathy Peiss provides important insights into how culture can be transmitted from the bottom up. See Kathy Peiss, *Cheap Amusements: Working Women and Leisure in Turn-of-the-Century New York* (Philadelphia: Temple University Press, 1986).

31. For discussion of the conservative wing of the 1920s Democratic Party and its cultural and ideological divisions, see Douglas B. Craig, *After Wilson: The Struggle for the Democratic Party, 1920–1934* (Chapel Hill: University of North Carolina Press, 1992).

32. "Rabble Rouser of the Right," *New Republic*, October 4, 1939.

33. Horowitz, *Beyond Left and Right*, xi.

34. Horowitz's contention is additionally present in Robert D. Johnston's analysis of Portland, Oregon's petit bourgeoisie, who often identified and organized along with the working class against concentrated authority. Johnston, *Radical Middle Class*. Thelen and Lears quoted in Horowitz, *Beyond Left and Right*, xii; David Thelen, *Paths of Resistance: Tradition and Democracy in Industrializing Missouri* (Columbia: University of Missouri Press, 1991); T. J. Jackson Lears, *No Place of Grace: Antimodernism and the Transformation of American Culture, 1880–1920* (Chicago: University of Chicago Press, 1991). See also Christopher Lasch, *The True and Only Heaven: Progress and Its Critics* (New York: W. W. Norton, 1991).

35. "Favors Overall Movement," *Cincinnati Enquirer*, April 26, 1920.

36. Glickman, *Buying Power*, 7.

37. For an example of scholarship in the field of communications that explores the role of media in shaping a national discursive space characterized by controlled nationalistic discussion and a limited public sphere, see Andrew Calabrese and Barbara Ruth Burke, "American Identities: Nationalism, the Media, and the Public Sphere," *Journal of Communication Inquiry* 16, no. 2 (1992): 52–73; Benedict Anderson, *Imagined Communities: Reflections on the Origin and Spread of Nationalism* (New York: Verso, 2006); see also T. H. Breen, *The Marketplace of Revolution: How Consumer Politics Shaped American Independence* (New York: Oxford University Press, 2005); Jon Butler, *Becoming America: The Revolution before 1776* (Cambridge: Harvard University Press, 2001).

38. For examples of anthropological discussions of how the category of race, as symbolic space in cultural discourse, can play a strong role in shaping or reproducing power relationships along class, nationalistic, professional, and other lines, see John Russell, "Race and Reflexivity: The Black Other in Contemporary Japanese Mass Culture," in *Rereading Cultural Anthropology*, ed. George Marcus (Durham: Duke University Press, 1992), 296–318, and Helán Page and R. Brooke Thomas, "White Public Space and the Construction of White Privilege in U.S. Health Care: Fresh Concepts and a New Model

of Analysis," *Medical Anthropology Quarterly* 8, no. 1 (March 1994): 109–16. At times, the racial component of the discursive space of consumer activism discussed in this book enabled *both* middle and working-class activists to claim victimhood against the supposed unfair practices of nonwhite people, but their local organizing still largely took place in class-segmented spaces (see chapter 2).

39. For additional discussion of the interplay between discursive space and physical places or historical contexts, or both, see Sue Thomas, "Reconfiguring the Public Sphere: Implications for Analyses of Educational Policy," *British Journal of Educational Studies* 53, no. 3 (September 2004): 228–48; Wilson, *White Collar Fictions*, 7–8. Christopher P. Wilson notes how historical context should be considered more than a backdrop for analysis of literary expressions. Rather, as Wilson suggests, "it is necessary to scuttle back and forth between cultural forms and their social situating. Literary forms often pose a cultural horizon or set of historical givens to be interrogated, brought into conflict with each other, dramatized in dreamlike explorations; through these imaginary transformations, sense and nonsense are made of new social determinants and their possibilities." Nan Enstad, *Ladies of Labor, Girls of Adventure: Working Women, Popular Culture, and Labor Politics at the Turn of the Twentieth Century* (New York: Columbia University Press, 1999), 51; "A Nation in Overalls," *Literary Digest*, May 1, 1920; "A New Dawn for the Middle Classes," *CT*, April 25, 1920.

## Chapter 1

1. Los Angeles U.S. Food Administration LMC/M to the American Protective League, Los Angeles, October 26, 1918, California Food Administration Records, National Archives, San Bruno, CA (hereinafter CFAR); Helen R. Kenealy to Louis M. Cole, October 20, 1918, CFAR; American Protective League Report in re: Dr. W. S. Thompson, 1319 Fifth Avenue, September 28, 1918, CFAR; 1920 U.S. Census, Los Angeles, Los Angeles County, California, digital image, s.v. "Helen R. Kenealy," *Ancestry.com.*

2. "Voice of the People," *CT*, June 24, 1917; 1910 U.S. Census, Chicago, Cook County, Illinois, digital image, s.v. "Jean Roberts Albert," *Ancestry.com.*

3. Michael McGerr, *A Fierce Discontent: The Rise and Fall of the Progressive Movement in America, 1870–1920* (New York: Free Press, 2003), 68; Richard Hofstader, *The Progressive Movement, 1900–1915* (Englewood Cliffs, NJ: Prentice Hall, 1963); Horowitz, *Beyond Left and Right*, 14.

4. See, for example, Dana Frank, "Where Are the Workers in Consumer-Worker Alliances? Class Dynamics and the History of Consumer-Labor Campaigns," *Politics & Society* 31, no. 3 (2003): 363–79; Sybil Lipschultz, "Hours and Wages: The Gendering of Labor Standards in America," *Journal of Women's History* 8, no. 1 (Spring 1996): 114–36; Landon Storrs, *Civilizing Capitalism: The National Consumers' League, Women's Activism, and Labor Standards in the New Deal Era* (Chapel Hill: University of North Carolina Press, 2000), 14.

5. Henry Bournes Higgins, National Consumers' League, *A New Province for Law and Order: Industrial Peace through Minimum Wage and Arbitration* (New York: National Consumers' League, 1915); National Consumers' League, *The Waste of Industry, Overworked Women and Girls, Ill Health, Danger, Low Wages: Some Reasons Why Protective Laws for Women in Industry Are Necessary* (New York: National Consumers' League, 1915).

6. Kathleen G. Donohue, *Freedom from Want: American Liberalism and the Idea of the Consumer* (Baltimore: Johns Hopkins University Press, 2003), 8; "Where Does the Consumer Come In?," *Atlanta Jeffersonian*, July 15, 1909; "How to Lighten the Burden to the Consumer," *Tucson Daily Citizen*, September 6, 1911; "Robbing the Consumer," *Kalamazoo Gazette*, December 12, 1911.

7. Joe Sullivan, *Marxists, Militants, and Macaroni: The IWW in Providence's Little Italy* (Kingston, RI: Rhode Island Labor History Society, 2001), 9; U.S. Department of Commerce, Bureau of Foreign and Domestic Commerce, *Statistical Abstract of the United States 1918* (Washington, DC: Government Printing Office, 1919), 578–79; U.S. Department of Commerce, Bureau of the Census, *Historical Statistics of the United States: Colonial Times to 1970 Part I* (Washington, DC: Government Printing Office, 1975), 578.

8. William Frieburger, "War, Prosperity and Hunger: The New York Food Riots of 1917," *Labor History* 25, no. 2 (1984): 238; Dana Frank, "Housewives, Socialists, and the Politics of Food: The 1917 New York Cost of Living Protests," *Feminist Studies* 11, no. 2 (Summer, 1985): 255–85; Bureau of the Census, *Historical Statistics of the United States*, 578; "Food Riot 'Plot' Being Trailed," *CT*, February 23, 1917; "Food Riots on West Side Land Fifty in Cells," *CT*, May 30, 1917; "The Story of the United States Grain Corporation, April 5, 1920," Folder: Politics . . . plan of operations, information booklets, Box 7, United States Food Administration Records, Herbert Hoover Presidential Library, West Branch, IA (hereinafter USFAR).

9. "House and Senate Debate Food Riots," *NYT*, February 22, 1917; "The Story of the United States Grain Corporation, April 5, 1920," Folder: Politics . . . plan of operations, information booklets, Box 7, USFAR.

10. This particular boycott also included a number of working-class residents. Records of the Los Angeles City Council, May 8, 1917, and March 11, 1917, LACCR; Letter to the Editor, *CT*, June 14, 1917; "Spud Boycott, Also Onions," *Miami Herald*, March 18, 1917. The East Jefferson Improvement Association had a white-collar leadership. Their president, for example, was a pharmacist. 1920 U.S. Census, Los Angeles, Los Angeles County, California, digital image, s.v. "Charles H. V. Lewis," *Ancestry.com*.

11. "President Discusses the Food Problem," *NYT*, April 12, 1917.

12. "Resume of Letters . . . to all Federal Food Administrators, 1917–1918 Proclamations," part 9, Box 3, USFAR; Food Control Act of 1917, Public Law 41, 65th Cong., 1st sess. (August 10, 1917).

13. "Fears Social Upheaval," *LAT*, May 19, 1917.

14. Rep. Lever, speaking on H.R. 4961, on June 18, 1917, 65th Cong., 1st sess., *Congressional Record* 55, pt. 4: 3795, 3797; Rep. Anderson, speaking on H.R. 4961, on June 18, 1917, 65th Cong., 1st sess., *Congressional Record* 55, pt. 4: 3809; Rep. Knutson, speaking on H.R. 4961, on June 18, 1917, 65th Cong., 1st sess., *Congressional Record* 55, pt. 4: 3820.

15. "Assails Food Bill as Dictatorial," *NYT*, June 15, 1917; Sen. Reed, speaking on H.R. 4961, on June 14, 1917, 65th Cong., 1st sess., *Congressional Record* 55, pt. 4: 3596; Arthur S. Link, ed., *The Papers of Woodrow Wilson*, vol. 43 (Princeton: Princeton University Press, 1983), 210.

16. Rep. Lever, speaking on H.R. 4961, on June 18, 1917, 65th Cong., 1st sess., *Congressional Record* 55, pt. 4: 3795, 3798; Rep. Anderson, speaking on H.R. 4961, on June 18, 1917, 65th Cong., 1st sess., *Congressional Record* 55, pt. 4: 3809; Rep. Knutson, speaking on H.R. 4961, on June 18, 1917, 65th Cong., 1st sess., *Congressional Record* 55, pt. 4: 3819.

17. Rep. Anderson, speaking on H.R. 4961, on June 18, 1917, 65th Cong., 1st sess., *Congressional Record* 55, pt. 4: 3809; Rep. James, speaking on H.R. 4961, on June 18, 1917, 65th Cong., 1st sess., *Congressional Record* 55, pt. 4: 3830; "Food Control," *CT*, June 23, 1917.

18. Sen. Kellogg, speaking on H.R. 4961, on June 28, 1917, 65th Cong., 1st sess., *Congressional Record* 55, pt. 5: 4418; Sen. Reed, speaking on H.R. 4961, on August 8, 1917, 65th Cong., 1st sess., *Congressional Record* 55, pt. 6: 5921

19. Alexander Trachtenberg and Benjamin Glassberg, eds., *The American Labor Year Book 1921–1922* (New York: Rand School of Social Science, 1922), 430; Rep. Fess, speaking on H.R. 4961, on June 18, 1917, 65th Cong., 1st sess., *Congressional Record* 55, pt. 4: 3801; "Business as Usual," *Piqua Daily Call*, July 16, 1917.

20. In the postwar period, the Lever Act was used against striking railroad workers. See Trial Transcript, "In the District Court of the United States, Southern District of California, Southern Division, *United States v. Henry W. Crumrine et al.*," National Archives, Laguna Niguel, CA; Link, *Papers of Woodrow Wilson*, vol. 43, 20–23; Rep. Keating, speaking on H.R. 4961, on June 23, 1917, 65th Cong., 1st sess., *Congressional Record* 55, pt. 4: 4184–86.

21. "To Discourage Sale of Hens," *New York Produce Review and American Creamery* 45, no. 14 (February 6, 1918), 459. See also "Food Board to Ask That Hens Be Not Killed," *San Francisco Chronicle*, February 11, 1918.

22. Helen Zoe Veit also underscores how Americans' experiences with the USFA led them to think about conservation in moral terms. Helen Zoe Veit, "'We Were a Soft People': Asceticism, Self-Discipline and American Food Conservation in the First World War," *Food, Culture and Society: An International Journal of Multidisciplinary Research* 10, no. 2 (Summer 2007): 169, 181; United States Food Administration Home Card, Folder: Home Cards, Box 8, USFAR; "United States Food Administration Suggestions for Enlisting the Active Support of Religious Organizations," March 1918, CFAR.

23. Link, *Papers of Woodrow Wilson*, vol. 43, 160–61; William Clinton Mullendore, *History of the United States Food Administration, 1917–1919* (Palo Alto: Stanford University Press, 1941), 80; Press Release No. 133, Food Administration Public Information Department, July 28, 1917, p. 2, Folder: Press Releases 100–150, Box 10, USFAR.

24. Los Angeles Chamber of Commerce Members' Annual 1918, p. 15, Carton 40, Records of the Los Angeles Chamber of Commerce, University of Southern California Special Collections; Los Angeles Chamber of Commerce Board of Directors Minutes, October 14, 1917, Carton 24, ID 9, Los Angeles Chamber of Commerce Records, University of Southern California Special Collections.

25. "Defense Women to Meet Here for Convention," *CT*, June 20, 1917. Professions taken from the 1920 United States Census. See note 23 in chapter 5 for a discussion of the limitations of using Census data in this context. Kentucky Council of Defense, *Report of the Activities of the Kentucky Council of Defense to January 1, 1920* (Frankfort, KY: State Journal Co., 1920), 81; "Food Administration: Ten Lessons for Conservation, Lessons I to V," Folder: Bulletins #1–17, Box 7, USFAR; "Schedule of Bulletins," Folder: Bulletins #1–17, Box 7, USFAR.

26. See previous note; Report of the State Council of Defense of California to Governor William D. Stephens (June 1, 1917–January 1, 1919), pp. 12–13, Los Angeles Public Central Library; Mrs. H. H. Hartley to Ralph Merritt, March 1, 1918, CFAR; J. W. Hunt

(6805 Bonsallo) to Los Angeles Food Administration, April 8, 1918, CFAR; *Los Angeles City Directory* (Los Angeles: Los Angeles Directory Company, 1918), 947, 1050.

27. Card beginning with "Go back to the simple life . . . ," Cards, Small Display Pieces, Box 7, USFAR.

28. "Thinking the War Through," *House and Garden* 33, no. 4 (April 1918): 24.

29. Frank Willing Leach, "How Our Forefathers Checkmated the Food Profiteers during the Revolution," *Washington Post*, January 6, 1918.

30. Resume of Letters . . . To All Federal Food Administrators, 1917–1918 Proclamations, Box 3, USFAR; Marsha Gordon, "Onward Kitchen Soldiers: Mobilizing the Domestic during World War I," *Canadian Review of American Studies* 29, no. 2 (1999): 61–87.

31. Letter to Louis M. Cole, February 20, 1918, CFAR; Myron McNeal to Louis M. Cole, August 20, 1918, CFAR; U.S. Food Administration to American Protective League (Los Angeles), August 13, 1918, CFAR.

32. Letter to Louis M. Cole, February 20, 1918, CFAR; Myron McNeal to Louis M. Cole, August 20, 1918, CFAR.

33. Frank Wilson to Louis Cole, August 7, 1918, CFAR.

34. Joan M. Jensen, *The Price of Vigilance* (Chicago: Rand McNally, 1968), 22, 46; Emerson Hough, *The Web* (Chicago: Reilly & Lee Co., 1919), 13; American Protective League, *American Protective League: Organized with the Approval and Operating under the Direction of the United States Department of Justice, Bureau of Investigation* (Washington, DC: American Protective League, 1918), 30–33; Los Angeles American Protective League Report, Case #5795, CFAR.

35. The Minutemen were an expression of the APL in Washington into the postwar period. "Public Reserve Precinct 1," Box 10, Charles Frey Papers, UCLA Special Collections, Charles Young Library; Hough, *The Web*.

36. "County Republicans Named on State Body," *LAT*, September 21, 1918; "Women's Work, Women's Clubs," *LAT*, June 18, 1920; "The Friday Morning Club, November 14, 1919, 940 South Figueroa Street, Los Angeles, Topic—'Causes and Cures for the High Cost of Living,' Ralph P. Merritt," Folder 3, Box 32, John R. Haynes Papers, UCLA Special Collections; Jane Apostol, "Why Women Should Not Have the Vote: Anti-Suffrage Views in the Southland in 1911," *Southern California Quarterly* 70 (Spring 1988): 32; Jane Apostol, *South Pasadena: A Centennial History 1888–1988* (Pasadena: South Pasadena Public Library, 1987), 66.

37. Grace C. Simons to Louis Cole, June 5, 1918, CFAR; City Administrator to Mrs. Seward A. Simons, June 6, 1918, CFAR; City Administrator to American Protective League, CFAR; American Protective League Report In re: Chris Paul, 1766 La Brea Ave., Hollywood, Cal., CFAR; W. A. Hammel to Louis Cole, June 29, 1918, CFAR.

38. American Protective League Report In re: Chris Paul, 1766 La Brea Ave., Hollywood, Cal., CFAR; W. A. Hammel to Louis Cole, June 29, 1918, CFAR.

39. Records of *United States vs. Hulett C. Merritt*, Criminal No. 1558, National Archives Division, Laguna Niguel, CA; "Raid Houses Owned by Rich Man; Seize Sugar," *Los Angeles Evening Herald*, July 25, 1918.

40. Bureau of the Census, *Historical Statistics of the United States*, 211; Editorial, *NYT*, October 29, 1918; "The Imperishables," Folder 3, Box 1, Powell Family Papers, UCLA Special Collections.

41. Priebe to Harold Powell, November 13, 1919, Folder 3, Box 1, Powell Family Papers, UCLA Special Collections; R. H. Switzler to Harold Powell, November 22, 1919, Folder 3, Box 1, Powell Family Papers, UCLA Special Collections; see also EWJH to Harold Powell, November 10, 1919, Folder 3, Box 1, Powell Family Papers, UCLA Special Collections; W. R. Dadson to Harold Powell, November 21, 1919, Folder 3, Box 1, Powell Family Papers, UCLA Special Collections.

42. "The Price-Boosters," *LAT*, September 4, 1919; MFL to Hiram Johnson, April 17, 1919, Folder 14, Box 2, Katherine Philips Edson Papers, UCLA Special Collections.

## Chapter 2

1. "Objects to Profiteering," *LAT*, July 25, 1919.

2. Americans had increasingly tied consumption practices to their notions of citizenship in the pre–World War I decades. See Charles F. McGovern, *Sold American: Consumption and Citizens, 1890–1945* (Chapel Hill: University of North Carolina Press, 2006), 3.

3. The percentage of the male labor force in Los Angeles holding white-collar professions was approximately 15 percent higher than that of the United States as a whole. Clark Davis, *Company Men: White-Collar Life and Corporate Cultures in Los Angeles, 1892–1941* (Baltimore: Johns Hopkins University Press, 2000), 77.

4. "Relative Retail Prices of Food," in Department of Commerce, Bureau of Foreign and Domestic Commerce, *Statistical Abstract of the United States 1921* (Washington, DC: Government Printing Office, 1922), 631; Letters to the editor, *CT*, May 30, 1919, *Boston Daily Globe*, August 10, 1919, *Washington Post*, August 15, 1919.

5. "The Strike of a Mother," *NYT*, September 16, 1919.

6. Editorials, *LAT*, July 19, 1919 and May 30, 1920; "Middle Class Woes," *Oxnard Daily Courier*, May 16, 1919.

7. "Questions That Interest Women," *Woman's Journal*, August 16, 1919; "Tackle the Cost of Living," *LAT*, July 19, 1919; Louis Cole to B. F., June 5, 1918, CFAR; Entry for April 29, 1920, Diary of Fred Alton Haight, Medford, Oregon, 1918 and 1920–21, Ms. 338, Southern Oregon Historical Society, Medford, Oregon.

8. Edmund Vance Cook, "The Middlemen," *Harrisburg (PA) Evening News*, May 31, 1919; "Georgia to Act as Middle Man," *Atlanta Constitution*, August 20, 1919.

9. Editorial, *LAT*, July 19, 1919; Records of the City Council of Los Angeles, August 5, 1919, LACCR.

10. "Every Backyard in Los Angeles Is a Potential Producer," *LAT*, February 19, 1917.

11. "Woman Sets Garden Mark," *Los Angeles Examiner*, March 29, 1917.

12. *Fall Garden Bulletin*, Municipal Reference Collection, Harold Washington Public Library, Chicago, IL; Charles Lathrop Pack, *Urban and Suburban Food Production: Its Past and Its Future* (Washington, DC: National Emergency Garden Commission, 1917); Charles Lathrop Pack, *The War Garden Victorious* (Philadelphia: J.P. Lippincott, 1919), 1–23.

13. One individual home garden meeting even drew 2,500 people. "Cut Food Cost and Win Prize," *Los Angeles Examiner*, February 26, 1917; "Home Garden Idea Spreads Like Wildfire," *Los Angeles Examiner*, March 6, 1917; "School of Gardening Interests Thousands," *LAT*, May 6, 1917.

14. The *St. Petersburg (FL) Independent* characterized Cowles as a "strong Republican." "New President of Women's Clubs Possesses a Fine Personality," *St. Petersburg Evening Independent*, June 17, 1916; Horowitz, *Beyond Left and Right*, xii.

15. Woodman ran for reelection on a probusiness Republican platform. He proclaimed that the city "must have a business executive as its head," that "it is good business" to have him in office, and called for industrial improvements. The *Los Angeles Times* further praised him and his constituents' antiunion credentials, referring to their opposition to "lawless forms of labor unionism" (though, as Tom Sitton notes, Woodman had also been considered a progressive in certain respects). Woodman additionally claimed, "Los Angeles is clean," yet he had been under indictment for alleged graft. Meanwhile, the *Los Angeles Examiner* was in opposition to Woodman in the lead-up to the election of 1919. "It Is Good Business to Re-Elect Woodman," *LAT*, May 5, 1919; "Who Are the 'Gang'?" *LAT*, May 31, 1919; "Snyder Mayor of Los Angeles," *Lexington (NC) Dispatch*, June 18, 1919; Tom Sitton, *John Randolph Haynes: California Progressive* (Stanford: Stanford University Press, 1992), 124–25, 166–67.

16. Records of the City Council of Los Angeles, June 19, 1917, LACCR; Records of the City Council of Los Angeles, June 20, 1917, LACCR; Records of the City Council of Los Angeles, June 29, 1917, LACCR; Records of the City Council of Los Angeles, July 2, 1917, LACCR; "Water at Half-Rate to Raise City-Lot Crops," *LAT*, February 13, 1918; "Team Work," *LAT*, April 26, 1917.

17. "Release Feb. 22nd—United Stated Food Administration—Lucas," CFAR. For images of white-collar gardening, see editorial cartoons/images, *LAT*, May 11, 1917, February 13, 1918; *Los Angeles Examiner*, March 7, 1917; "28. Home Garden, 'How's That War Garden Progressing?,'" CFAR; "The Patriotic Garden: Making a Nation of Garden Cities," CFAR; Pamphlet: "Raking the Gardener," CFAR; "Raking the Gardener and Canning the Canner," National Emergency Food Garden Commission, CFAR.

18. 1920 U.S. Census, Chicago, Cook County, Illinois, digital image, s.v. "Perry Holden," *Ancestry.com*; 1920 U.S. Census, Los Angeles, Los Angeles County, California, digital image, s.v. "Luther G. Brown," *Ancestry.com*; 1920 U.S. Census, Winona, Winona County, Minnesota, digital image, s.v. "Samuel L. Wright," *Ancestry.com*; *Fall Garden Bulletin*, Municipal Reference Collection, Harold Washington Public Library, Chicago, IL; *Winona Republican-Herald*, March 14, 1918; "Farm Instructors Wanted for City," *LAT*, April 28, 1917; "Organization Plans for City War Gardens . . . ," CFAR; "I-3 . . . 'Melt the fat, add flour mixed with seasoning . . . A War-Garden Exhibit," CFAR.

19. U.S. Food Administration, for RELEASE, War Gardens and Sugar Supply, IV-3 and III-3, CFAR; "City's Idle Land . . . ," *LAT*, April 22, 1917; "Get Busy in Your . . . ," *LAT*, February 13, 1918; "Garden Brigades . . . ," *Los Angeles Examiner*, March 13, 1917.

20. "For Laggards but Not Slackers," CFAR; "Making a Nation of Garden Cities," *The Patriotic Garden*, undated, p. 188, CFAR; clipping of *Los Angeles Examiner*, December 27, 1918, CFAR; "Venice in Food Campaign," *Los Angeles Examiner*, April 26, 1917.

21. "To Unite Middle Class," *NYT*, December 14, 1919.

22. See chapters 4 and 5.

23. "'War Garden' Needed Now," *Jackson (MI) Citizen Patriot*, May 18, 1920.

24. Southern California boosters, such as Charles Fletcher Lummis, a photographer for the magazine *Land of Sunshine*, attempted to lure middle-class migrants to Los Angeles by depicting the city as a haven for healthy middle-class babies and a Garden of Eden. See Jennifer A. Watts, "Photography in the Land of Sunshine: Charles Fletcher

Lummis and the Regional Ideal," *Southern California Quarterly* 87, no. 4 (2005): 339–76; for an analysis of migration patterns to Los Angeles in the late nineteenth and early twentieth centuries, see Robert M. Fogelson, *The Fragmented Metropolis: Los Angeles, 1850–1930* (Cambridge: Harvard University Press, 1967), 63–84 and 189. For census records on Anderson, see 1920 U.S. Census, Los Angeles, Los Angeles County, California, digital image, s.v. "Mary Anderson," *Ancestry.com*; 1910 U.S. Census, Los Angeles, Los Angeles County, California, digital image, s.v. "Mary Anderson," *Ancestry.com*. Data on midwestern migration to Los Angeles reflects percentages from 1910, printed in table 8 in Fogelson, *Fragmented Metropolis*, 81.

25. Louis S. Lyons and Josephine Wilson, eds., *Who's Who among Women of California* (San Francisco: Security Publishing, 1922), 131; "Readily Sign Food Pledge," *LAT*, November 1, 1917; "Lauds Southland Women," *LAT*, October 28, 1917; 1920 U.S. Census, Los Angeles, Los Angeles County, California, digital image, s.v. "Mary Anderson," *Ancestry.com*.

26. Anderson also participated in the postwar campaign of the United States Department of Justice High Cost of Living Division to use middle-class women to bring down high prices (see chapter 3). See, for example, Special Assistant to the Attorney General to Mrs. J. T. Anderson, October 7, 1920, DOJ-HCL.

27. The Women's Committee of the U.S. Department of Justice High Cost of Living Division (1919–20) (see chapter 3) did encourage home gardening as a solution to high food prices, but focused most of its efforts elsewhere.

28. "Daylight War at City Hall," *LAT*, May 11, 1920; "Farmer and Daylight Saving," *Indiana Farmer's Guide*, February 22, 1919; see also "Daylight Saving Arrangements," *Indiana Farmer's Guide*, March 13, 1920.

29. Records of the City Council of Los Angeles, October 1, 1918, LACCR.

30. Records of the City Council of Los Angeles, February 11, 1919, LACCR; Records of the City Council of Los Angeles, February 14, 1919, LACCR.

31. Editorial, *LAT*, February 8, 1920; Letters to the editor, *CT*, August 19, 1919.

32. "Victory Garden Best Bolshevik Antidote," *North Adams (MA) Transcript*, March 4, 1919.

33. "The Public Pulse," *Grand Rapids (MI) Press*, December 8, 1920.

34. "Sees Boon in High Rent," *Kansas City Star*, September 7, 1919.

35. "Mrs. Sherman Asks Georgia Women to Aid School Gardens," *Atlanta Constitution*, January 12, 1919.

36. U.S. Department of the Interior, Bureau of Education, *The Garden Army in 1919* (Washington, DC: Government Printing Office, 1919), 1; J. H. Francis, "The United States School Garden Army," *Bulletin* 26 (1919), 3 (Washington, DC: U.S. Department of the Interior, Bureau of Education).

37. Records of the City Council of Los Angeles, March 18, 1919, LACCR; City of Los Angeles Commission of Social Service Annual Report, July 1, 1918–July 1, 1919, pg 38, LACCR; "Victory Garden Best Bolshevik Antidote."

38. Becky M. Nicolaides, *My Blue Heaven: Life and Politics in the Working-Class Suburbs of Los Angeles, 1920–1965* (Chicago: University of Chicago Press, 2002), 3, 34.

39. Ibid., 28–29.

40. For instance, see *Torrance (CA) Herald*, April 21, 1922; Nicolaides, *My Blue Heaven*, 34; For examples of union periodicals offering gardening advice, see "Work Your

Garden," *The Labor World* (Duluth, MN), April 24, 1920; "Plan What You Will Can before You Plant a Garden," *Labor Journal* (Everett, WA), April 28, 1922.

41. "S.P. Employees Are Hooverizing," *Napa Daily Journal*, January 10, 1918.

42. Trial Transcript, "In the District Court of the United States, Southern District of California, Southern Division, *United States v. Henry W. Crumrine et al.*," p. 135–37, *United States v. Henry W. Crumrine et al.* file, National Archives, Laguna Niguel, CA.

43. A number of scholars have discussed working-class neighborhoods in this period, focusing on a variety of themes. In Southern California, for instance, Becky M. Nicolaides explores life in the working-class suburb of South Gate in *My Blue Heaven*. Mark Wild discusses the social and political dynamics of multiethnic neighborhoods in the working-class areas of Los Angeles central city. Mark Wild, *Street Meeting: Multiethnic Neighborhoods in Early Twentieth-Century Los Angeles* (Berkeley: University of California Press, 2005).

44. Nicolaides, *My Blue Heaven*, 33–35.

45. Letter to the editor, *LAT*, March 11, 1919; World War I Draft Registration Cards, 1917–1918, images, *Ancestry.com*, card for James Henry Spillane, serial no. 1765, order no. 530, Local Draft Board 9, Los Angeles, Los Angeles Co., CA.

46. "Educators Who Need Instruction," *Railway Trainman* 37, no. 1 (Jan. 1920), 15–16.

47. "U.S. War on Japanese Potato Pool," *Los Angeles Evening Herald*, January 17, 1920.

48. According to United States Census data, the number of Asian-born residents of Los Angeles increased from 1,881 in 1890 to 11,028 in 1920. The number of Mexican-born residents of Los Angeles increased from 493 to 21,653 in the same period. See Fogelson, *Fragmented Metropolis*, 76.

49. See Matthew Frye Jacobson, *Whiteness of a Different Color: European Immigrants and the Alchemy of Race* (Cambridge: Harvard University Press, 1999), 7–9 and 39–90.

50. "U.S. War on Japanese Potato Pool."

51. "Potato Banned by Club Women," *LAT*, March 5, 1920. These railroad shops did include white-collar employees.

52. "Housewives Join in Big Fight to Force Down Potato Prices," *Los Angeles Evening Herald*, January 22, 1920; "2000 Women of the Ebell Club Fight High Spud Prices," *Los Angeles Evening Herald*, February, 3, 1920.

53. "U.S. War on Japanese Potato Pool"; "Potato Boycott May Be Extended," *Los Angeles Evening Herald*, January 26, 1920.

54. "Probe of Jap 'Potato King' Is Ordered," *Los Angeles Evening Herald*, March 13, 1920.

55. Donald Hata and Nadine Hata, "George Shima: 'The Potato King of California,'" *Journal of the West* 25, no. 1 (January 1986): 59.

56. "A Horrifying Suggestion," *LAT*, July 15, 1920.

57. "Latest News of Food Prices," *LAT*, March 25, 1920.

58. "Newport Women Urge Potato Boycott," *Santa Ana Register*, March 12, 1920; Records for Della M. and Frank Corwin, Index to Register of Voters, Los Angles Precinct 84, California Voter Registrations, California State Library.

59. Records of the City Council of Los Angeles, June 3, 1920, LACCR.

60. One important factor in the consideration of why food prices declined at this point is an overproduction of farm commodities both domestically and abroad. For dis-

cussion of this problem, its origins, and its impact on farmers, see Gilbert C. Fite, "The Farmers' Dilemma, 1919–1929," in *Change and Continuity in Twentieth-Century America: The 1920s*, ed. John Braeman, et al. (Columbus: Ohio State University Press, 1968), 67–102; Records of the City Council of Los Angeles, March 10, 1919, LACCR; price changes calculated from *Bulletin of the United States Bureau of Labor Statistics* 315 (January 1923): 44–47 (Retail Prices 1913 to December 1921); "Protest Free Seeds," *LAT*, March 1, 1919.

61. "Jurisprudence and Jujubes on a Suburban Acre," *LAT*, April 10, 1921.

62. The city's municipal markets reemerged in the mid-1910s after a 52-year absence.

63. See Helen Tangires, *Public Markets and Civic Culture in Nineteenth-Century America* (Baltimore: Johns Hopkins University Press, 2003); Karen J. Friedmann, "Urban Food Marketing in Los Angeles, 1850–1885," *Agricultural History* 54, no. 2 (1980): 433–34.

64. "Throngs Attend Market Opening," *LAT*, May 4, 1913.

65. Fitting to his skill set and his white-collar consumer identity, an attorney coordinated the acquisition of signatures of "approximately 6000 voters, taxpayers and property owners" for a petition that aimed to expand the markets and the power of their operators. Records of the City Council of Los Angeles, October 26, 1917, LACCR; Records of the City Council of Los Angeles, October 30, 1917, LACCR; 1920 U.S. Census, Los Angeles, Los Angeles County, digital image, s.v. "Henry H. Roser," *Ancestry.com*; "Food Protests by Housewives," *LAT*, December 15, 1916. The secretary of the Housewives League was married to a newspaper solicitor. 1920 U.S. Census, Monterey Park, Los Angeles County, digital image, s.v., "George W. Graydon," *Ancestry.com*; Tangires, *Public Markets and Civic Culture*, 181.

66. Records of the City Council of Los Angeles, May 14, 1917, LACCR; Records of the City Council of Los Angeles, July 10, 1917, LACCR; Records of the City Council of Los Angeles, July 18, 1917, LACCR; Records of the City Council of Los Angeles, October 10, 1917, LACCR; Records of the City Council of Los Angeles, September 20, 1918, LACCR; Records of the City Council of Los Angeles, October 7, 1918, LACCR; "Public Deceived about Markets," *Municipal League Bulletin* (Los Angeles) 10 (1917): 4; "Money Leak in City Markets," *LAT*, April 1, 1917, "Municipal Fad Is Near Death," *LAT*, May 20, 1919.

67. Records of the City Council of Los Angeles, July 3, 1918, LACCR; Records of the City Council of Los Angeles, December 18, 1918, LACCR.

68. Clark Davis, "An Era and Generation of Civic Engagement: The Friday Morning Club in Los Angeles, 1891–1931," *Southern California Quarterly* 84, no. 2 (2002): 135–68; the quotation "strongly in favor of maintaining the public markets" refers to the support of public markets by both the Friday Morning Club and the Hollywood Women's Club. Records of the City Council of Los Angeles, November 11, 1918, LACCR; Records of the City Council of Los Angeles, November 28, 1918, LACCR; Records of the City Council of Los Angeles, January 24, 1919, LACCR; Letter from Councilman Cleveland to the Los Angeles City Council, read on January 24, 1919, Records of the City Council of Los Angeles, January 24, 1919, LACCR.

69. "Washingtonians Voice Protests against Food Pirates," *Washington Post*, June 22, 1917; "Surplus U.S. Army Food Sold . . . ," *Rockford (IL) Morning Star*, July 6, 1919.

70. For an influential treatment of how geographic, discursive, and oppositional spaces have led to community identification (focusing on nationalism), see Anderson,

*Imagined Communities*. "If the Middle Class Should Strike," *Outlook*, November 12, 1919; and see editorial cartoons (reprinted in the chapter), *Los Angeles Evening Herald*, May 25, June 12, and June 14, 1920.

71. See Jacobson, *Whiteness of a Different Color*, 7–9 and 39–90.

72. Natalia Molina, *Fit to Be Citizens? Public Health and Race in Los Angeles, 1879–1939* (Berkeley: University of California Press, 2006), 2, 35.

73. Records of the City Council of Los Angeles, August 9, 1920, LACCR.

74. United States Census data lists an increase in the number of Japanese-born residents of Los Angeles from 40 in 1890 to 8,536 in 1920. Fogelson, *Fragmented Metropolis*, 76–77 (census table printed in Fogelson).

75. A racially charged letter to the U.S. Secretary of State from governor William D. Stephens reported that in California, "Japanese agricultural labor has developed to such a degree that at the present time between 80 and 90 per cent of most of our vegetable and berry products are those of the Japanese farms." Stephens's letter transmitted (and drew on data from) a 1920 report by the State Board of Control of California titled, *California and the Oriental*, which, he argued, showed a growing "Japanese problem." California State Board of Control, *California and the Oriental: Japanese, Chinese, and Hindus: Report of the State Board of Control of California to Gov. WM D. Stephens* (Sacramento: California State Printing Office, 1920), 7–8; "American Truck Growers Ready to Step into Jap's Place," *LAT*, August 15, 1920.

76. "Women Strike at Potato Profiteers," *Los Angeles Evening Herald*, March 8, 1920.

77. In September 1919, Arthur Lee, secretary of the Retail Grocers' Association of Southern California, noted, "Contrary to the popular opinion of the public, the grocers deplore the high cost of living." "Grocers Deplore H.C.L.," *LAT*, September 2, 1919.

78. Records of the City Council of Los Angeles, June 2, 1919, LACCR.

79. Ibid.

80. Ibid.; "Not Profiteers Claim Japanese," *LAT*, September 18, 1919; "Keeping a Market," *LAT*, August 15, 1920.

81. "The High Cost of Living," *Ladies' Home Journal*, March, 1920; Records of the City Council of Los Angeles, August 17, 1920, LACCR.

82. "The City Market," *Indiana Farmer's Guide*, January 3, 1920; "City Market Problems," *Indiana Farmer's Guide*, March 13, 1920; Records of the City Council of Los Angeles, August 17, 1920, LACCR.

83. Seventy-nine percent of people held white-collar positions among those listed on a sample of two census sheets for residents living in direct vicinity to the market on Vermont and 48th (ambiguous classifications omitted from data). 1920 U.S. Census, Los Angeles, Los Angeles County, Supervisor Distinct 8, Enumeration District 366, Precinct 563, digital images, sheets 3–4, *Ancestry.com*; Records of the City Council of Los Angeles, June 1, 1920, LACCR; Records of the City Council of Los Angeles, September 1, 1920, LACCR; Records of the City Council of Los Angeles, August 25, 1920, LACCR; Records of the City Council of Los Angeles, August 19, 1920, LACCR.

84. Records of the City Council of Los Angeles, September 3, 1920, LACCR; Records of the City Council of Los Angeles, September 8, 1920, LACCR; Records of the City Council of Los Angeles, September 10, 1920, LACCR; Records of the City Council of Los Angeles, October 13, 1920, LACCR; Records of the City Council of Los Angeles, October 14, 1920, LACCR; Records of the City Council of Los Angeles, September 2, 1920, LACCR.

85. Brown authored the original State Market Act in 1915 and intended for it to benefit both producers and consumers by providing for, according to the *LAT*, "opening State markets and selling food products at public auction directly to the consumer," but the market director instead focused on organizing producers to attain better prices for them. Brown hoped to rectify this problem though a new initiative. Mansel G. Blackford, *The Politics of Business in California, 1890–1920* (Columbus: Ohio State University Press, 1977), 29–39; "State Market Fiasco," *LAT*, January 13, 1917; "For State Markets," *LAT*, July 11, 1920.

86. For Sterling Boothe's support of Brown's ideas, see Records of the City Council of Los Angeles, August 17, 1920, LACCR; "Would Abolish City Markets," *LAT*, August 17, 1920.

87. Blackford, *Politics of Business in California*, 29–39.

88. "Consumers Get Busy," *LAT*, May 27, 1920; "Start Market Act Drive," *LAT*, June 24, 1920; "Politics," *LAT*, July 7, 1920; 1920 U.S. Census, Los Angeles, Los Angeles County, California, digital image, s.v., "Katherine A. James," *Ancestry.com*.

89. "Says More Laws to Stop Profiteering Is Greatest Need," *Oxnard (CA) Daily Courier*, January 22, 1920; "Start War on Middlemen," *LAT*, June 20, 1920; "Start Market Act Drive," *LAT*, June 24, 1920.

90. Blackford, *Politics of Business in California*, 29–39.

91. "Consumers Get Busy"; "Sees Drop in Costs if Market Act Wins," *LAT*, June 25, 1920, "Denim Deluge Downs Our Dudes," *LAT*, April 25, 1920; "Divorce Evil Is No Danger to America," *Salt Lake Telegram*, April 7, 1920.

92. "For State Markets"; "Women's Work, Women's Clubs," *LAT*, June 22, 1920.

93. "6 Days to Get 40,000 Market Act Signers," *Los Angeles Evening Herald*, July 16, 1920; "State Market Commission" (1920), Initiative and Referendum Petition Files (Proposed Ballot Measures), Secretary of State Elections Division, California State Archives, Sacramento, CA. I would like to thank Linda Johnson at the California State Archives for her correspondence on this matter.

94. Price changes calculated from *Bulletin of the United States Bureau of Labor Statistics* (Retail Prices 1913 to December 1921) 315 (January 1923): 44–47; Department of Commerce, Bureau of Foreign and Domestic Commerce, *Statistical Abstract of the United States 1921* (Washington, DC: Government Printing Office, 1922), 631; and Department of Commerce, Bureau of Foreign and Domestic Commerce, *Statistical Abstract of the United States 1922* (Washington, DC: Government Printing Office, 1923), 507; "Order Marketmen to Vacate Stalls," *Hartford (CT) Courant*, January 14, 1922; "The Municipal Market Case," *Oshkosh (WI) Daily Northwestern*, August 11, 1921.

## Chapter 3

1. Frederic Haskin column, *Bridgeport (CT) Standard Telegram*, August 21, 1919.

2. Edith Strauss to "Madam," November 8, 1919 (form letter to leaders of women's organizations), DOJ-HCL.

3. Arthur S. Link, ed., *The Papers of Woodrow Wilson*, vol. 25 (Princeton: Princeton University Press, 1978), 10–12. Figures represent wholesale prices; Bureau of the Census, *Historical Statistics of the United States*, 200.

4. "A War Budget for the Household," *Independent*, August 4, 1917; "The Only Solution," *Life*, August 2, 1917; "Wages and the Cost of Living," *Forum*, September, 1918.

5. Bureau of the Census, *Historical Statistics of the United States*, 200.

6. Letter to the Editor, *CT*, August 19, 1919; "The Middle-Class Protest," *NYT*, August 6, 1919; "When Will War Be Over?" *Riverside (CA) Independent Enterprise*, September 2, 1919.

7. For data and sources, see the appendix.

8. Freemasons, Grand Lodge of Illinois, *Proceedings of the Grand Lodge of the Most Worshipful Grand Lodge: Ancient and Free Accepted Masons of the State of Illinois: Eighteenth Annual Meeting, Held at Chicago, October 14, 15, and 16, 1919* (Bloomington, IL: Pantagraph, 1920), 112; "Wages and the Cost of Living," *Forum*, September, 1918; "Dirge of a Member of the Middle-Classes," *Life*, June 5, 1919.

9. L. R. Livingston to Howard Figg, December 6, 1919, DOJ-HCL; Transcript, *U.S. vs. Antwerp Diamond Inc.*, *U.S. vs. Antwerp Diamond Inc.* File, National Archives Northeast Division-NYC; Mrs. H. H. Hartley to Ralph Merritt, March 1, 1918, CFAR.

10. Meltzer, "Intermediate Millions."

11. Sen. La Follette, speaking on H.R. 8624, on August 30, 1919, 66th Cong., 1st sess., *Congressional Record* 58, pt. 5: 4590.

12. "Wilson Refuses Food Curb Delay," *NYT*, August 7, 1919; Arthur S. Link, ed., *The Papers of Woodrow Wilson*, vol. 62 (Princeton: Princeton University Press, 1990), 171, 209.

13. Link, *Papers of Woodrow Wilson*, vol. 62, 209–19.

14. Ibid., 210, 213, 214, 219.

15. For Committee discussion, see U.S. Senate Committee on Agriculture and Forestry, *Hearings before the U.S. Senate Committee on Agriculture and Forestry, 66th Congress, first session, on August 19, 1919* (Washington, DC: GPO, 1919); Sen. Harrison, speaking on H.R. 8624, on August 30, 1919, 66th Cong., 1st sess., *Congressional Record* 58, pt. 5: 4589, 5165.

16. Rep. Newton, speaking on H.R. 8624, on August 23, 1919, 66th Cong., 1st sess., *Congressional Record* 58, pt. 4: 4208; Rep. Blanton, speaking on H.R. 8624, on August 23, 1919, 66th Cong., 1st sess., *Congressional Record* 58, pt. 4: 4208–09.

17. Rep. Summers, speaking on H.R. 8624, on August 22, 1919, 66th Cong., 1st sess., *Congressional Record* 58, pt. 4: 4221; Rep. Campbell, speaking on H.R. 8624, on August 22, 1919, 66th Cong., 1st sess., *Congressional Record* 58, pt. 4: 4209; Rep. Young, speaking on H.R. 8624, on August 22, 1919, 66th Cong., 1st sess., *Congressional Record* 58, pt. 4: 4209.

18. Rep. Campbell, speaking on H.R. 8624, on August 22, 1919, 66th Cong., 1st sess., *Congressional Record* 58, pt. 4: 4209.

19. Rep. Venable, speaking on H.R. 8624, on August 22, 1919, 66th Cong., 1st sess., *Congressional Record* 58, pt. 4: 4225; Rep. Griffin, speaking on H.R. 8624, on August 22, 1919, 66th Cong., 1st sess., *Congressional Record* 58, pt. 4: 4220.

20. While the DOJ-High Cost of Living Division often focused on clothing, it also worked to reduce the prices of other commodities. U.S. Senate Committee on Agriculture and Forestry, *Hearings before the U.S. Senate Committee on Agriculture and Forestry*, 63.

21. U.S. Senate Committee on Agriculture and Forestry, *Hearings before the U.S.*

*Senate Committee on Agriculture and Forestry*, 79; "Statement of the Work of the Cost of Living Division of the Bureau of Investigation for the Fiscal Year 1919–20," DOJ-HCL; Special Assistant to the Attorney General to Lee Brock, February 27, 1920, DOJ-HCL.

22. United States Department of Justice, *Annual Report of the Attorney General of the United States* (Washington, DC: Government Printing Office, 1919), 17–18.

23. U.S. Senate Committee on Agriculture and Forestry, *High Cost of Living. Hearing before the United States Senate Committee on Agriculture and Forestry, and House Committee on Agriculture, Sixty-Sixth Congress, First Session, on Aug. 16, 1919. Part 1* (Washington, DC: Government Printing Office, 1919), 58.

24. Attorney General's Office to Francis Caffey, DOJ-HCL.

25. Figg to Neely, January 5, 1920, DOJ-HCL.

26. Indictment, *U.S. vs. F.G. Collins* File, National Archives Northeast Division, Waltham, MA.

27. "F.G. Collins Shoe Company Indicted," *Providence Journal*, December 13, 1919; "Two Shoe Dealers Are Arraigned in U.S. Court," *Providence Journal*, December 17, 1919; "Shoe Men to Go On Trial Here Monday," *Providence Journal*, January 20, 1920; "Shoe Firm Seeks to Kill Indictment," *Providence Journal*, January 21, 1920; "Indictment Against Shoe Firm Upheld," *Providence Journal*, January 24, 1920; "F.G. Collins Shoe Co. Denies Charge of Profiteering," *Providence Evening Bulletin*, December 17, 1919; "Motion to Quash Indictment Filed," *Providence Evening Bulletin*, January 20, 1920.

28. Figg to Baker, December 12, 1919, DOJ-HCL; Figg to Baker, January 12, 1920, DOJ-HCL.

29. Indictment, *U.S. vs. F.G. Collins* File, National Archives Northeast Division, Waltham, MA; "Shoe Men Plead Nolo," *Providence Evening Bulletin*, January 26, 1920; "Two Shoe Dealers Are Arraigned in U.S. Court," *Providence Journal*, December 17, 1919.

30. Figg to Baker, January 15, 1920, DOJ-HCL; Figg to Baker, January 24, 1920, DOJ-HCL.

31. No actual amount is listed in DOJ records.

32. Motion to Quash, *U.S. vs. F.G. Collins Shoe Company* File, National Archives Northeast Division, Waltham, MA.

33. Ibid.

34. Criminal Docket, *U.S. vs. F.G. Collins Shoe Company* File, National Archives Northeast Division, Waltham, MA; a letter from Assistant Attorney General Howard Figg to a U.S. attorney makes reference to the fact that Brown rendered no written opinion; Figg to Flynn, February 3, 1920, DOJ-HCL.

35. "Shoe Profiteers Are Heavily Fined," *Pawtucket Times*, January 27, 1920.

36. For a few examples of the case's publicity outside of New England, see "Collins Shoe Firm Chiefs Fined," *CT*, January 27, 1920; "Fined for Profiteering," *Sun and New York Herald*, January 27, 1920; "Profiteering Law Upheld," *Monroe (LA) News-Star*, January 24, 1920.

37. "The Merchant's Point of View," *NYT*, February 1, 1920.

38. Those listed are only a sampling of Lever Act decisions in federal district courts in early 1920. To All Fair Price Commissioners re: constitutionality of Lever Act, April 12, 1920, DOJ-HCL; Opinion by Judge Faris, *U.S. v. L.L. Cohen Grocery*, Supreme Court Opinion delivered, February 28, 1921, 255 U.S. 81, 41 S. Ct. 298, 65 L. Ed. 516; Opinion by

Judge Tuttle, *Detroit Creamery Co. et al. v. Kinnane et al.*, No. 331 District Court, E.D. Michigan, S.D. 264 F. 845, 1920 U.S. LEXIS 1281; "Cases in which the United States Attorney was Restrained by Action of the District Judge," DOJ-HCL.

39. Figg to L.A. Sarrow, February 9, 1920, DOJ-HCL.

40. Letter to the editor, *Boston Herald*, August 5, 1919.

41. Montgomery, *Workers' Control in America*, 97; "If the Middle Class Should Strike"; "How the Forgotten Man Lives," *Boston Herald*, September 19, 1919; 1920 U.S. Census, Durham, Stafford County, New Hampshire, digital image, s.v. "Ernest R. Groves," *Ancestry.com*.

42. Buffalo also seemed to be a promising place to prosecute, because it had a well-regarded fair price commissioner. Indictment, *U.S. vs. Antwerp Diamond Inc.*, *U.S. vs. Antwerp Diamond Inc.* File, National Archives Northeast Division, NYC; Transcript, *U.S. vs. Antwerp Diamond Inc.*, *U.S. vs. Antwerp Diamond Inc.* File, National Archives Northeast Division-NYC; "Buffalo Firm Is Fined $18,000," *Oneonta (NY) Daily Star*, June 4, 1920; Figg to Stafford, December 13, 1919, DOJ-HCL.

43. Petition of writ of error, *U.S. vs. Antwerp Diamond Inc.* File, National Archives Northeast Division-NYC.

44. Transcript, *U.S. vs. Antwerp Diamond Inc.*, *U.S. vs. Antwerp Diamond Inc.* File, National Archives Northeast Division-NYC.

45. "Women's Wear Retail Trade to Be Probed," *Women's Wear*, February 21, 1920; 1910 U.S. Census, Buffalo, Erie County, New York, digital image, s.v. "James B. Stafford," *Ancestry.com*.

46. Transcript, *U.S. vs. Antwerp Diamond Inc.*, *U.S. vs. Antwerp Diamond Inc.* File, National Archives Northeast Division-NYC.

47. Transcript, *U.S. vs. Antwerp Diamond Inc.*, *U.S. vs. Antwerp Diamond Inc.* File, National Archives Northeast Division-NYC.

48. "Buffalo Firm Is Fined $18,000"; Transcript, *U.S. vs. Antwerp Diamond Inc.*, *U.S. vs. Antwerp Diamond Inc.* File, National Archives Northeast Division-NYC.

49. For the Supreme Court declaration of the unconstitutionality of the Lever Act, see *U.S. v. L.L. Cohen Grocery Company*, Supreme Court opinion delivered February 28, 1921, 255 U.S. 81, 41 S. Ct. 298, 65 L. Ed. 516.

50. "Is Cloth Apparel?," *Sandusky (OH) Star Journal*, June 18, 1920; "War Profiteers Backing G.O.P. with 'Slush Fund,'" *Sandusky (OH) Star-Journal*, September 8, 1920.

51. "War Profiteers Backing G.O.P. with 'Slush Fund'"; "Wool Men Are Alleged Profiteers," *Altoona Tribune*, May 27, 1920.

52. "Shawsheen Village: A Fantasy Unfulfilled," Box 5, Roddy Papers, American Textile Museum Library.

53. See, for example, David Goldberg, *A Tale of Three Cities: Labor Organization and Protest in Patterson, Passaic, and Lawrence, 1916–1921* (New Brunswick: Rutgers University Press, 1989), or Edward Roddy, *Mills, Mansions, and Mergers: The Life of William M. Wood* (North Andover, MA: Merrimack Valley Textile Museum, 1982).

54. Oral history interview with J. W. Dairymple, Box 3, Roddy Papers, American Textile Museum Library; C. A. Wood Autobiography, p. 150, Box 4, Roddy Papers, American Textile Museum Library.

55. C. A. Wood Autobiography, p. 289–90, Box 4, Roddy Papers, American Textile Museum Library; "American Woolen Profit 15,513,415," *NYT*, April 28, 1920.

56. "Woolen Mill President Says Public Will Pay," *CT*, May 20, 1920; Goldberg, *A Tale of Three Cities.*

57. "Wood Fails to Give Any Names," *Boston Daily Globe*, December 18, 1919; "Union Leaders Suspect Wood's Company Store," *Women's Wear*, January 16, 1920; "Woolen Industry to Hit H.C.L." *Literary Digest*, January 3, 1920.

58. "Where the Consumer Comes In," *Reno Evening Gazette*, April 27, 1920.

59. "The Forum," *Duluth News-Tribune*, December 23, 1919.

60. In January of 1920, the DOJ encouraged Wood to be mindful of his profits before he set prices. Howard Figg expressed his hope to Wood that "your opening prices may not be based upon an anticipated increase but upon actual operating cost to carry only a reasonable profit." After Wood set his prices, he offered to allow DOJ investigators to examine his books. However, when they arrived, Wood was far from accommodating. Figg wrote him an angry reply: "If I have enlarged the scope of your offer or misunderstood the spirit of same, namely that you welcomed investigation and unbiased judgment of the reasonableness of your prices and were content to rest your justification before the public and the law on that basis, I beg you will correct me." Figg to William Wood, January 29, 1920, DOJ-HCL; Figg to William Wood, March 12, 1920, DOJ-HCL.

61. "Profiteering in Wool Is Charged," *Placerville (CA) Mountain Democrat*, June 5, 1920; "Demonstration at Arden," *Andover (MA) Townsman*, June 4, 1920.

62. "Shawsheen Village: A Fantasy Unfulfilled," Box 5, Roddy Papers, American Textile Museum Library.

63. "Who Backs Wood?," *New York Call*, May 30, 1920.

64. United States v. American Woolen Co. et al., 265 F.404 (7th Cir. 1920); "Shawsheen Celebration," *Andover (MA) Townsman*, June 18, 1920. The U.S. government appealed the decision to the Supreme Court, but this was a slow process. In 1921, the Supreme Court dismissed the case along with other Lever Act appeals after finding the Lever Act unconstitutional.

65. "Cloth and Clothes," *Modesto (CA) Evening News*, June 18, 1920; "Dangerous Precedent," *Atlanta Constitution*, June 14, 1920; "Legal Technicalities," *Buffalo News*, June 7, 1920; "One End of Profiteering," *CT*, July 17, 1920.

66. "Interpretations Given to Curtailment by Wool Manufacturers," *Bulletin of the National Association of Wool Manufacturers* 50 (October 1920): 410, 412.

67. Ibid., 405, 406, 409; "Gompers Roars as Mills Close," *LAT*, July 29, 1920; "Textile Workers Threaten to Overtake Woolen Wills," *CT*, December 22, 1920.

68. "American Woolen Cuts Hands' Pay," *Washington Post*, January 11, 1921; for a reflection of many historians' periodization of the 1920s as the lean years, see Melvyn Dubofsky and Foster R. Dulles, *Labor in America: A History* (Wheeling, IL: Harlan Davidson, 2004).

69. "Is Cloth Apparel?"; "Interpretations Given to Curtailment by Wool Manufacturers," *Bulletin of the National Association of Wool Manufacturers* 50 (October 1920): 402.

70. "Women Organizing to Fight H.C.L.," *Altoona (PA) Tribune*, January 14, 1920.

71. Edith Strauss to "Madam," November 8, 1919 (form letter to leaders of women's organizations), DOJ-HCL.

72. "Enlisting Women to Cut Living Cost," *NYT*, October 18, 1919; "Women Organizing to Fight H.C.L."

73. A. Mitchell Palmer to Edna White, October 31, 1919, DOJ-HCL; Edith Strauss to "Madam," November 9, 1919, DOJ-HCL; for other examples of letters seeking the advice

and cooperation of women, see "Form Letter to Fair Price Commissioners," November 6, 1919; Edith Strauss to Evelyn Ellsworth, November 10, 1919; Asst. Attorney General to Lee Brock, March 1, 1920; all DOJ-HCL.

74. Untitled chart, DOJ-HCL; Clubs Co-Operating with H.C.L. in Various States, DOJ-HCL.

75. Edith Strauss to "Madam," November 8, 1919, DOJ-HCL; *Annual Report of the Attorney General of the United States for the Year 1920* (Washington, DC: Government Printing Office, 1920), 182; Dept. of Justice, Division of Women's Activities, H.C.L., Information of Value in Choosing Material for Blouse, DOJ-HCL; 21, Reg 5091, Dept. of Justice Division of Women's Activities, H.C.L., Committee of Women's Organizations, "It shall be the duty of this committee . . . ," DOJ-HCL.

76. Daniel Horowitz, "Frugality or Comfort: Middle-Class Styles of Life in the Early Twentieth Century," *American Quarterly* 37 (Summer 1985): 239–59; Enstad, *Ladies of Labor.*

77. Report of Activities of Women's Organization, H.C.L. in Different States, Exhibit C., DOJ-HCL; Dept. of Justice Division of Women's Activities, H.C.L. Wearing Apparel Do's and Don'ts, DOJ-HCL.

78. *Oracle*, Duvall High School Yearbook (Jacksonville, FL, 1920), 88, Florida Collection, Jacksonville Public Library; "One Girl's Ideas on the Old Clothes Problem," *Ladies' Home Journal*, May 1920; "Made-Over Gowns in Crusade against H.C.L." *Women's Wear*, January 31, 1920.

79. Circular Letter to Advisory Committee Members and Others re Status of Misbranding and Other Textile Legislation, DOJ-HCL; Truth in Fabric Law, H.R. 11641, 66th Cong., 2nd sess.

80. For Immediate Release, Reel 84, National Consumers League Records (hereinafter NCLR); untitled document beginning with "Social Justice by Congressional Action . . . ," Reel 84, NCLR; Statement of Mrs. Raymond Robins—Presenting the Delegation of Women, on Social Justice Women's Day, Reel 84, NCLR.

81. Memo to Governor Cox, Oct. 1920, Reel 84, NCLR; Proposed Planks for National Party Platforms, Reel 84, NCLR; Summary of Interviews with Presidential Candidates, Reel 84, NCLR.

82. "Minnesota Women Talk on How to Cut Prices," *Women's Wear*, February 16, 1920.

83. Zella E. Bigelow, "Suggestions for a Demonstration of the Selection of Clothing," *Journal of Home Economics* 12, no. 2 (February 1920): 69–76; "Recent Work of the Committee on the Standardization of Textiles," *Journal of Home Economics* 12, no. 3 (March 1920): 101–8; "News from the Field," *Journal of Home Economics* 12, no. 4 (April 1920): 191–92; "The Present Status of Misbranding Acts and Other Textile Legislation," *Journal of Home Economics* 12, no. 5 (May 1920): 221–23; Evelyn M. Hickmans, "The Price and Value of Textiles," *Journal of Home Economics* 12, no. 8 (August 1920): 359–63; Ethel L. Phelps, "A Study of Clothing Purchasing Habits," *Journal of Home Economics* 12, no. 11 (November 1920): 491–95.

84. Joseph Feiss to National Consumers League, October 31, 1919, Reel 50, NCLR; F. Kelley to B. Smith, December 20, 1919, Reel 84, NCLR; Suggestions for A Truth in Fabric Campaign, Reel 50, NCLR.

85. National Association of Wool Manufacturers, "Arguments Against the 'Truth in Fabric' Bills Pending in the United States Congress, Sixty-Sixth Congress, Second Session," p. 13, New York Public Library.

86. "The Merchant's Point of View," *NYT*, March 28, 1920; "Textile Men Condemn Truth in Fabric Bill," *Women's Wear*, January 7, 1920; for an example of an article discussing contradictory messages regarding thrift with Truth in Fabric legislation, see "Worthy Cause Badly Handled," *Manitowoc (WI) Herald-Times*, August 23, 1920.

87. "Women's Leader in War on Prices Rebels," *Women's Wear*, January 30, 1920.

88. In Re Senate Investigation of Department of Justice Women's Organization in Connection with Campaign Expenditures, DOJ-HCL; Figg to Fair Price Commissioners, August 2, 1920, DOJ-HCL; Figg to Van Anda, May 19, 1920, DOJ-HCL; for analysis of women's clothing prices from mid-1919 to mid-1920 as advertised at three department stores, see Mark W. Robbins, "Awakening the 'Forgotten Folk': Middle Class Consumer Activism in Post-World War I America" (PhD diss., Brown University, 2009), 352–54. Wholesale prices, calculated from averaging price changes (Bureau of Labor Statistics) of articles designated as women's clothing, indicate an average price increase of 30.15 percent from 1919 to June 1920. U.S. Department of Labor, Bureau of Labor Statistics, "Wholesale Prices 1890 to 1920," *Bulletin of the Bureau of Labor Statistics* 296 (June 1922): 116–23. It is worth noting that Figg and Strauss became romantically involved, perhaps further discouraging Figg from declaring the Women's Division a failure.

89. Attorney General Assistant to Mrs. J. T. Anderson, October 7, 1920, DOJ-HCL; "Statement of the Work of the Cost of Living Division for the Bureau of Investigation, for the Fiscal Year 1919–1920," DOJ-HCL; U.S. Department of Labor, Bureau of Labor Statistics, *Bulletin of the Bureau of Labor Statistics* 300 (May 1922): 57. Another survey cites an increase of 21 percent from August 1919 to June 1920: Eugene Rotwein, "Post–World War I Price Movements and Price Policy," *Journal of Political Economy* 53 (September 1945): 249.

90. Untitled speech in W. V., DOJ-HCL; *The Fraternal Record: A Monthly Magazine Devoted to Secret Orders Everywhere* 23 (May 1920): 52; *The Fraternal Record: A Monthly Magazine Devoted to Secret Orders Everywhere* 23 (June 1920): 15.

91. Edith Strauss, summary of activity in individual states, DOJ-HCL.

## Chapter 4

1. "Double War Time Romance Wedding Held in Overalls," *Daily Oklahoman*, April 29, 1920.

2. "Lawyer Pleads Case in Denim," and "Boy Is Forced into Overalls at High School," *Daily Oklahoman*, April 29, 1920.

3. Hereinafter called "overall movement" in keeping with the phrasing of most historical sources.

4. "Overalls Parade Almost Gets Lost," *NYT*, April 25, 1920; Henry W. Macrosty, "Inflation and Deflation in the United States and the United Kingdom, 1919–23," *Journal of the Royal Statistical Society* 90 (1927): 52.

5. "Overalls Signal for America to Return to Work"; "One Value of Overalls," *Bridgeport (CT) Telegram*, April 23, 1920; "Wearing 'Em in Birmingham," *Charlotte (NC) Observer*, April 13, 1920.

6. "Overall Clubs Being Formed to Force King High Cost of Clothing Abdicate to Queen of Reason," *Florida Times-Union* (Jacksonville), March 28, 1920; "Overall Club Plans Parade Next Monday," *Florida Metropolis* (Jacksonville), March 31, 1920.

7. "Overall Clubs Being Formed to Force King High Cost of Clothing Abdicate to Queen of Reason"; "Overall Ass'n Will Stage Parade April 8," *Florida Times-Union*, April 4, 1920; occupational data determined from newspaper articles and the 1920 U.S. Census.

8. "Overall Club Plans Parade Next Monday."

9. "Overall Clubs Being Formed to Force King High Cost of Clothing Abdicate to Queen of Reason"; "'Overall Club' Parade Thursday," *Florida Metropolis*, April 5, 1920; "Rudy Grunthal Goat in Frame-Up," *Florida Metropolis*, April 7, 1920; records of the Jacksonville City Council, April 7, 1920, Jacksonville City Hall, Jacksonville, Florida.

10. "Overall Club Plans Parade Next Monday"; "'Overall Club' to Make Parade Plans Tonight," *Florida Metropolis*, April 3, 1920.

11. "Overall Club Plans Parade Next Monday"; "Overall Parade Will Be Staged in City Today," *Florida Times-Union*, April 8, 1920; "Overall Paraders Traversed Streets of City Yesterday," *Florida Times-Union*, April 9, 1920.

12. For discussion of the organizing implications of shared consumer identity, see Glickman, *Buying Power*, 18–19; "Overall Paraders Traversed Streets of City Yesterday."

13. See Nancy Hewitt, *Southern Discomfort: Women's Activism in Tampa, Florida, 1880s–1920s* (Urbana: University of Illinois Press, 2003).

14. See Robert Ingalls, *Urban Vigilantes in the New South: Tampa, 1882–1936* (Knoxville: University of Tennessee Press, 1988).

15. "Overall Club Being Formed in Tampa to Combat High Prices," *Tampa Tribune*, March 31, 1920; 1920 U.S. Census, Tampa, Hillsborough County, Florida, digital image, s.v. "Hafford Jones," *Ancestry.com*.

16. "Overall Club Being Formed in Tampa to Combat High Prices"; "'Overall Concert for Folks Easter Morning," *Tampa Tribune*, April 1, 1920; "Would Cut Cost of Graduating Dresses," *Tampa Tribune*, April 2, 1920.

17. "Firemen First to Don 'Conventional' Blue," *Tampa Tribune*, April 3, 1920; "'Overalls Club' Will Appear This Morning," *Tampa Tribune*, April 4, 1920; "Overall Club Hands Mayor Its Petition," *Tampa Tribune*, April 5, 1920.

18. "Firemen First to Don 'Conventional' Blue"; "Overall Club Hands Mayor Its Petition."

19. For examples of national press coverage of the Tampa overall movement, see "Refuses Appeal to Suppress News of Overall Movement," *NYT*, April 13, 1920; "How Tampa Idea Started," *NYT*, April 19, 1920, "Easter Parade in Tampa," *CT*, April 5, 1920; "Overalls Club Is Tampa Idea," *LAT*, April 19, 1920; "Overall Movement Spreads in South," *Christian Science Monitor*, April 13, 1920; "Wear Overalls Till Prices Drop," *Record-Journal* (Douglas County, CO), April 9, 1920; "Tampa Idea of Wearing Denim Sweeps Country," *Albuquerque Journal*, April 19, 1920.

20. For the composition of the Tampa overall club, names were taken from a report on the formation of the overall club, and their professions were determined through the 1920 U.S. Census; Karl H. Grismer, *Tampa: A History of the City of Tampa and the Tampa Bay Region of Florida* (St. Petersburg: St. Petersburg Printing Company, 1950), 397; "Overall Club Being Formed in Tampa to Combat High Prices"; "'Overall Concert for Folks Easter Morning"; "'Tampa Idea' Is Spreading Fast," *Tampa Times*, April 12, 1920; Letter to the editor, *Tampa Times*, April 20, 1920.

21. "How Tampa Idea Started," *NYT*, April 19, 1920.

22. "Firemen First to Don 'Conventional Blue"; "Overall Association Will Ask Min-

isters to Preach on H.C.L.," *Florida Times-Union*, April 14, 1920; "Morse Addresses Overall Club," *Columbia (SC) State*, May 8, 1920.

23. Luke 3:10–3:14, quoted in *The Holy Bible Containing the Old and New Testaments* (King James version) (New York: American Bible Society, 1963), 878; "Jax Business Men in Overall Parade," *Tampa Tribune*, April 10, 1920.

24. Raymond Arsenault, *St. Petersburg and the Florida Dream, 1888–1950* (Gainesville: University Press of Florida, 1996).

25. Ibid., 120, 139, 145.

26. "There Was None Wilder Than Mitchell," *St. Petersburg Times*, May 22, 1960; Karl Grismer, *The Story of St. Petersburg: The History of Lower Pinellas Peninsula and the Sunshine City* (St. Petersburg: P. K. Smith, 1948), 300–301; Scott Taylor Hartzell, *St. Petersburg: Voices of America* (Mount Pleasant, SC: Arcadia, 2002), 52–53.

27. Arsenault, *St. Petersburg and the Florida Dream*, 136–40; Grismer, *Story of St. Petersburg*, 300–301.

28. "There Was None Wilder Than Mitchell"; Grismer, *Story of St. Petersburg*, 300–301; Hartzell, *St. Petersburg*, 52–53; Arsenault, *St. Petersburg and the Florida Dream*, 136–40.

29. "There Was None Wilder Than Mitchell"; Hartzell, *St. Petersburg*, 53.

30. "There Was None Wilder Than Mitchell"; Arsenault, *St. Petersburg and the Florida Dream*, 136; Hartzell, *St. Petersburg*, 53.

31. Hartzell, *St. Petersburg*, 53; "There Was None Wilder Than Mitchell."

32. "Vote for Mitchell," *St. Petersburg Independent*, April 3, 1920; "Vote for Mitchell; To the Voters of St. Petersburg," *St. Petersburg Times*, April 4, 1920; Records of the St. Petersburg City Council, April 1920, St. Petersburg City Hall.

33. "The New Mayor," *St. Petersburg Independent*, April 8, 1920; Hartzell, *St. Petersburg*, 53.

34. "Overall Philosophy," *St. Petersburg Times*, April 27, 1920.

35. "Overall Clubs," *St. Petersburg Independent*, April 14, 1920; "Overalls—The New Purple," *Elyria (OH) Chronicle-Telegram*, April 24, 1920; *Lowell (MA) Sun*, April 25, 1920; "Business Men Here Look With Favor on New 'Overall Club,'" *Appleton (WI) Post-Crescent*, April 17, 1920.

36. "Mitchell Sells Two Hundred Overalls," *St. Petersburg Times*, May 5, 1920; "Offer Overalls 50 Cents Pair," *St. Petersburg Independent*, April 15, 1920; "Members of Club Organized Here Buy No New Clothes in 6 Months," *St. Petersburg Independent*, April 16, 1920.

37. Letter to the editor, *St. Petersburg Times*, April 29, 1920; 1920 U.S. Census, St. Petersburg, Pinellas County, Florida, digital image, s.v. "William J. Carpenter," *Ancestry.com*; "Overalls and Aprons," *St. Petersburg Independent*, April 24, 1920.

38. "Mayor Elect Puts in Big Order for Meat," *Tampa Tribune*, April 25, 1920; "Old Indian Trail Will End at St. Petersburg," *Tampa Tribune*, May 8, 1920.

39. See *St. Petersburg Times* coverage, April–May, 1920.

40. "There Was None Wilder Than Mitchell"; Records of the St. Petersburg City Council: June 9, 1920, date unknown, May 9, 1921, and December 20, 1921, St. Petersburg City Hall; Hartzell, *St. Petersburg*, 53; Arsenault, *St. Petersburg and the Florida Dream*, 189.

41. "Noel Mitchell Freed," *St. Petersburg Times*, May 1, 1936; "There Was None Wilder Than Mitchell."

42. "Norfolk Brethren Form Overalls Club," *Federal Employee* 5, no. 17 (April 24, 1920): 2; "Employees of County Decide for Overalls," *Oakland Tribune*, April 20, 1920; "Overalls and Old Clothes," *London* (UK) *Times*, April 20, 1920; "Parisians to Don Overalls," *London Times*, June 19, 1920; "A Sumptuary Problem," *London Times*, June 19, 1920; "British M.P. Wears Overalls in Commons," *Manitoba Free Press*, May 8, 1920; "Gaiety to Feature Next Week 'Let's Be Fashionable,'" *Manitoba Free Press*, September 18, 1920.

43. "Use of Overalls Spreads Rapidly," *Bridgeport (CT) Telegram*, April 20, 1920; Lakeview High School Collection, Folder 1–4, Box 4, Sulzer Regional Library Special Collections, Chicago Public Library; "Overalls Rebellion Will Never Be Popular with the Boy on the Farm," *Boston Daily Globe*, April 25, 1920; Sen. Dial, speaking on "The High Cost of Living," on April 19, 1920, 66th Cong., 2nd sess., *Congressional Record* 59, pt. 6: 5823.

44. See, for example, "Bits of New York Life," *Atlanta Constitution*, April 25, 1920; "To Wear Overalls in Broadway Today," *NYT*, April 16, 1920; "Police to Lead Overalls Parade," *NYT*, April 21, 1920.

45. Assorted Materials, scrapbook "Cheese Club," "1920, re overall parade" MWEZ X n.c., Billy Rose Theatre Collection, New York Public Library; Cheese Club File and Harry Hershfield File, Billy Rose Theatre Collection, New York Public Library; "Police to Lead Overalls Parade"; "The Joker in the Overalls," *Lake Park (IA) News*, May 6, 1920.

46. On the tendency of consumer movements to become commodified or co-opted, or both, see David Steigerwald, "All Hail the Republic of Choice: Consumer History as Contemporary Thought," *Journal of American History* 93, no. 2 (September 2006): 385–403; Assorted Materials, scrapbook "Cheese Club," "1920, re overall parade" MWEZ X n.c., Billy Rose Theatre Collection, New York Public Library; "Back to Old Clothes Movement Hits Film Colony at Hollywood," *New Orleans Item*, May 2, 1920; "Flashes," *LAT*, April 29, 1920; "Girls from Theater Rap HCL with Fords," *Los Angeles Evening Herald*, June 12, 1920.

47. Gus Kahn, *Overalls and Calico* (New York: Jerome H. Remick, 1920); Assorted Materials, scrapbook "Cheese Club," "1920, re overall parade" MWEZ X n.c., Billy Rose Theatre Collection, New York Public Library; "Comments on Short Subjects," *Moving Picture World*, May 29, 1920.

48. "Denim and Gingham," *Independent* (magazine, New York), May 1, 1920; *Newark Evening News*, quoted in "A Nation in Overalls," *Literary Digest*, May 1, 1920.

49. "Birmingham Sets Pace in Crusade against the High Cost of Clothes," *St. Petersburg Independent*, April 13, 1920; "Overalls Over All," *Woman Citizen*, April 24, 1920.

50. In many localities men encouraged women to organize gingham clubs.

51. "Women in Calico Join Overall Band," *NYT*, April 17, 1920; Letter to the editor, *Columbia State*, April 20, 1920; *Lowell Sun*, April 22, 1920.

52. "Wear Overalls to Oppose H.C.L.," *Columbia State*, April 13, 1920; letter to the editor, *Richmond Times*, April 12, 1920.

53. See examples: "Suggests Overalls," *Columbia State*, April 22, 1920; "Overall Clubs Formed in Ogden," and "Mayor Urged Overall Wear," *Ogden Standard-Examiner*, April 18, 1920; "Overalls Go Skyward in Big Demand," *Oakland Tribune*, April 18, 1920.

54. "Our First Overall Club," *LAT*, April 20, 1920; "Wear Your Old Clothes," *LAT*, April 25, 1920.

55. Records of the Common Council of the City of San Diego, April 19, 1920, City

Clerk's Office, San Diego; "Overalls and Old Clothes, Omens of Lower Prices," *NYT*, April 25, 1920; Letter to the editor, *Columbia State*, April 22, 1920; "Mayor Takes Office in Suit of Overalls," *Detroit Free Press*, April 21, 1920.

56. "Mayor Urged Overall Wear"; "Overalls Go Skyward in Big Demand," *Oakland Tribune*, April 18, 1920; "A Nation in Overalls."

57. Rep. Upshaw, speaking on H.R. 13432, on April 17, 1920, 66th Cong., 2nd sess., *Congressional Record* 59, pt. 6: 5808; "Congress Plans to Wear Denim," *Charlotte News*, April 18, 1920.

58. Sen. Dial, speaking on "The High Cost of Living," on April 19, 1920, 66th Cong., 2nd sess., *Congressional Record* 59, pt. 6: 5823.

59. Ibid.

60. Sen. Thomas, speaking on H.R. 11892, on April 24, 1920, 66th Cong., 2nd sess., *Congressional Record* 59, pt. 6: 6113; for an overview of Thomas's political philosophy, see Charles S. Thomas, "Without a Friend," *American Bar Association Journal* 7, no. 10 (October 1921): 547–52.

61. Sen. Kenyon, speaking on Profiteering and the High Cost of Living, on May 19, 1920, 66th Cong., 2nd sess., *Congressional Record* 59, pt. 7: 7291.

62. "Overalls? 'Well You Tell 'em,'" *Lima (OH) Daily News*, April 18, 1920; "Faddism Will Fail," *Portsmouth (NH) Herald*, April 23, 1920; "The Overalls Folly," *Charleston (WV) Daily Mail*, April 13, 1920; "Unnecessary Overalls," *Kingsport (TN) Times*, April 16, 1920; *Perry (IA) Daily Chief*, May 21, 1920; 1920 U.S. Census, Lima, Allen County, Ohio, digital image, s.v. "Austin Potter," *Ancestry.com*.

63. "Business Men Here Look with Favor on New 'Overall Club,'" *Appleton (WI) Post-Crescent*, April 17, 1920.

64. Entries for April 23, 1920 and June 7, 1920, Diary of Fred Alton Haight, Medford, Oregon, 1918 and 1920–21, Ms. 338, Southern Oregon Historical Society.

65. "The Overall Movement in Russia," *Life*, July 1, 1920; "Niland in Overalls, Scores Profiteers," *Boston Globe*, April 26, 1920.

66. "Chronica Semanal," *El Heraldo de Mexico*, April 25, 1920; "Overalls Not for Harlem," *Chicago Defender*, May 1, 1920; "Southern White 'Ge'mmen' to Wear Overalls," *Tulsa Star*, April 17, 1920.

67. Samuel Gompers, "Labor's Protest against a Rampant Tragedy," *Our Journal* (Metal Polishers International Union) 29 (June 1920): 6; for discussion of early twentieth-century working-class consumer organizing, see Dana Frank, *Purchasing Power: Consumer Organizing, Gender, and the Seattle Labor Movement, 1919–1929* (New York: Cambridge University Press, 1994).

68. "News, Notes, and Comments," *Steam, Shovel and Dredge* 27, no. 6 (June 1920): 408; William M. Leiserson, "The Meaning of Labor Representation: The Agreement in the Clothing Industry," *Annals of the Academy of Political and Social Science* 90 (July 1920): 23.

69. Special Assistant to the Attorney General to Mrs. A.A. Adams, May 4, 1920, DOJ-HCL.

70. "Put Boycott on Firms," *Ironwood (MI) Daily Globe*, May 7, 1920; "The Overall Craze," *Labor World* (Duluth, MN), May 1, 1920; "The Overall Warriors," *Shoe Workers' Journal* 21, no. 5 (May 1920): 14; "Celebrating the Silly Season," *New York Call*, April 23, 1920.

71. *New England Farms*, April 24, 1920; "Wearing Overalls," *Indiana Farmer's Guide*,

May 8, 1920; Letter to the editor, *Plattsburgh (NY) Sentinel*, May 11, 1920; *Iowa Homestead*, May 20, 1920.

72. "Asked at Random," *Michigan Daily*, April 21, 1920; "Campus Ready to Combat High Cost of Living Monday," *Michigan Daily*, April 25, 1920; "2500 Students Sign Up for Old Clothes and Display Green Tags," *Michigan Daily*, April 27, 1920; "Will Organize Old Clothes Movement," *The Tech* (MIT), April 23, 1920; "Governor in Old Shoes," *NYT*, April 28, 1920.

73. "Wear Your Old Suit," *Ogden Standard-Examiner*, April 28, 1920; Sen. Reed, speaking on S. Res. 358, on May 10, 1920, 66th Cong., 2nd sess., *Congressional Record* 59, pt. 7: 6800; "Upshaw Caught a Cold, So He Quit Wearing Overalls," *Boston Daily Globe*, April 21, 1920.

74. Thomas Pegram, *One Hundred Percent American: The Rebirth and Decline of the Ku Klux Klan in the 1920s* (Lanham, MD: Rowman and Littlefield, 2011), 149; "'Billy Sunday of Congress Speaks in Fredericksburg," *Richmond (VA) Times-Dispatch*, January 10, 1925.

75. Jerry L. Slaunwhite, "The Public Career of Nathaniel Barksdale Dial" (PhD diss., University of South Carolina, 1978), ix, 4, 146, 150, 159, 197.

76. Sen. Dial, speaking on The High Cost of Living, on April 19, 1920, 66th Cong., 2nd sess., *Congressional Record* 59, pt. 6: 5823–5824.

77. Stephen J. Leonard notes Thomas's "knack for offending the right, the left, and a good part of the middle." While in many respects Thomas's ideology and career in politics defy easy political categorization, he did support significant conservative positions. Sewell Thomas, *Silhouettes of Charles S. Thomas: Colorado Governor and United States Senator* (Caldwell, ID: Caxton Printers, 1959), 191–92, 212–22; Stephen Leonard, "Swimming Against the Current: A Biography of Charles S. Thomas, Senator and Governor," *Colorado Heritage* (Autumn 1994): 29–34.

78. "Senator Harding Advises Simplicity," *San Diego Union*, April 18, 1920.

79. Frederick E. Schortemeier, *Rededicating America: Life and Recent Speeches of Warren G. Harding* (Indianapolis: Bobbs-Merrill, 1920), 227–29.

80. "But Why the Placard?," *Lexington (KY) Herald*, June 4, 1920.

81. "Prices Falling, Palmer Declares," *NYT*, April 24, 1920.

82. Lawrence Glickman has underscored how consumer activists throughout American history have sought to exercise "economic power and moral responsibility" (for the benefit of others or themselves); Glickman, *Buying Power*, 6; "Overalls Signal for America to Return to Work"; "The Gospel of More Work and More Production," *LAT*, May 12, 1920.

83. Glickman, *Buying Power*.

84. Carl Roden scrapbook, Chicago Public Library Archives, Harold Washington Library Special Collections, Chicago, IL; "He Leads Fight on Profiteering," *Muskogee (OK) Times-Democrat*, August 9, 1920; "Council Acts Today to Punish Rent Gougers," *CT*, August 12, 1920.

## Chapter 5

1. Population statistics based on the 1900 and 1920 U.S. Censuses. For discussion of the single-family home ideal, see Margaret Garb, *City of American Dreams: A History of*

*Home Ownership and Housing Reform in Chicago, 1871–1919* (Chicago: University of Chicago Press, 2005), 1–10; Perry R. Duis, *Challenging Chicago: Coping with Everyday Life, 1837–1920* (Urbana: University of Illinois Press, 1998), 72, 74.

2. "Rent Hog Is Slander on Pig," *Chicago Daily News*, March 19, 1920.

3. Chicago Association of Commerce, *Survey of the Construction Industries and Physical Development of Chicago, Twenty-first Anniversary of the Chicago Association of Commerce* (Chicago: Chicago Association of Commerce, 1925), 12 (held at the Newberry Library, hereinafter NL); "Public Committee of 50 on Housing," Folder 1938, Box 36, Graham Taylor Papers, NL; Report of the Illinois Housing and Building Commission to the Governor and General Assembly, February 11, 1920, p. 13, Frank Lowden Papers, Illinois State Archives, Springfield, IL; "A Basic Principle," *Chicago Herald-Examiner*, May 6, 1920; "Validity of Rent-Fixing Statutes," *Central Law Journal* 91 (1920): 459; building permit data from *Report of the Illinois Building Investigation Commission Authorized by the 52nd General Assembly* (Springfield: Illinois State Register Printers, 1923) (hereinafter *RIBIC*), 4.

4. G. M. Hitchcock to Attorney General, January 28, 1920, DOJ-HCL; Paul V. Perry to Charles Merriam, December 19, 1918, Folder 11, Box 73, Charles Merriam Papers, University of Chicago Special Collections Library (hereinafter University of Chicago Special Collections Library, UCSCL); "New Dawn for the Middle Classes"; Royal E. Montgomery, "Graft in the Building Trades," *University Journal of Business* 4 (October 1926): 327; *RIBIC*, 8.

5. "Hammond Killing Taken Up," *Chicago Day Book*, July 11, 1914.

6. David Witwer, *Shadow of the Racketeer: Scandal in Organized Labor* (Urbana: University of Illinois Press, 2009), 9.

7. See also Andrew Wender Cohen, *The Racketeer's Progress: Chicago and the Struggle for the Modern American Economy, 1900–1940* (New York: Cambridge University Press, 2004).

8. "To the President and Members of the Chicago Real Estate Board," *Chicago Real Estate Board Bulletin* 27 (August 16, 1919): 652–54.

9. "200 a Day Join Fight on Rent Profiteers," *CT*, September 18, 1919.

10. *Proceedings of the City Council of the City of Chicago* 88 (August 5, 1919): 1110; John Lowling to Frank Lowden, January 20, 1921, Folder 6, Box 39, Series III, Frank Lowden Papers, UCSCL; Rep. Huddleston, speaking on H.R. 8624, on August 22, 1919, 66th Cong., 1st sess., *Congressional Record* 58, pt. 4: 4206.

11. Bureau of the Census, *Historical Statistics of the United States*, 40–51 and 135–66; data (including table) calculated from U.S. Department of Labor, Bureau of Labor Statistics, *Bulletin of the Bureau of Labor Statistics* 357 (May 1924): 457.

12. See Richard Ohmann, *Selling Culture: Magazines, Markets, and Class at the Turn of the Century* (New York: Haymarket Press, 1996); Horowitz, *Morality of Spending*, 83–84; Garb, *City of American Dreams*; William Tuttle, *Race Riot: Chicago in the Red Summer of 1919* (New York: Atheneum, 1970); for worries about families (middle class or otherwise) having to share residences with other people, see, for example, "May Take City Decade to Catch Up on Housing," *CT*, December 28, 1919; *Report of the Illinois Housing and Building Commission* (Springfield: Illinois State Printers, 1921), 5–12.

13. Julian Yurmen to Harry Olsen, January 10, 1919, Folder 6, Box 3, Harry Olsen Papers, Northwestern University Archives, Northwestern University Library.

14. "Most New-Weds Now Go to 'Live with Mother,'" *CT*, August 3, 1920; "Cupid Studies the Dollar Market," *Providence Journal*, April 4, 1920.

15. Letter to the editor, *CT*, February 9, 1921.

16. "Come Brethren, Let Us Get Together," *Englewood Times*, July 25, 1919; "The Merchant's Point of View," *NYT*, February 15, 1920.

17. The council also passed a resolution 42–1 asking Gov. Lowden to call a special session of the state Assembly to address high rents. *Proceedings of the City Council of the City of Chicago* 88 (August 5, 1919), 1110; "Rents Raised; Relief Sought; None in Sight," *CT*, February 4, 1920; "Council Asks Power to Halt Rent Raises," *Chicago City Club Bulletin*, August 16, 1920.

18. "Landlords Get Chance to Tell Why Rent Soars," *CT*, August 15, 1919.

19. The white-collar orientation of the CTPA is based on how the organization represented itself and how others (particularly the press) characterized it on various occasions, as well as on the professions of a number of CTPA leaders determined through newspaper coverage and the 1920 United States Census; "Chicago," *Louisiana Planter and Sugar Manufacturer* 73, no. 18 (November 1, 1924): 358; United States Senate, Select Committee on Reconstruction and Production, *Reconstruction and Production* (1921), 942.

20. For an example of the regular activities of a tenant association outside of Chicago, see Minutes of the Germantown (Philadelphia) Tenants Protective Association, Pennsylvania Historical Society, Philadelphia. "Punishment for Rent Boosters Taken Up Today," *CT*, August 13, 1919; "Landlords Get Chance to Tell Why Rent Soars," *CT*, August 15, 1919; "Tenants Resent Landlords' Talk of 'Deadbeats,'" *CT*, August 18, 1919; "Tenants Adopt Constitution for Rent Fights," *CT*, August 29, 1919.

21. Perry R. Duis notes that May 1, as "moving day," had become "an annual ritual" in Chicago by the 1870s. Specific reference to moving day on May 1 in Chicago dates back to at least 1847; Duis, *Challenging Chicago*, 75.

22. For working-class tenant activism, see Ronald Lawson and Stephen E. Barton, "Sex Roles in Social Movements: A Case Study of the Tenant Movement in New York City," *Signs* 6, no. 2 (1980): 232–33; Ronald Lawson and Mark Naison, eds., *The Tenant Movement in New York, 1904–1984* (New Brunswick: Rutgers University Press, 1986); Andrew Wood and James A. Bear, "Strength in Numbers: Urban Rent Strikes and Political Transformation in the Americas, 1904–1925," *Journal of Urban History* 32 (2006): 867; Ronald Lawson, "The Rent Strike in New York City, 1904–1980: The Evolution of a Social Movement Strategy," *Journal of Urban History* 10, no. 3 (1984): 235–58; for a book-length discussion of New York tenant activism in the postwar period, see Robert M. Fogelson, *The Great Rent Wars: New York, 1917–1929* (New Haven: Yale University Press, 2013).

23. This endnote relates to a similar type of demographic data used in chapters 1 and 5. For chapter 1, the data reflects only locatable names in the 1910 or 1920 U.S. Censuses. Some names were missing and other names presented too many options. Generally speaking, illegible professions and professions listed as "none," "retired," or difficult to classify were omitted, except when a husband's profession was listed. In these cases, the husband's profession was used. The charts thus represent only a sampling of the actual demographics. Discussing the class makeup of organizations or spatially mapping/analyzing residence patterns by class presents the problem of how to define what is to a large

extent a culturally constructed concept. It would be nearly impossible to empirically determine the class identification of individuals in (enough) specific households based on other methodology, thus categorizing by profession (the best demographic data available) is the best mapping/empirical option. This book does not argue that class can be defined solely by profession. Data on professions is used in this instance (and a few others) only because it is locatable (and it is worth emphasizing that white-collar families did often exhibit similar cultural behavior, for example, patterns of consumption). For a discussion on the drawbacks of defining class by profession, see Burton Bledstein and Robert D. Johnston, eds., *The Middling Sorts: Explorations in the History of the American Middle Class* (New York: Routledge, 2001); Chicago residential pattern charts constructed using data in the 1910 (Morse/Lunt) and 1920 (Wilson/Windsor and Morse/Lunt) U.S. Censuses, Chicago, Cook County, digital images, *Ancestry.com*. Two census sheets corresponding with the addresses listed on the charts served as samples to construct each table and chart. Professions that were difficult to categorize as white or blue collar were omitted from the charts. "Tenants Form Round Robins on Big Rent Boosts," *CT*, February 14, 1920.

24. "Forty Tenants Combine for First Strike," *CT*, February 28, 1920; "City-Wide Union to Fight Unjust Rents Demanded," *CT*, March 1, 1920; the 1920 U.S. Census lists H. S. Standish's occupation as "lawyer," a white-collar profession; 1920 U.S. Census, Chicago, Cook County, Illinois, digital image, s.v. "H. S. Standish," *Ancestry.com*.

25. "Courts Delay Evictions and Tenants Stick," *CT*, May 2, 1920.

26. "Reviving the Rent War," *CT*, August 4, 1920; see, for instance, "Show How City Can Discipline Rent Profiteers," *CT*, March 10, 1920.

27. Despite reports of joint arbitration with the CTPA, later newspaper articles referenced an arbitration board with no mention of collaboration with the CTPA. "Realtors Open Battle against Rent Gougers," *CT*, February 3, 1921; "Fifty Boards to Arbitrate All Rent Troubles," *CT*, March 24, 1920; "Realty Board Arbitrates 25 Rent Wrangles," *CT*, April 8, 1920; "Report of the Renting Division, April 7, 1920," *Chicago Real Estate Board Bulletin* 28 (April 28, 1920): 316.

28. "Rents and Investment Building," *Chicago Real Estate Board Bulletin* 27 (June 1919): 498–99; "Two Issues Which Must Be Settled," *Chicago Real Estate Board Bulletin* 27 (August 19, 1919): 625; "August 15, 1919, to the Honorable William Hale Thompson," *Chicago Real Estate Board Bulletin* 27 (August 1919): 652–54.

29. "Realty Board Arbitrates 25 Rent Wrangles"; "Arbitrate Rent Rows," *CT*, May 6, 1920; "To the Presidents and Members of the Chicago Real Estate Board [December 18, 1920]," *Chicago Real Estate Board Bulletin* 28 (December 1920/January 1921): 882; "Address Delivered before the Chicago Real Estate Board's Weekly Luncheon, Thursday Noon, February 26th, 1920, by Gerhardt F. Meyne . . . ," *Chicago Real Estate Board Bulletin* 28 (March 15, 1920): 189–205; "To the President and Members of the Chicago Real Estate Board," *Chicago Real Estate Board Bulletin* 27 (September 25, 1919): 726–28; J. Clarkson to Frank Lowden, April 13, 1920, and "Resolution Adopted at the First Annual Meeting of the National Federation of Construction Industries, Chicago, IL, March 25, 1920," Box 38, Series III, Frank Lowden Papers, UCSCL.

30. Each of Rockwood's examples summarized the outcomes of arbitration over rent values that would be in a typically middle-class rent range. Edith Rockwood, "Rent Profiteers," *Women's City Club Bulletin* article, March 1920, Folder 12, Box 2, Records of the

Chicago Women's City Club, University of Illinois–Chicago Special Collections; "Realtors Open Battle against Rent Gougers."

31. Across Chicago, the cost of housing rose by 21 percent between December 1919 and June 1920. Data calculated from U.S. Department of Labor, Bureau of Labor Statistics, *Bulletin of the Bureau of Labor Statistics* 357 (May 1924): 457.

32. See, for example, 1910 United States Census, Chicago, Cook County, Roll: T623_276, p. 126, which lists a grocery clerk, journalist, salesman, physician, school teacher, minister, musician, bank clerk, stenographer, real estate agent, grocery dealer, bookkeeper, and three clerks.

33. Interview with Walter Prigge, March 1926, quoted in Neal Samoors, Michael Williams, and Mary Jo Doyle, *Neighborhoods within Neighborhoods: Twentieth Century Life on Chicago's Far North Side* (Chicago: Rogers Park/West Ridge Historical Society, 2002), 173.

34. See "Revolt of the Consumer." Samoors, Williams, and Doyle, *Neighborhoods within Neighborhoods*, 62; interview with Sr. Ann Ida Gannon, college administrator, quoted in Samoors, Williams, and Doyle, *Neighborhoods within Neighborhoods*, 71.

35. "Names and salaries of employees, April 26, 1916," Committee on Administration, Chicago Public Library Archives, Harold Washington Library Special Collections, Chicago, IL; "names and salaries of employees, April 4, 1913," Committee on Administration, Chicago Public Library Archives, Harold Washington Library Special Collections, Chicago, IL; "names and salaries of employees, April 2, 1914," Committee on Administration, Chicago Public Library Archives, Harold Washington Library Special Collections, Chicago, IL; Carl Roden Scrapbook, Harold Washington Library Special Collections, Chicago, IL; Letter from Patterson to Roden, December 24, 1934, Chicago Public Library Archives, Harold Washington Library Special Collections, Chicago, IL; "Last Day to See Exhibit of Lincoln Relics," *CT*, February 26, 1916; "Country Circus at Austin," *CT*, May 29, 1909; "Veteran Worker," *CT*, October 16, 1932; Advertisement, "Today at Mandels," *CT*, March 20, 1936; "Statues for Our Squares," *CT*, September 5, 1939.

36. Carl Roden scrapbook, Chicago Public Library Archives, Harold Washington Library Special Collections, Chicago, IL; "He Leads Fight on Profiteering."

37. "Ask Legislative Candidates to Tell Rent Views," *CT*, September 25, 1920; "Tenants Throw Battle Gauge in Political Arena," *CT*, October 29, 1921.

38. "Overseas Hero Cheers Tenants on in Rent War," *CT*, March 9, 1920; "Revolt of the Consumer."

39. "10,000 Defy Landlords in Chicago," *Chicago Herald-Examiner*, May 2, 1920; "Landlords Fail to Have Joyous Time in Court," *Chicago Evening Post*, May 3, 1920.

40. No Illinois law gave the court the power to decide what level of rent would be exorbitant.

41. Mrs. Edith Byrne, Appellee, v. Mrs. J. A. McCarthy, Gen. No. 26,520, Decisions of the Appellate Courts of Illinois, Chicago, First District, May, 1921, University of Chicago Law Library; Charles M. Case, Appellee, v. Joseph E. Fagin, Appellant, Gen No. 26,623, Decisions of the Appellate Courts of Illinois, Chicago, First District, July, 1921, University of Chicago Law Library; "Landlords and Equity," *Chicago Herald-Examiner*, May 11, 1920.

42. "Rent 'Rebels' Win Victory," *Chicago Herald-Examiner*, May 5, 1920.

43. *Proceedings of the City Council of the City of Chicago* 90 (May 3, 1920): 103; Gov. B.

Clarkson, Director of the Council and of the Field Divisions, Washington, DC, to the several State Councils of Defense, January 9, 1919, Box 36, Series III, Frank Lowden Papers, UCSCL.

44. "Profiteering Landlord 'Cycle' or 'Cockroach,'" *CT*, October 2, 1920.

45. Editorial, *Chicago Evening Post*, May 4, 1921.

46. "Tenant Gets Trial by Jury despite Lease," *Chicago Daily Journal*, April 27, 1921; "Judges Confer on Rent Suits," *Chicago Daily Journal*, April 26, 1921; 1930 U.S. Census, Chicago, Cook County, Illinois, digital image, s.v. "Charles S. MacCubbin," *Ancestry.com*.

47. According to a Chicago Municipal Court report, "owing to the housing shortage and rent increases," a jump in "forcible entry" cases after May "deserves special mention." Leading up to moving day, some landlords used aggressive techniques to convince their tenants to vacate. For instance, in Lake View, after his tenant refused to pay a $35 rent increase, landlord Emil Welky removed the back door of the apartment, wrongly believing that it would force him to vacate. "Fifteenth Annual Report of The Municipal Court of Chicago for the Year December 6 to December 4 Inclusive," p. 9, Municipal Reference Collection, Harold Washington Library, Chicago Public Library; Records of *Howard F. Bishop v. Emil Welky*, Superior Court of Cook County, 1921 (S365369), Cook County Clerk of Courts Archives; "Tenants Make Stubborn Fight to Hold Flats," *Chicago Journal of Commerce*, May 2, 1921; "Tenants Sit Tight; Await Writ Servers," *Chicago Daily Journal*, May 2, 1921; "Strike of 20,000 Tenants," *Chicago Daily Journal*, April 25, 1921; "Tenants' Unfair Rent Signs Are Declared Legal"; the 1920 U.S. Census lists Behan's profession as "Lawyer," 1920 U.S. Census, Chicago, Cook County, Illinois, digital image, s.v. "C. D. Behan," *Ancestry.com*.

48. See chapter 2. "Landlords File Ouster Suits in Tenant War," *Chicago Evening Post*, May 2, 1921; "Strike of 20,000 Tenants"; "Tenants Set for May Strike," *Chicago Daily Journal*, April 29, 1921; "'Beware! Watch for Trickery' League's Advice," *Chicago Daily Journal*, April 30, 1921; "Renters Storm Capitol in War on Landlords," *CT*, March 17, 1921.

49. See introduction.

50. "Strike of 20,000 Tenants"; "Renters Storm Capitol in War on Landlords"; "'Beware! Watch for Trickery' League's Advice"; "Anti-Rent Profiteering Bill Now Pending in Legislature," *Chicago Real Estate* 1, no. 2 (March 1921): 6, 9.

51. "Anti-Eviction Bill Is Passed by Legislature," *Chicago Evening Post*, May 3, 1921; "Governor Signs Bonus Act," *Illinois State Journal* (Springfield), May 4, 1921; "Tenant League to Hold Three-Day Jubilee," *Chicago Evening Post*, May 4, 1921; "Play Fair Is Advice of Rent League Chief," *Chicago Daily Journal*, May 4, 1921; "Tenant Dance Will Celebrate Rent Victories," *Chicago Evening Post*, May 6, 1921.

52. "Judge Rooney Uses New Rent Law to Aid Evicted Tenants," *Chicago Daily Journal*, May 5, 1921, "Judges Delay Eviction Cases," *Chicago Daily Journal*, May 7, 1921; "Tenants Hold Up Rent Cases."

53. "Graft Ruined Him, Former Builder Sobs," *CT*, March 27, 1921; "Claim Realtors Curbed Building to Keep Rents Up," *CT*, April 25, 1921.

54. Barbara Warne Newell, *Chicago and the Labor Movement: Metropolitan Unionism in the 1930s* (Urbana: University of Illinois Press, 1961), 81.

55. Cohen, *Racketeer's Progress*, 209–32.

56. See Cohen, *Racketeer's Progress*, for discussion of how Chicago craftsmen contested the corporatization of the city's economy. For quotation, see ibid., 1.

57. Sen. Harold Kessinger, for instance, reiterated that "rents will not come down until buildings go up." Newspapers printed headlines, such as "Contractor Bares Union Extortions" and "Daily Probers Call Builders; Give Contractors Another Opportunity to Tell Story of Graft 'Shakedown'"; "U.S. Indicts 110 Builders in Graft War," *CT*, May 1, 1921; "Chicago's Building Situation," *Chicago City Club Bulletin*, October 10, 1921; "The Building Lockout," *Chicago Evening Post*, April 29, 1921; "Three Unions Found in Ring to Get Graft," *Chicago Journal of Commerce*, May 7, 1921; "Contractor Bares Union Extortions," *Chicago Daily Journal*, May 14, 1921; "Daily Probers Call Builders," *Chicago Daily Journal*, May 19, 1921; *RIBIC*, 3.

58. "U.S. Told How Graft Boosts Building Cost," *CT*, December 31, 1920.

59. "Tenants Urge Crowe to Smash Builder 'Trust,'" *CT*, February 17, 1921.

60. Data taken from Royal E. Montgomery, "Graft in the Building Trades," *University Journal of Business* 4, no. 4 (October 1926): 326–27. The *Chicago Herald-Examiner* and the Dailey Commission final report referred to more than 200 defendants "awaiting trial." Whereas these reports were published relatively early in the legal process, Royal E. Montgomery wrote about the Commission and its ultimate results six years after the end of its activities. Presumably not all of these defendants were taken to trial, which might explain the discrepancy in numbers. *RIBIC*, 4; Chad Wallin, *The Builders' Story: An Interpretive Record of the Builders' Association of Chicago, Inc., an Organization Co-existent with the Chicago Chapter of the Associated General Contractors of America* (Chicago: Builders' Association of Chicago, 1966), 42–43.

61. "End of Building Tieup Expected within 10 Days," *CT*, May 16, 1921.

62. "Tenants Urge Crowe to Smash Builder 'Trust.'"

63. Royal E. Montgomery, "The Landis Arbitration and Award," *University Journal of Business* 4, no. 3 (July 1926): 260–64.

64. For discussion of how Landis was influenced by the Dailey Commission, see ibid., 260–93. It is also worth noting that discord between builders and labor reached extreme levels. After the Landis Award, a series of bombings occurred that resulted in destruction of buildings, deaths, and arrests of labor leaders.

65. In many cases Landis established a greater reduction in wages than contractors had asked.

66. "The Landis Award," *New Majority*, January 14, 1922.

67. Cohen, *Racketeer's Progress*, 245–54; Wallin, *Builders' Story*, 47; Montgomery, "Landis Arbitration and Award," 263, 269, 273, 289; James Merriner, *Grafters and Goo Goos: Corruption and Reform in Chicago, 1833–2003* (Carbondale: Southern Illinois University Press, 2004), 106; see also Sidney Fine, *'Without the Blare of Trumpets': Walter Drew, the National Erectors' Association, and the Open Shop Movement, 1903–57* (Ann Arbor: University of Michigan Press, 1995), 216–19.

68. Sylvester J. Konenkamp, "Chicago District Carpenters and the Landis Award," *Life and Labor Bulletin* 7, no. 3 (February 1929): 1; Chicago Association of Commerce, *Survey of the Construction Industries*; "Your Opportunity to Perform a Great Service to Your Community" (pamphlet), Landis Award Mic. Clippings and Pamphlets, Landis Papers, Chicago History Museum Archives.

69. Cohen, *Racketeer's Progress*, 248.

70. *Directory of Directors in the City of Chicago* (Chicago: Audit Co. of New York, 1903); "Your Opportunity to Perform a Great Service to Your Community" (pamphlet), Landis Award Mic. Clippings and Pamphlets, Landis Papers, Chicago History Museum Archives.

71. Henry K. Holsman and Ralph Parlette, *Giant We-The-People and Judge Landis' Award* (Chicago: Parlette-Padget Company, 1922), 6, 11, 22, 28, 43; "Your Opportunity to Perform a Great Service to Your Community"; "Talking Points," Landis Award Mic. Clippings and Pamphlets, Landis Papers, Chicago History Museum Archives; "A Criminal Conspiracy," *New Majority*, March 4, 1922.

72. Andrew Wender Cohen also notes that "[b]y presenting [the] open shop drive as a war against corruption, collusion, and inefficiency, executives cast themselves as representative of the public interest." Cohen, *Racketeer's Progress*, 245; "White Collars Going to Work," *Spokane Daily Chronicle*, May 12, 1923; "Landis Trade School Proves Big Success," *Chicago Commerce*, September 16, 1922; clipping from *Chicago Commerce*, February 17, 1923, Landis Award Mic. Clippings and Pamphlets, Landis Papers, Chicago History Museum Archives; "Talking Points"; "The Disappearing Apprentice," *Saturday Evening Post*, September 1, 1923.

73. Fine, *'Without the Blare of Trumpets'*, 216–19; Rosenwald to "Mr. Stern," June 19, 1928; Thomas Donnelly to Rosenwald, June 11, 1927; Rosenwald to Louis Eckstein, January 5, 1927; Rosenwald to Thomas Donnelly, December 14, 1925; Rosenwald to T. E. Donnelly, December 17, 1926, all Folder 8, Box 10, Rosenwald Papers, UCSCL; Newberry Library Financial Agent to Mr. F. W. Armstrong, CCELA, December 14, 1921, Box 22, Records of the Newberry Library Financial Agent, NL.

74. "Three Large Chicago General Contractors Repudiate Landis Award," *Amalgamated Sheet Metal Workers' Journal* 23 (September 15, 1923): 13.

75. "Banker Resigns from 'Citizens,'" *New Majority*, January 28, 1922.

76. Economist C. Lawrence Christenson came to this percentage by examining building insurance records. C. Lawrence Christenson, *Collective Bargaining in Chicago: 1929–30* (Chicago: University of Chicago Press, 1933), 24.

77. Rosenwald to Atkins, July 27, 1922, Folder 8, Box 10, Rosenwald Papers, UCSCL; "Chicago to Boost Package Car Plan," *Philadelphia Inquirer*, September 4, 1922.

78. After an adverse decision by the Illinois Supreme Court curtailed many of its practices in 1929, the Committee fell apart. The Landis Award Employers' Association took its place, but it controlled far fewer construction projects. Fine, *'Without the Blare of Trumpets'*, 219.

79. Drawing on statistics from Christenson, *Collective Bargaining in Chicago*, Barbara Warne Newell summarizes that 90 percent of the Chicago construction industry was unionized in 1929. Newell, *Chicago and the Labor Movement*, 200.

## Epilogue

1. "A Manifesto to the Middle Classes," *London Times*, May 10, 1919.

2. "Middle Class Union Formed," *London Times*, March 7, 1919; "Manifesto to the Middle Classes"; "Chats with Visitors in Washington," *Washington Post*, February 29, 1920; "Clad in Overalls, Newman Appears in the Commons," *Atlanta Constitution*, May 8, 1920.

3. "Tenants Will Form 'Middle Class' Union," *CT*, April 6, 1921.

4. Speech, June 1, 1921, p. 5, Folder 7, Box 8, Series 5, Frank Lowden Papers, UCSCL.

5. "Middle Class Union Formed in New York," *Pittsburgh Press*, February 9, 1920; "Public's Union Is Incorporated," *Christian Science Monitor*, April 24, 1920; "Middle Class Union Charter Granted in N.Y.," *CT*, February 8, 1920; "Depew Urges Formation of 'Middle Class' Union," *CT*, April 15, 1920; "Chats with Visitors in Washington," *Washington Post*, February 29, 1920.

6. Glickman, *Buying Power*.

7. "New Dawn for the Middle Classes"; "Topics of the Times," *NYT*, April 16, 1920; "Chauncey M. Depew on the Middle Class Union," *NYT*, April 25, 1920; "The New 'Middle Class' Union," *Ogden Standard-Examiner*, May 9, 1920.

8. See Marjorie Murphy, *Blackboard Unions: The AFT and the NEA, 1900–1980* (Ithaca: Cornell University Press, 1990); ibid., 5; "Middle Class Unions," *Survey*, May 15, 1920; "New Dawn for the Middle Classes"; "'White Collar Union' Launched at Rallies Here," *CT*, July 13, 1921; "Chauncey M. Depew on the Middle Class Union."

9. See "No. 346—Cost of Living in the United States: Index Numbers," in United States Department of Commerce, Bureau of Foreign and Domestic Commerce, *Statistical Abstract of the United States 1929* (Washington, DC: Government Printing Office, 1929).

10. According to Lizabeth Cohen, a subtle form of organizing was taking place beneath the surface. Industrial workers in Chicago, who had been divided in the strikes of 1919, participated in a common consumer culture and welfare capitalism that led them to have more in common with each other by the 1930s. According to Cohen, during the New Deal Era, which saw federally sanctioned collective bargaining, workers became "effective as national political participants." Lizabeth Cohen, *Making a New Deal: Industrial Workers in Chicago, 1919–1939* (New York: Cambridge University Press, 1990), 5.

11. "Middle Class to Have Huge Union to Gain Justice," *Appleton (WI) Post-Crescent*, February 2, 1920; "Socialists Stand for One Big Union," *NYT*, May 13, 1920.

12. "Tenants Will Form 'Middle Class' Union,'" *CT*, April 7, 1921.

13. Robert Zieger, *Republicans and Labor, 1919–1929* (Lexington: University of Kentucky Press, 1969), 74–76; "Delirious Dawes Dents Democracy," *New Majority*, March 3, 1923.

14. United Garment Workers of America, "Anti-Union Shop Favored by Swashbuckler Dawes," *Garment Worker* 22, no. 24 (March 30, 1923): 2.

15. "Minute Men Win First Fight, They Show in Booklet," *CT*, December 16, 1923; Minute Men of the Constitution (MMC), *The First Fight of the Minute Men of the Constitution*, 1924, pamphlet, held at the Widener Library, Harvard University, 4.

16. Data refers to identifiable names and professions in the 1920 U.S. Census. MMC, *First Fight of the Minute Men of the Constitution.*

17. MMC, *First Fight of the Minute Men of the Constitution*, 10.

18. "G.O.P. Candidate Answers Davis Acceptance Speech," *Billings (MT) Gazette*, August 24, 1924.

19. MMC, *First Fight of the Minute Men of the Constitution*, 4–5, 10–11; "Voice of the People," *CT*, May 9, 1923.

20. MMC, *First Fight of the Minute Men of the Constitution;* "Dawes Deals Out 'Hell-Maria' to Minute Men's Foe," *CT*, April 29, 1923; "Dawes Forms Minute Men to Uphold U.S.," *CT*, April 26, 1923.

21. "Proposes Pact to Halt Building Strikes 3 Years," *CT*, November 17, 1922; "Citizen Board Answers Legal Sally of Labor," *CT*, January 6, 1922; "Delay Hearing on Carpenters' Injunction Plea," *CT*, December 16, 1921; "Mill Carpenter Strike Ties Up More Building," *Chicago Evening Post*, May 7, 1920; "The Chicago Situation," *Carpenter*, April 1922. See also Mitchell Newton-Matza, "Intelligent and Honest Radicals: The Chicago Federation of Labor and the Illinois Legal System, 1919–1933" (PhD diss., Catholic University of America, 1999), 119–49.

22. See "Labor Protests Rule by Judges," *New Majority*, August 25, 1923; "The Chicago Federation of Labor Meeting Held at the Musicians Hall," *New Majority*, October 13, 1923; "Injunction Fighters Pick Judicial Ticket," *New Majority*, November 3, 1923; "'Injunction Dennie,'" *New Majority*, November 10, 1923; MMC, *First Fight of the Minute Men of the Constitution*, 6.

23. *Bridgemen's Magazine* 24 (1924): 197; "Coming Events," *Amalgamated Sheet Metal Workers' Journal* 27–28 (1923): 11–13; International Brotherhood of Electrical Workers, "The American Revolution of 1923," *Journal of Electrical Workers and Operators* 22, no. 8 (May 15, 1923): 419; "'Open Shop' Campaign in Chicago," *New Majority*, October 13, 1923; "'Injunction Dennie,'" *New Majority*, November 10, 1923.

24. "Minute Men Denounced by Labor Leader," *Rockford Morning Star*, August 28, 1923.

25. November 14, 1923 entry, Dawes Diary, Box 119, Folder 32, Dawes Papers, Northwestern University Special Collections; Phalen to Dawes, undated, Box 119, Folder 19, Dawes Papers, Northwestern University Special Collections.

26. "A Startling Statement," *Monroe (LA) News-Star*, May 3, 1923; "Now the Minute Men!," *Uniontown (PA) Morning Herald*, April 3, 1923; "Minute Men of the Constitution United in Common Bond of Patriotism," *Graham (NC) Alamance Gleaner*, September 27, 1923.

27. "Tells Why He Distrusts J. W. Davis and Gen. Dawes," *Urbana (IL) Daily Courier*, August 7, 1924. For examples of newspapers lauding the Dawes nomination, see "Coolidge and Dawes," *San Bernardino County Sun*, June 13, 1924; "Charles Gates Dawes," *Franklin (PA) News-Herald*, June 14, 1924.

28. Timmons, *Portrait of an American*, 215.

29. For discussion of declining union power in the 1920s, see Irving Bernstein, *The Lean Years: A History of the American Worker, 1920–1933* (New York: Penguin, 1960).

30. Cohen, *Consumers' Republic*, 28–31; Jacobs, *Pocketbook Politics*, 156; "Consumers Want a Federal Bureau," *NYT*, February 17, 1938; "Agency to Aid Consumers Urged on President," *NYT*, February 25, 1938.

31. Glickman, *Buying Power*, 189; Jacobs, *Pocketbook Politics*.

32. Gilbert Seldes, *Your Money and Your Life: A Manual for the "Middle Classes"* (New York: Whittlesey House, 1938), 3–4, 7, 120. For an example of one of many newspaper articles that suggested the need for middle-class organization, see "Shall the Middle Class Organize?," *Mason City (IA) Globe-Gazette*, April 28, 1937.

33. Walter B. Pitkin, *Capitalism Carries On* (New York: McGraw Hill, 1935), 24–25, 241–42.

34. "Are We to Have a Middle Class Union?," *Elyria (OH) Chronicle-Telegram*, May 1, 1920; "Overall Spirit Is Admirable . . . ," *Cincinnati Enquirer*, April 20, 1920; "Educator to Launch Middle Class League," *Reading (PA) Eagle*, June 29, 1939; "A New League?,"

*New Orleans Times-Picayune*, June 29, 1939; "Prof. Pitkin Proposes Use of Existing Tools to Make Voice of 'Great Majority' Effective," *Elyria Chronicle-Telegram*, June 30, 1939.

35. "Questionnaires to Be Delivered to Elyrians," *Elyria Chronicle-Telegram*, August 12, 1939; "Pitkin Says War Imperils Middle Class," *Elyria Chronicle-Telegram*, September 13, 1939; "Now on Sale, March Issue of Everybody's Business," *Elyria Chronicle-Telegram*, February 20, 1945.

36. "Bulletin Issued by American Majority," *Elyria Chronicle-Telegram*, October 4, 1939; "American Majority Brings Intimate County Details," *Elyria Chronicle-Telegram*, February 27, 1940; "Million Dollars Spent for $358,000 School," *Elyria Chronicle-Telegram*, March 25, 1940; "American Majority Criticizes Cost of Election Supplies for Lorain County," *Elyria Chronicle-Telegram*, May 7, 1940; "Suggests Ways County Might Save Money," *Elyria Chronicle-Telegram*, October 11, 1939.

37. "Pitkin Summons the Middle Class for a 'Revolution,'" *Milwaukee Journal*, June 29, 1939; "United Movement Growing to Save Middle Class from Destruction," *Dallas Morning News*, September 24, 1939; "American Majority Groups to Be Organized in Three Other States," *Elyria Chronicle-Telegram*, September 19, 1939; "It Takes Courage to Publish These Facts," *Mansfield (OH) News-Journal*, April 16, 1942; "Butler Public Schools Strange Interlude," *Mansfield News-Journal*, July 8, 1942.

38. "Rabble Rouser of the Right," *New Republic*, October 4, 1939; "Announcement to the Public," *Mansfield News-Journal*, January 7, 1942; "Everybody's Business," *Elyria Chronicle-Telegram*, October 25, 1944.

39. Cohen, *Consumers' Republic*, 8–9.

40. "Increase Is Urged in Labor Output," *NYT*, January 13, 1947.

41. See Jacobs, *Pocketbook Politics*, 250–61.

42. Quote taken from Cohen, *Consumers' Republic*, 121.

43. Joseph Basco, "Protesters Occupy Hemming Plaza in Downtown Jacksonville," *Spinnaker* (University of North Florida), October 12, 2011; Adam Kealoha Causey, "Occupy Jacksonville Protest Held in Hemming Plaza," *Florida Times-Union*, October 10, 2011, accessed July 18, 2015 (article: http://jacksonville.com/news/florida/2011-10-08/story/occupy-jacksonville-protest-held-hemming-plaza; photo gallery with pictures of protest signs: http://photos.jacksonville.com/mycapture/folder.asp?event=1338365&CategoryID=57821).

44. Overall club members at Hemming Park had marched with signs calling on people to help "deport the profiteer" and "demand value for your money"; "Overall Paraders Traversed Streets of City Yesterday," *Florida Times-Union*, April 9, 1920.

45. Ann Spanier, letter to the editor in *Oakland Tribune* Talk Back, *Contra Costa Times*, October 21, 2011.

46. Ruth Milkman, Stephanie Luce, and Penny Lewis, *Changing the Subject: A Bottom-Up Account of Occupy Wall Street in New York City* (New York: Murphy Institute, City University of New York, 2013), accessed July 17, 2015, https://media.sps.cuny.edu/filestore/1/5/7/1_a05051d2117901d/1571_92f562221b8041e.pdf. The study mainly analyzed the Occupy movement in New York City, with survey data focusing on attendees of a rally at Union Square.

47. See Elizabeth Flock, "Occupy Wall Street Protesters Decry 'Corporate' Black Friday, Call Off Egypt Trip," *Washington Post*, November 23, 2011; and "Barney Jopson, "US Shoppers Ignore Pleas by Protesters," FT.com (*Financial Times*), November 25, 2011.

48. Abby Scher and Chip Berlet, "The Tea Party Moment," in *Understanding the Tea Party Movement*, ed. Nella Van Dyke and David S. Meyer (Burlington, VT: Ashgate, 2014), 109. See also Vanessa Williamson, Theda Skocpol, and John Coggin, "The Tea Party and the Remaking of Republican Conservatism," *Perspectives on Politics* 9, no. 1 (March 2011): 25–43; John B. Judis, "Tea Minus Zero," *New Republic*, May 19, 2010, accessed July 16, 2015, http://www.newrepublic.com/article/politics/tea-minus-zero

49. Video clip of Nancy Ripley, "Voices of the Tea Party," *New York Times*, April 14, 2010, accessed July 16, 2015, http://www.nytimes.com/interactive/2010/04/14/us/teaparty.html?_r=0

50. Clarence Y. H. Lo, "Astroturf versus Grass Roots: Scenes from Early Tea Party Mobilization," in *The Precipitous Rise of the Tea Party*, ed. Lawrence Rosenthal and Christine Tost (Berkeley: University of California Press, 2012), 98–129.

51. Shereen Siewert, "Who Is Funding Wisconsin's Fight for Governor?," *Fond du Lac (WI) Reporter*, September 7, 2014; Matthew Payne, "Who's Funding Scott Walker?," *Wall Street Journal*, May 4, 2012; Janet Hook, "First Three Political Candidates Share Tea Party Roots," *Wall Street Journal*, April 12, 2015.

52. See Scott Walker, "Striking the Right Bargain in Wisconsin," *Washington Post*, March 16, 2011; Jeremy W. Peters, "G.O.P. Hopefuls Now Aiming to Woo the Middle Class," *New York Times*, May 3, 2015.

53. For a discussion of the role of corporate leaders in early Tea Party organizing and funding, see Lo, "Astroturf versus Grass Roots: Scenes from Early Tea Party Mobilization."

# Index